DE LUDO GLOBI
(THE GAME OF SPHERES)

NICHOLAS DE CUSA • De Ludo Globi

The Game of Spheres

TRANSLATION, AND INTRODUCTION BY PAULINE MOFFITT WATTS

ABARIS BOOKS • NEW YORK

International Standard Book Number 0-89835-068-9
First published 1986 by Abaris Books, Inc.
24 West 40th Street, New York, New York 10018
Printed in the United States of America

To

F. Edward Cranz

Paul Oskar Kristeller

In admiration of their erudition
and humanity

Woodcut of Nicholas de Cusa from title page to *Des Bapsts Hercules Wider die Deudschen* by Johann Kymeus, Wittenberg 1538

TABLE OF CONTENTS

1. Preface 9

2. A Note on the Translation 11

3. Introduction to the *De ludo globi* 13

4. Text and Translation 53

5. List of Variants 123

6. Bibliography of Works Cited 131

1. PREFACE

There is currently a revival of interest in the 15th-century speculative thinker and reformer, Nicolaus Cusanus, amongst English-speaking scholars. An outgrowth of this interest, one which will play an important role in sustaining it, is the recent publication of new translations of several of Cusanus' writings. Jasper Hopkins has made a translation of the *De docta ignorantia*, probably Cusanus' most fundamental work, which will undoubtedly supplant the not altogether satisfactory 1954 version of Germain Heron. Hopkins has also translated the *Apologiae doctae ignorantiae*, Cusanus' defense of the *De docta ignorantia*, and two important late works, the *De non-aluid* and the *De possest*. Clyde Lee Miller has lately published a new translation of one of the three dialogues of the *Idiota*, the *Idiota de mente*. This translation, like the present one, appears in Abaris Books' Janus Series. Miller's English translation is the first since an anonymous 1560 version. There exist in addition several versions of the *De visione dei*, and John P. Dolan has published selections from various works in his *Unity and Reform* (for complete citations of all the translations mentioned above see the Bibliography). The translation of a number of important works, notably the *De coniecturis* and the *De beryllo*, remains to be undertaken.

This book renders the *De ludo globi* into English for the first time in the hope that it will stimulate further study of Cusanus, especially of his late thought. I am grateful to The Huntington Library for permission to reproduce an illustration from S.K. Heninger's *The Cosmographical Glass*. I would like to thank Professors F. Edward Cranz, Paul Oskar Kristeller, Nicholas Steneck, and Charles Trinkaus for their continued encouragement and for their readings of all or parts of this book. I am particularly indebted to Professor Kristeller. These scholars have together saved me from many errors; the mistakes and shortcomings that remain are my own.

2. A NOTE ON THE TRANSLATION

The *De ludo globi* consists of two parts, or books. It survives in two manuscripts; *Cod. Cusan. 219* (138r-162v) and *Krakow 682* (3r-33r).[1] The earliest printed edition of Cusanus' works, the Strasbourg *incunabulum* of 1488, contains the *De ludo globi*, relying upon the Cues manuscript for its text.[2] In 1514, Jacques Lefèvre D'Étaples published an edition of Cusanus' *Opera Omnia* in Paris. Lefèvre D'Étaples' text of the *De ludo globi* follows the Strasbourg *incunabulum* with, however, some variations in style, some corrections of printing errors in the *incunabulum*, some new errors of its own and, significantly, the addition of a number of illustrations of the *ludus globi*. Neither of the two surviving manuscripts nor the Strasbourg *incunabulum* had contained any illustrations. In the 1514 edition, Lefèvre D'Étaples also added two poems in praise of the *ludus globi*—one at the conclusion of each of the work's two parts. These poems are not considered to be by Cusanus himself, but rather were added later by a friend or admirer. There also exists a 1565 edition of Cusanus' *Opera Omnia*, produced in Basel. This is essentially a reprint of the Paris 1514 edition and contains the text of the *De ludo globi*, but with illustrations that differ somewhat from those that accompany Lefèvre D'Étaples' edition. In fact, the Basel illustrations seem to involve a game that differs from the one that Cusanus describes and may have been a later invention. The modern edition of Cusanus' *Opera Omnia*, appearing seriatim under the auspices of the Heidelberg Academy of Sciences, has not yet to my knowledge produced its text of the *De ludo globi*. However, the text of the *De ludo globi* in Leo Gabriel's fairly recent *Nikolaus von Kues: Philosophisch-Theologische Schriften* follows the Cues and Krakow manuscripts, rather than any of the subsequent printed editions.[3]

Following the request of the editors of the Janus Series, I have based this translation on the text of the *De ludo globi* which appears in the Paris, 1514 edition of Cusanus' *Opera Omnia*. The Latin text and English translation appear on opposite pages. I have also consulted the Latin text established in the Leo Gabriel edition, which contains variations from the Paris, 1514 edition. The variants between the Paris, 1514 edition and the Leo Gabriel edition are listed in an appendix to the translation. When I follow Gabriel rather than Lefèvre D'Étaples, I point it out in the notes to the translation.

In making this translation, I have tried to render Cusanus' Latin as closely and literally as possible. I have striven for clarity and consistency, but have also wanted to respect the deliberateness of Cusanus' ambiguities. There are general and specific problems involved in the translation of Cusanus' Latin. Generally, he employs a vocabulary and ideas that were alive and vibrant for him but were difficult for even his contemporaries and are in many ways obscure to us. He was part of an intellectual and spiritual world that we no longer easily recognize, though we remain its heirs. More specifically, it is often difficult to render the words and phrases that Cusanus coins into English. And it is also true that Cusanus intends that the same word have different meanings or at least different connotations at different points in his argument. Indeed, the richness and the layered quality of his thought depend upon such intentional ambiguities. But this is not an excuse for a paraphrastic translation and I have striven to avoid one. Where substantive questions of meaning arise, I discuss them in the notes. There are places in the translation where I use English words or phrases that have no exact correspondents in the Latin text. This occurs principally where I have replaced pronouns that Cusanus uses with their antecedent nouns in order to trace his meaning more clearly. But there are also difficult passages where some interpolation seemed necessary. I have put such words and phrases in brackets in order to alert the reader.

My translation of the Latin word *globus* deserves some preliminary explanation. I have used two different English words—*ball* and *sphere*—to distinguish what seemed to me to be two essentially different, though closely related, contexts. Where Cusanus speaks of the game that he and his students are playing I translate *globus* as *ball*. But, as the introduction to the *De ludo globi* shows, the projectile with which the *ludus globi* is played is not really round but is rather a kind of scooped-out sphere. Hence the use of the word *ball* to refer to this object is perhaps slightly misleading. On the other hand, alternatives such as *globe* or *spheroid* seemed too awkward. There really is no single satisfactory English word; the reader needs always to bear in mind the description of this curious projectile that Cusanus provides at the onset of the *De ludo globi*. Where Cusanus speaks of the *ludus globi* in a symbolic sense, I translate *globus* as *sphere* which I believe conveys this second connotation most appropriately.

As the poems in praise of the *ludus globi* which occur at the end of each of the two books of the dialogue are generally considered to be spurious, I have not translated them.

NOTES

1. For much of the information contained in this paragraph I rely upon Gerda von Bredow's *Vom Globusspiel (De ludo globi), Schriften des Nikolaus von Kues*, ed. Ernst Hoffmann, Vol. 13, Hamburg: Felix Meiner, 1952, p. 123.

2. There is a modern edition of the Strasbourg *incunabulum*: Paul Wilpert ed., *Nikolaus von Kues Werke, Quellen und Studien zur Geschichte der Philosophie*, Vol. V, Berlin: Walter De Gruyter & Co., 1967.

3. See Leo Gabriel, editor, *Nikolaus von Kues: Philosophisch-Theologische Schriften*, Vol. I, Vienna: Herder & Co., 1964, p. xxvi sqq. The *De ludo globi* text appears in Vol. III, pp. 221-355 of this edition, published in 1967.

3. INTRODUCTION

1.

The *De ludo globi* and the Problem of Cusanus' Late Thought

During the last several years of his life Nicolaus Cusanus (1401-1464) wrote a cluster of works which he intended to be taken as cumulative statements of his lifetime of speculation. These include the *De possest* (1460), *De non-aliud* (1461-62), *De venatione sapientiae*, *De ludo globi*, *Compendium* (all written in 1462-63), and the *De apice theoriae*, composed shortly before Cusanus' death in August of 1464. In each of these works, Cusanus, sensing that the end of his life approaches, strives to summarize or epitomize his thoughts. For example, in the *De venatione sapientiae*, he says:

> I have resolved to leave for posterity notes summarizing those hunts for knowledge that I have always mentally intuited to be truer, even in my old age. I don't know whether a longer and better time for contemplation will be granted me; indeed, I have already passed through my sixty-first year.[1]

Curiously, these late works have been little studied. Cusanus scholars have paid a great deal of attention to such earlier admittedly key works as the *De docta ignorantia* (1440), the dialogues of the *Idiota* (1450), and the *De visione dei* (1453). Other major pieces (the *De coniecturis* comes first to mind) are, relatively speaking, untouched. There have been few attempts to study the problem of development in his thought and through this, to assess him comprehensively as a thinker.

On the other hand various important thematic studies have been made. These are usually focused upon the more formal aspects of Cusanus' thought, such as his trinitarianism and his Christology. In addition, quite a number of detailed source studies have appeared, establishing Cusanus' contacts with certain individual thinkers and schools of thought. Though these important contributions add to the minute understanding of Cusanus' sources, they also in a sense further fragment the effort to grasp his more general historical significance as a thinker. There has been no attempt to place Cusanus within the larger context of late medieval and Renaissance intellectual and religious history since Ernst Cassirer's fascinating but dated interpretation, *Individuum und Kosmos in der Philosophie der Renaissance* (1927).[2] The following essay seeks both to illustrate aspects of development in Cusanus' thinking and to address the more general problem of Cusanus' historical significance, though it necessarily does these things in only a preliminary way.

If we take Cusanus himself as our guide we quickly see that he views his own thought as developing through his life-long contemplation of certain basic problems. To his mind the private, individual development of his own thought occurred within the larger context of previous and contemporary intellectual and spiritual histories and he is always concerned to relate his own thought to these traditions. These basic tendencies in his thought are especially apparent in the late works.

In these works, Cusanus repeatedly emphasizes the importance of the ordinary individual's search for truth. Philosophizing and theologizing are not the only means to be used, nor are they to be confined to the formally trained academics, as he first makes clear in the dialogues of the *Idiota*. All men innately desire to know the truth and search for it through the whole range of human activities and creations. In fact, the proper fulfillment of humanity demands this search for truth. But at the same time that Cusanus probes the singularity of the individual hunt, he stresses that men must establish their own personal truths in relation to commonly held traditions and cultural experiences.

The historical development of ideas preoccupies Cusanus in such late works as the *De non-aliud* and *De venatione sapientiae*. In the *De non-aliud*, for example, he dialectically explores certain aspects of the Platonic tradition in a dialogue between himself and several friends, each an expert on the thought of a specific Platonist. And in his letters to the young monk Nicolaus Albergati, written during this same period, Cusanus engages in a poignant contemplation of his own mind and spirit. He clearly conceives of both common traditions and individual minds as undergoing continual change and development, and as constantly interacting with one another.

He himself is stimulated by the realization of the imminence of his own death to explore once again the basic problems with which he has been concerned throughout his life. He also feels that he has made some significant advances in his thinking towards the end of his life and he wants to record these while he is still able. Each of the works mentioned at the beginning of this essay is then an important facet in the prism of Cusanus' late thought. As a group these works provide an important key to the overall understanding of Cusanus' thought. They are also essential to the placement of Cusanus within the larger context of late medieval/Renaissance intellectual and religious history and to the assessment of his historical significance as a speculative thinker. Among them, it is perhaps the *De ludo globi* that shines forth most brightly and with the greatest complexity.

2.

Anticipations of the *De ludo globi* in Cusanus' Earlier Works

Cusanus himself tells us that the early turning point in his speculations occurred as the result of a vision that he experienced in 1438 while at sea returning from a voyage to Constantinople. In that vision the transcendent principle of "learned ignorance" (*docta ignorantia*) was revealed to him by God—"The Father of Lights."[3] In grasping the principle of "learned ignorance" Cusanus was convinced that he had found that which he had long sought unsuccessfully through various academic *viae*. He believed that his vision of "learned ignorance" was not simply a private experience but that it could provide the basis for a more common solution to the intellectual and spiritual problems that confounded his contemporaries as well as himself. In the several years following the vision, he composed two seminal works devoted to the explication of "learned ignorance." These were the *De docta ignorantia* of 1440 and the *De coniecturis* completed after the *De docta ignorantia*, sometime before 1443.

For Cusanus the essential tension lay in the fact that while man's natural desire to know was the proper end of his earthly existence, he was incapable of knowing the external world—"the precision of combinations in material things"—directly. Beyond this, man could never hope to know his creator—God—directly, since, according to Cusanus, "there is no proportion between the finite and infinite." (*infiniti ad finitum proportionem non esse*). Given the finite and contingent nature of his mind and his disjunction from God and creation, man's proper goal then must be the knowledge of his own ignorance:

> ...since the desire [to know] within us is not in vain, we desire to know that we are ignorant. If we shall fully attain this, then we shall attain learned ignorance. For nothing more perfect will happen even to the man most devoted to learning than to be found most learned in that ignorance itself that is peculiar to him; and he will become more learned to the extent that he knows his own ignorance.[4]

This is the principle of *docta ignorantia*.

Cusanus' principle of *docta ignorantia* leads him to reject the scholastic *viae* of his contemporaries. In the *Apologia doctae ignorantiae* of 1448, Cusanus defends the *De docta ignorantia* against the strong critique of the Heidelberg realist, Johannes Wenck. Wenck's attack, the *De ignota litteratura*, and Cusanus' *Apologia* together supply something of a contemporary context for the *De docta ignorantia*.[5]

In the *Apologia*, Cusanus severely criticizes his contemporaries for their overreliance on what he calls the "properties of words." Words are finally the tools of reason and they must ultimately be transcended by the intellect, which alone can bring man closer to the "vision" of God:

> Mystical theology leads to solitude and silence, where there is the vision of the invisible God that is ceded to us. Knowledge, however, which lies in agitations leading to contention, is that which desires the victory of words and is inflated. It is far from that which hastens us to God Who is our peace.[6]

Cusanus advises Wenck that if he wishes "to be transferred from blindness to light, he must read with his intellect" the *Mystical Theology* of pseudo-Dionysius the Areopagite and various commentaries on it.[7]

Throughout both the *De docta ignorantia* and the *Apologia* Cusanus makes his allegiances clear. He dismisses the possibilities provided by logic and discursive reasoning in the hunt for knowledge, for "vision." Men who use logic and "all philosophical inquisition" are like hunting dogs who follow their noses about, running back and forth in search of their prey:

> ...logic and all philosophical inquiry does not yet arrive at vision. Hence, just as a hunting dog uses the 'discourse' native to him in following footprints through sensible experience, in order that finally in this way (*via*) he may reach what he seeks, ...so man uses logic.[8]

Such men will always be confined by the contraries, the oppositions that govern reason:

> Reasoning seeks and runs about through discourse. Discourse is necessarily bound by the limits of from what and to which, and those things which are opposites to each other, we call contradictory.[9]

For Cusanus, the truer forms of speculation begin at exactly the point where reason, upon which the scholastic *viae* are based, reaches its limitations.

It is the intellect, the seat of *docta ignorantia*, that leads man to "vision":

> ...learned ignorance raises a person to vision as does a high tower. When placed there, he sees that which a person who roams through a field seeks vestigially through various foragings; and he perceives the extent to which the seeker approaches and distances himself from that which he seeks. Learned ignorance, existing from the high region of the intellect, judges discursive reasoning in this way.[10]

Through the power of intellectual "vision" man is able to transcend the limited and conflicting perspectives proffered by reason. This power of intellectual "vision" rests upon the conviction which Cusanus believes has always been shared by the wisest of men, that "the visible universe is a reflection of the invisible one" and that all things "have some kind of relationship to one another, however occult and incomprehensible it seems to us." But no matter how accurate and apt man's speculations might seem, they could always be infinitely more accurate and apt because "there is no proportion between the finite and the infinite."[11]

Cusanus' recognition of the disjunction between the finite, visible world and the infinite, invisible one leads him to the realization that the symbols that man uses in his speculations concerning the latter of these two worlds are necessarily disproportionate ones. These symbols are, in a word, *metaphors* – they designate unknown and hidden aspects of the infinite, invisible world but they may very possibly in no way resemble them. In any case, man has no way of judging the certainty of his metaphors. To a very great extent, this is not crucial anyway, for the speculative thinker chooses his metaphors precisely for their paradoxical and enigmatic power. This process is antithetical to that of the reason, which "runs from what to which."

In his emphasis upon the hidden nature of the divine and belief that divinity can only be discussed through riddles and paradoxes—disproportionate metaphors—Cusanus can be associated with the negative theology of Neoplatonists such as Proclus and Pseudo-Dionysius the Areopagite, both of whom influenced him significantly. Proclus, for example, stated in his commentary on Plato's *Republic* that:

> Symbols are representations of those things of which they are symbols. For that which is the contrary of something else cannot be a representation of that thing, such as the ugly of the beautiful or that which is contrary to nature of that which is natural. For symbolic wisdom hints at the nature of reality through the medium of elements totally contrary in their nature.[12]

And Pseudo-Dionysius the Areopagite observed in the *Celestial Hierarchy* that the best way to speculate concerning the invisible world of divinity was through "dissimilar signs" or "sacred fictions."[13] However, in the *Apologia*, Cusanus, on the basis of his principle of 'learned ignorance,' explicitly went beyond Dionysius in emphasizing the radical discontinuity between human speculations concerning the divine and the divinity itself that these speculations designate:

> For all likenesses that the holy men, *even the most divine Dionysius*, posit, are wholly disproportionate and useless rather than useful to all those lacking learned ignorance—that is, the knowledge of this; *that they [the likenesses] are wholly disproportionate.*[14] (my emphases) .

As Part 3 of this Introduction will demonstrate, the *De ludo globi* is an especially rich example of Cusanus' creative use of metaphor to discuss humanity and divinity, an approach based upon his own brand of negative theology, first elaborated in the 1440s.

According to Cusanus, man could do no better than to employ symbols derived from "most firm" and "most certain" mathematics in his search for the divine. Here Cusanus consciously links himself with the Pythagorean and Platonic traditions in his conviction of the "incorruptible certitude" of mathematics. Pythagoras himself, whom Cusanus calls the first true philosopher, Boethius, "the most learned of the Romans," Plato and the Platonists, Augustine, and even Aristotle, shared the belief that divinity is most effectively pursued through the symbolic power of number:

> Here we walk the road of the ancients, as we concur with them in saying that since it appears to us that there is no other way of approaching divine things except through symbols, then we can more fittingly use mathematical signs because of their incorruptible certitude.[15]

Cusanus maintained his belief in the special symbolic powers of mathematics throughout his life. The philosophical and theological arguments of such late works as the *De ludo globi* and the *De apice theoriae* are set forth through various numerical and geometrical metaphors.

It is in the *De docta ignorantia* that Cusanus first introduces some of the seminal metaphors of this type. These are metaphors that he will consistently return to and expand in subsequent writings. A particularly compelling one occurs in the first book of the *De docta ignorantia*, where Cusanus calls God, as had the pseudo-Hermetic *Book of the XXIV Philosophers* and Meister Eckhart before him, an infinite sphere whose center is everywhere and nowhere, a sphere whose center is identical with its circumference.[16] In the second book of the *De docta ignorantia*, he extrapolates from this metaphor of Book I that the *universe* too is spherical (but not a perfect sphere) and it too has a center that is everywhere and nowhere.[17] These discussions of sphericity in the *De docta ignorantia* prefigure the later, more complex ones of the *De ludo globi*. In that work Cusanus sees God, the universe, *and man* all as spheres of a certain sort and traces out their interrelationships through a meditation on the shapes and movements of circles and globes.

Such metaphors, apt though they may be, do not however provide man with certain knowledge of either God or his creation. In the first book of the *De docta ignorantia*, Cusanus, after having posited that God is an infinite circle, argues that man's attempts to know God are, in effect, always polygonal. Though man may approach knowledge of God more closely through symbolic thought, he will never know him precisely—just as no matter to what extent the sides of a polygon are multiplied, it will never coincide with the circumference of a circle. Perspective—the angle of perception—the "from what to which" always constricts man.[18]

Man is likewise incapable of precisely understanding the sphere of the universe. He always remains the prisoner of his location in time and space. This location fixes him at a point that he easily deceives himself into thinking is stationary and, moreover, the *center* of the universe. Again in the *De docta ignorantia*, Cusanus explains:

> We do not apprehend motion unless through some comparison with a fixed point. For if someone in a boat in the middle of the water ignored the flow of the water and didn't see the shores, how would he understand that the boat was moving? And on account of this, it would always appear to each person, whether he was on earth or on the sun or another star, that he himself would be in the center—as if it were immobile—and that everything else was moving. He certainly would always place the poles in relationship to himself and other [beings] existing on the sun, on [other parts of] the earth, on the moon and on Mars would place the poles in relationship to themselves.[19]

It is on the basis of his conviction of the absolute relativity of the human terrestrial situation that Cusanus constructs his conception of the universe as infinite and in perpetual motion. His infinite, centerless, whirling universe seems far from the elementally stratified, earth (and man) centered universe usually associated with medieval Christian Aristotelianism:

> Therefore the earth, which cannot be the center [of the universe], cannot be lacking in all motion. For actually it is necessary that it be moved in such a way that it could be moved infinitely less. Therefore just as the earth is not the center of the universe, so the sphere of the fixed stars is not its circumference, although in actually comparing the earth to the heavens, the earth itself seems to be closer to the center and the heavens to the circumference. Therefore the earth is not the center of the eighth or of any other sphere, nor does the appearance of the six signs of the zodiac above the horizon lead to the conclusion that the earth is in the center of the eighth sphere.[20]

The two passages quoted above and others in the second book of the *De docta ignorantia* are well-known and have long struck scholars. These apparently singular statements regarding the infinity and constant movement of the universe, coupled with a skeptical treatment of what is regarded as the commonly held medieval belief that the earth is located at the center of the universe, have given rise to the debate regarding Cusanus' place in the "scientific revolution," particularly his relation to Copernicus. This debate has tended to deflect scholarly attention from another very real and important historical problem; that of placing Cusanus within the context of late medieval and Renaissance cosmology.

For example, Cusanus' application of Hermetic dictums drawn from the *Book of the XXIV Philosophers* to cosmological speculation is not by any means unique. As Edward Grant has shown, at least one influential fourteenth-century thinker, Thomas Bradwardine (c. 1290-1349), used propositions drawn from the *Book of the XXIV Philosophers* to support his argument for what Grant calls God's "infinite ubiquity." In his *De causa Dei*, in the course of discussing the problem of the possible existence of an infinite extracosmic void, Bradwardine advanced the argument that God existed everywhere within and without the cosmos:

> For He is infinitely extended without extension and dimension. For truly, the whole of an infinite magnitude and imaginary extension, and

> any part of it, coexist fully and simultaneously, for which reason He can be called immense, since He is unmeasured; nor is He measurable by any measure; and He is unlimited because nothing surrounds Him fully as a limit; nor, indeed, can He be limited by anything, but rather He limits, contains and surrounds all things.[21]

In support of his argument Bradwardine cited three propositions from the *Book of the XXIV Philosophers*, listing first the dictum also used by Cusanus that, "God is an infinite sphere whose center is everywhere and circumference nowhere." Cusanus owned an abbreviated version of Bradwardine's *De causa Dei* and in a note indicates that he was aware of its importance, especially for the "English."

I am not here making an argument for a direct link between Bradwardine and Cusanus but would suggest that both are part of the larger fabric of late medieval/Renaissance cosmological and theological speculation. One of the important strands in this fabric is the influence that the Hermetic *corpus* had upon medieval cosmological speculation; it has not been systematically analysed. But it seems that there is a certain pattern in the use to which these Hermetic and pseudo-Hermetic texts were put.

Bradwardine and Cusanus are both pursuing lines of thought that are in a certain sense anti-Aristotelian. Bradwardine wrote in the wake of the 1277 Condemnation of the Parisian Aristotelians by the Bishop of Paris and Cusanus, as we have seen, conceived of the *De docta ignorantia* as an alternative to the "Aristotelian sects that now prevail." Both thinkers are concerned in a general sense to defend God's absolute freedom and power to act in whatever way he wishes against the restrictions and limitations that they feel that contemporary Aristotelians have placed upon this divine power and freedom. More specifically, both Bradwardine and Cusanus use the same Hermetic dictum to underline divine power and freedom and to contest the notion of a finite, deterministic Aristotelian universe. As Grant argues in his assessment of Bradwardine and his contemporaries,

> The outcome was fourteenth-century nominalism and the concept of a God free to act independently of and even contrarily to Aristotelian metaphysics and natural philosophy.[22]

Though Cusanus adapts the pseudo-Hermetic metaphor of God as an infinite sphere in order to assure divine freedom and omnipotence as Bradwardine did, he did not enter into disputes involving the physics of space and void as Bradwardine and others also did. For example, Cusanus was not apparently concerned with the problem of an extra-cosmic void; for him the cosmos was an infinite continuum, mathematically proportioned and arranged. Cusanus' lack of concern with the problem of an extra-cosmic void links him with figures such as Bruno and Pascal and distinguishes him from others such as Bradwardine and Nicole Oresme, as Grant points out.

Cusanus' early explorations of the power of metaphor led him not only to make new speculations about the structure and movements of the universe but also to think differently about the nature of human thought and ultimately to develop a novel conception of man—one which reconciles a disjunctive metaphysic to a positive anthropology. It is in the very important companion piece to the *De docta ignorantia*, the *De coniecturis*, that Cusanus first sets forth the basis for a positive anthropology. Beginning with the disjunction that prevails between the finite and the infinite, he posits that any human assertion of the truth is therefore necessarily a *conjecture*:

> In the previous books of learned ignorance you [his friend Cardinal Cesarini] have understood that precise truth is unattainable much more deeply and clearly than I myself have done by my own efforts. The consequence is that any human positive assertion of the truth is conjecture, for the increase of the attaining of truth is inexhaustible. Since our science is in no way proportionate to this maximum knowledge itself which is humanly unattainable, the uncertain fall of our infirm apprehension from the purity of truth makes our positings conjectures of truth. Therefore, the

> unattainable unity of truth is known by conjectural otherness and the conjecture itself of otherness in the most simple unity of truth.[23]

This statement might lead one to think that human speculations are empty and pointless—that each of of us is a John the Baptist, "the voice of one crying in the wilderness." But Cusanus is here setting us up for what is, in effect, a "quantum leap" in his thought. In a few terse lines he projects a whole new basis for human speculation:

> Conjectures ought to come forth from our mind as the real world comes forth from the divine and infinite reason. When indeed the human mind, the high likeness of God, participates as it is able in the fecundity of the creative nature, it puts forth from itself as the image of the omnipotent form rational entities in the likeness of real beings. Thus, the human mind is the form of the conjectural world just as the divine mind is that of the real world. And, therefore, just as the absolute divine being is all that is in everything that is, so the unity of the human mind is the being of its conjectures.[24]

Cusanus has adopted as the basis of his anthropology the Biblical passage of *Genesis I:26*: "And God said, Let us make man in our image, after our likeness." This is the same passage that lay at the heart of many contemporary Italian humanists' speculations concerning humanity and divinity.[25]

Here in the *De coniecturis* Cusanus explicates the passage along traditional Platonist lines, calling the human mind the "form" of the conjectural world and the divine mind the "form" of the "real" world. Yet his emphasis upon the power and fecundity of both divine and human creativity is an essentially Christian one that goes beyond anything that can be found in Plato who regarded painting or the crafts as vicarious and obfuscated processes. At the beginning of the *De coniecturis*, Cusanus fundamentally transforms the dichotomies and tensions that dominate the *De docta ignorantia*. Though man still remains distanced from God and nature, his mind is now his link to his creator and his speculations are no longer the products of his disjunctive cosmic status. Man's mind, self-generating, and self-perpetuating in likeness of the divine mind, is now the source of his dignity and his god-like nature:

> Man therefore is God, but not absolutely, since he is man. Hence he is a human God. Man is also the world, but he is not everything by contraction, since he is man. Man is therefore a microcosm, or, in truth, a human world. Thus, the region of humanity itself encloses God and the universal region in its human power. Thus man is able to be a human god, and as god, he is able to be a human angel, a human beast, a human lion or bear, or anything else. Indeed, everything exists within the potentiality of humanity according to its mode.[26]

It was over forty years later (probably in 1486) that Giovanni Pico della Mirandola wrote his much more famous *Oration* (which only later came to be known as the *Oration on The Dignity of Man*). In that work Pico asserted that man alone of all creatures was created "to have that which he chooses and to be that which he will." In a manner similar, but not identical to that of Cusanus, Pico stressed that man was not bound by his created nature as were all the animals but could determine his own nature. God expressly told Adam this when He created him:

> Thou, like a judge appointed for being honorable, art the molder and maker of thyself; thou mayest sculpt thyself into whatever shape thou dost prefer. Thou canst grow downward into the lower natures which are brutes. Thou canst again grow upward from thy soul's reason into the higher natures which are divine.[27]

Though Cusanus too stresses man's special capacity to become that which he will, he directly links that capacity to man's being created in the divine image and likeness. In this, Cusanus can be most closely associated with a number of the early humanist treatises on man such as Antonio da Barga's *De dignitate hominis et excellentia humane vite* and Bartolomeo Facio's *De excellentia hominis* (both written in the 1440s), as well as Gianozzo Manetti's well known *De dignitate et excellentia hominis* (written in 1452 or 1453). Certainly, sections of the *De coniecturis* must be considered as important early examples of the developing genre of Renaissance discussions of the dignity of man.[28]

In the *De coniecturis* Cusanus goes on to assert that man, the "human god," creates and perpetuates his own microcosmic world—the world of culture and history:

> Therefore no other end exists for the active creativity of humanity than humanity. For it does not proceed beyond itself when it creates, but when it unfolds its virtue, it reaches toward itself alone. Nor does it bring about anything new, but discovers that everything that it creates through its unfolding already existed within itself, for we said that all things existed in it in a human way. Just as the power of humanity is powerful for humanly progressing into all things, so the universe progresses into [humanity]. Nor is that admirable virtue of proceeding to the illumination of all things anything other than to enfold the universe in itself humanly.[29]

It is the autonomous and inventive power of the human mind, acting in likeness of the divine mind, that Cusanus stresses in this passage. Man unfolds the power of his mind in various ways, one of which is in his creation of apt metaphors through which he explores his own sense of his relationship to God and the universe. As Cusanus' thought grows, his emphasis upon the creative power of the mind increases. His strongest statements regarding human creativity appear in his late works, a number of which are centered around the idea that thinking and acting are forms of play—serious games. And it is in the *De ludo globi* that Cusanus presents man as engaged in cosmic play, the inventor of games in which God and the universe are contained.

Although Cusanus believes that this creative activity of mind is shared by all men, he does not on that account believe that it is uniform. Man's inventions, his religions, his regimes, are subject to the same endless variations and movements that prevail in the celestial movements of the universe, and in the phenomena of nature:

> Observe also, that although any religion or regime in any nation of this world may appear to be stable, it is not precisely so. The Rhine River appears to flow steadily for a long time, but it never remains in the same state. Now it is more turbulent, now clearer, now rising and now receding.[30]

Cusanus sees these variations as the product of a kind of dialectic between unity and multiplicity, between the singularity and identity of the one and the infinity of othernesses. This dialectic has an ontological aspect; God is the unity from which the multiplicity, the *alteritas* of creation flows. It has also an epistemological and a psychic aspect; Man is the intellectual unity from which all human actions and inventions flow. The divine and human aspects of this dialectic preoccupy Cusanus from the *De coniecturis* on.

It is not coincidental, given his preoccupation with the dialectical and contrapuntal nature of thought and being, that Cusanus turns increasingly to the dialogue form. Beginning with the dialogues of the *Idiota* of 1450, Cusanus comes to use the dialogue almost exclusively. His preference for this form was shared by many fifteenth century humanists and has its historical antecedents most obviously in the works of Plato, whose works enjoyed their own "renaissance" during Cusanus' lifetime. Cusanus and his humanist contemporaries turned to the dialogue not simply out of admiration for Plato, or even as an alternative to the architectonic scholastic *summae*, but because they found it to be the most suitable form for dynamically confronting and testing the ideas and positions that they sought to integrate. The dialogue was the ideal vehicle for the expression of the personal and intrapersonal nature of thought and for displaying its spontaneous and improvisational power.[31]

In Cusanus' dialogues of the *Idiota*, the emphasis upon exactly this spontaneous and improvisational power of thought leads to his recognition and elaboration of a new ideal of lay wisdom, personified in the Idiot himself, who is not a professional thinker, neither a scholastic nor a humanist, but a craftsman. His world in not that of the academic disputation but rather the marketplace. In the dialogues the Idiot is interviewed first by an Orator and then a Philosopher, both initially sceptical of his claims to be able to instruct them on the problem of wisdom. But the Idiot shows them to be prisoners of their "book learning"; his authority is a different one. It is the wisdom that cries out in the streets of the marketplace:

> This is what I have said, that is, that you are led and deceived by authority. Somebody writes something, you believe him. Yet I say to you that wisdom cries out in the streets, and her cry is that she dwells in the highest.[32]

All the activities of the marketplace, the weighing and sorting of goods, the commercial exchanges, the creations of craftsmen, are manifestations of human wisdom. This human wisdom is the image of divine wisdom, and so the very multiplicity of activities of the marketplace is an expression of the single root of infinite wisdom:

> The infinite identity itself cannot be received in another, since it is received in another otherwise. And since it cannot be received in another unless in otherness, therefore it is received in the best way that it can be. But infinity, which cannot be multiplied, is best unfolded by reception in a variety of things, *for great diversity best expresses nonmultiplicity.*[33] (my emphasis)

The products of the human mind's creative activity include not only conjectures, but also an infinity of objects such as spoons (which the Idiot makes) and other products of the craftsman's art. Such objects have no exemplar in nature:

> Outside of the exemplar in our mind, the spoon has no other exemplar. For although the sculptor or painter takes exemplars from the things that he wishes to represent, I however do not. I bring forth spoons and bowls from wood and jars from mud. Indeed, in doing this, I imitate the form of no natural thing. In fact such forms as spoons, bowls, and jars are made by human art alone. Hence my art is more of a perfection than an imitation of created forms, and in this it is more similar to the infinite art.[34]

The craftsman does not imitate nature but creates new objects through his mental artistry in likeness of the way God created the universe. The craftsman creates through a fusion of his will with the mental concept of what he wants to make and in this too he is godlike:

> For, in omnipotence, willing and executing coincide, as when a glass-blower makes glass. For he blows in a breath, in which is a word or concept, and power (*potentia*), which executes his will. Indeed, unless the power and concept of the glass-blower were in the breath which he emits, such a glass would not come into existence.[35]

In the *De ludo globi* Cusanus expands upon the creative process of the craftsman, first set forth in the dialogues of the *Idiota*. In the *De ludo globi*, as we shall see below, he builds his discussion of creativity around an analysis of how a turner forms a ball out of wood on a lathe.

In the dialogues of the *Idiota*, Cusanus underlines the communal as well as the individual aspect of human creativity. Man bonds himself with other men, he forms societies, in the creation and exchange of such things as glass, spoons, bowls, jars and textiles. Man creates these objects and he also determines or "legislates" their meaning and value. This emphasis upon the communality of human inventions and the "legislated" quality of man's thinking is characteristic of Cusanus' late works.

They all, in one way or another, approach the problem of culture and history, seen as men's individual and collective attempts to construct meaning in the face of divine ineffability. A key discussion of this "legislated" quality of human creativity occurs in the course of Cusanus' concluding remarks to the *De ludo globi*. There he engages in a discussion of value as a cultural phenomenon through an analysis of how man invents and establishes coinage systems as a means of exchange.

In the two great contemplative pieces of the 1450s, the *De visione Dei* and the *De beryllo*, Cusanus emphasizes that man's conscious, willful thought and action is the key to his spiritual identity, his striving for a "vision" of his creator, as well as to his communal identity. Man's relationship to his creator is not a fixed one (as Cusanus already recognized in the *De coniecturis*) but one which grows or declines according to the extent to which man efficaciously applies his powers of will and intellect to the search for his maker. In the *De visione Dei* he asserts that each man sees God only through the "eyes of the mind," themselves colored by his own individuality and experience:

> As the eye of the flesh, when looking through a red glass, judges that everything it sees is red or, if it is looking through a green glass, that everything is green, so does the eye of each mind, muffled up in contraction and affect, judge you who are the object of the mind, according to the nature of its contraction and affect.[36]

Or, as Cusanus puts it in the *De beryllo*:

> Hence he [man] measures his own intellect through the power of his works and from this he measures the divine intellect, just as truth is measured in an image. And this is enigmatic knowledge. Moreover, he has the most subtle vision, through which he sees that the enigma is the enigma of truth, so that he knows that this is the truth, which is not imaginable in any enigma.[37]

For Cusanus then, man is the beginning and the end, the alpha and the omega of all thought and action; he is the ultimate riddle or enigma.

Edgar Wind has best expressed this sense of human power and freedom which Cusanus shared with other figures of the fifteenth and sixteenth centuries:

> In his adventurous pursuit of self-transformation man explores the universe as if he were exploring himself. And the farther he carries these metamorphoses, the more he discovers that all the varied phases of his experience are translatable into each other: for they all reflect the ultimate One, of which they unfold particular aspects. If man did not sense the transcendent unity of the world, its inherent diversity would also escape him.[38]

All thinking and action is circular, arising from and turning back upon itself in a kind of perfect and perpetual motion. In this way a man creates thoughts, objects, integrations, moral and monetary systems which in their larger scan become cultures and histories. He grasps not only his own, human world but also God and His creation, the universe, only through himself, the image of God. These insights, I have suggested, Cusanus built up over a lifetime. It can be argued that they find their most cohesive and imaginative expression in the *De ludo globi*.

3.

Central Themes of the *De ludo globi*

In his late works, those composed between 1460 and 1464, Cusanus strove for new ways to pull together his thoughts on man, God, and the cosmos. As Part 2 of this Introduction has demonstrated, his thought consistently revolved around the disjunctive metaphysic set forth in the *De docta ignorantia* and his growing stress upon the creativity of man, acting in the image of God, apparent from the *De coniecturis* on. In his late works these reciprocal themes led him consciously to explore the idea that all thinking and acting is a kind of *game*. In the *De possest* of 1460, for example, Cusanus discusses the way in which the example of a boy spinning a top can be applied to the problem of understanding how, "Eternal [Being] is all things at once and how the whole of eternity is within the present moment–so that when we leap forth, having left this image behind, we may be elevated above all sensible things."[39] And in the *De venatione sapientiae*, written at the same time as the *De ludo globi*, Cusanus compares the hunt for knowledge to the hunt for game. Hunters range over the fields in search for their prey in much the same way as philosophers and theologians range through "topics" in their search for truth.[40] It is however, in the *De ludo globi* that Cusanus presents his most extensive treatment of the theme that the dynamics of inventing and playing a game illuminate and demonstrate the nature of man and his relation to God and the universe.

The *De ludo globi* is a two part dialogue. The first part consists of a conversation between Cusanus himself and a young admirer and aspiring philosopher, Johannes, Duke of Bavaria. And the second part is a conversation between Cusanus and Johannes' cousin, Albertus. The use of the dialogue form is characteristic of Cusanus from 1450 on as already indicated. But it is worth noting here that in his late works Cusanus abandons the archetypal figures of the dialogues of the *Idiota* and instead makes himself and actual friends the participants. This is true of the *De ludo globi*, the *De possest*, and the *De non-aliud*. The practice of the injecting oneself and ones' friends (or sometimes enemies) into the dialogue is of course typical of the humanists. It serves to highlight further the spontaneous, improvisational, and personal nature of discourse discussed earlier in Part 2. There can be no doubt that Cusanus and the humanists intended this.

These qualities of spontaneity and improvisation, not coincidentally, also lie at the heart of play. But men enjoy playing games not simply for the sport and relaxation involved. In the first part of the *De ludo globi*, Johannes observes, as he and Cusanus rest from the "newly invented" game that they have been playing, that games have a deeper signficance for men. Cusanus agrees, saying:

> In fact some branches of knowledge have their instruments and games; arithmetic has its number games, music its monochord–nor is the game of chess or checkers lacking in the mystery of moral things. Indeed I think that no honest game is entirely lacking in the capacity to instruct. I think that this delightful exercise with the ball represents a significant philosophy for us (translation, p. 55).

Cusanus' belief in the pedagogical power of game links him to such thinkers as Plato and Plotinus. Plato observed in the *Laws* (which Cusanus knew through George of Trebizond's translation) that boys become men through playing games:

> ...he who is to be good at anything as a man must practice that thing from early childhood in play as well as in earnest, with all the attendant circumstances of the action. Thus, if a boy is to be a good farmer, or again, a good builder, he should play, in the one case at building toy houses, in the other at farming, and both should be provided by their tutors with miniature tools on the pattern of real ones. In particular, all necessary preliminary instruction should be acquired in this way. Thus, the carpenter should be taught by his play to use the rule and plumb line, and the soldier to sit a horse, and the like. We should seek to use games as a means of directing children's tastes and inclinations toward the station they are themselves to fill when adult. So we may say, in fact, the sum and substance of education is the right training which effectually leads the soul of the child at play on to the love of the calling in which he will have to be perfect, after its kind, when he is a man.[41]

And Plotinus (whose works Cusanus did not know) saw play as central to man's striving for Vision, which he considered to be the true end of all human, indeed, of all existent, activity:

> Suppose we said, playing at first before we set out to be serious, that all things aspire to contemplation, and direct their gaze to this end—not only rational but irrational living things, and the power of growth in plants, and the earth which brings them forth—and that all attain to it as far as possible for them in their natural state, but different things contemplate and attain their end in different ways, some truly, and some only having an imitation and image of this true end—could anyone endure the oddity of this line of thought? Well, as this discussion has arisen among ourselves, there will be no risk in playing with our own ideas. Then are we now contemplating as we play? Yes, we and all who play are doing this, or at any rate this is what they aspire to as they play. And it is likely that, whether a child or a man is playing or being serious, one plays and the other is serious for the sake of contemplation, and every action is a serious effort towards contemplation, compulsory action drags contemplation more towards the outer world, and what we call voluntary, less, but all the same, voluntary action, too, springs from the desire of contemplation.[42]

Cusanus too sees play as a peculiarly human activity which can lead ultimately towards God. All games spring from man's intelligence,· a "power" unique to him and one that distinguishes him from the animals:

> ...for no beast produces a ball and directs it motion to an end. Therefore you see that these works of man originate from a power which surpasses that of the other animals of this world (translation, p. 57).

Cusanus', Johannes', and Albertus' explorations of the spiritual and intellectual applications of the *ludus globi* inevitably revolve around the problem of man, his solitary and communal activities, his place in the cosmos and his relation to this creator.

The *ludus globi* is played on nine concentric circles drawn upon the ground. The *globus* used is in fact not really a ball, but a kind of spheroid that is, Cusanus says, "somewhat concave in the middle." It would then look something like this:

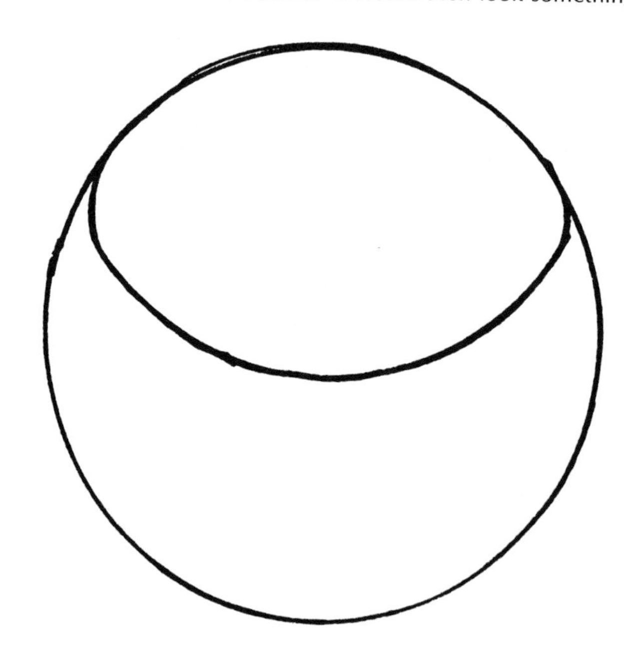

Because of its peculiar shape this spheroid does not roll the way a regular ball would, in a more or less straight line. Rather, it has what Cusanus calls a 'helical' (*elicus*), that is, a spiral or inwardly curving motion. The basic object of the game is to roll this spheroid in such a way that it enters the outermost of the nine concentric circles and travels around each of them, tracing out the circumferences of the progressively smaller circles as its impetus declines, finally coming to rest in their common center. Lefèvre D'Étaples diagrams the *ludus globi* in this way in his 1514 edition of Cusanus' *Opera Omnia*, Vol. I, *fol.* clii:

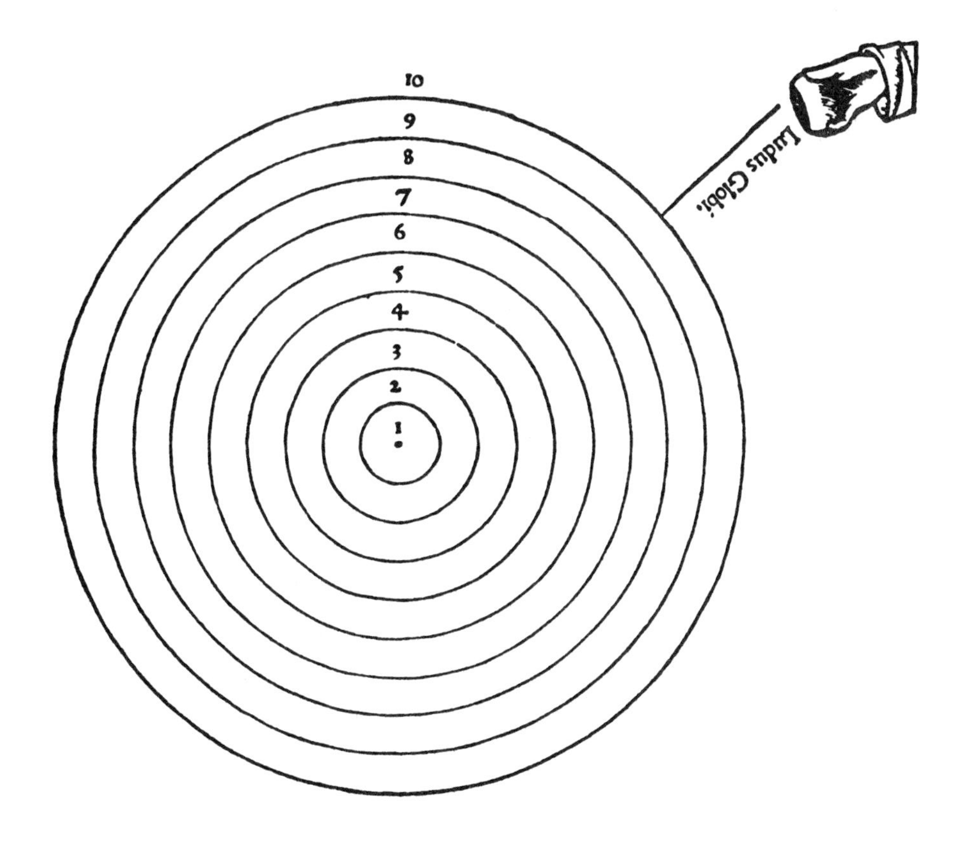

It is not clear whether Cusanus is here referring to an actual game. If he is, we do not know precisely what it was. The game he describes is somewhat akin to the European family of games that includes the Italian *bocce*, the French *pétanque*, and the English *bowls*. However, the first two games are played with round balls. The English *bowls* is played with a projectile made of wood "slightly oblate on one side and prolate on the other, so as to run with a bias."; this is not dissimilar to Cusanus' *globus*. On the other hand the game of *bowls* and the Italian *bocce* are both played on carefully manicured grounds and do not involve concentric circles. Cusanus' game is played on any available surface; this variation is part of the game itself. In this, the *ludus globi* is more like the French *pétanque*, which can be played anywhere. Cusanus' game does not precisely correspond to any known game then, but it does bear resemblances to these variations of a very old western European game. In fact it may be possible that Cusanus is not referring to an actual game, but rather that he is inventing a game for the purposes of his discussions with his two young friends. But it does seem likely that this game is derived from ones that were actually played in Cusanus' lifetime and still are today.[43]

Johannes contrasts the motion of the spheroid used in the *ludus globi* with the very straight line that an iron hoop would trace if it were rolled along a very flat, smooth surface such as a sheet of ice. Whereas the motion of the hoop would be a perfect, straight one, the movement of the *globus* in the game that they are playing is an imperfect, irregular, curved one. Cusanus also points out that the variation in the *ludus globi* stems not only from the peculiar shape of the *globus* itself but from other factors as well. First, the force with which the *globus* is thrown by each player enters in. A stronger throw (not necessarily a *desideratum* in this game) will result in a straighter trajectory, whereas a weaker one will produce a curved movement. When the *globus* is initially thrown, its impetus will be stronger and therefore straighter than it will be just before the *globus* comes to a halt (translation, p. 57).

The variability of the game is affected not only by the laws of motion but also by the endless differences among the abilities of the players themselves. Beginning in the *De docta ignorantia* Cusanus emphasized the endless variations among men; that no man could exactly imitate another in anything, no matter how long and hard he tried. Here in the *De ludo globi* he goes a step further and says that no man can ever precisely repeat his *own* actions, though he strives to play the game consistently and effectively:

> When someone throws the ball he does not hold it in his hand, release it, or place it on the ground in the same way twice, nor does he hurl it with equal power one time as he does another. It is not possible to do anything the same way twice . . . (translation, p. 57).

Finally, as Johannes observes, external factors, such as the condition of the ground or pavement upon which the game is played and the quality and condition of the *globus* itself, also contribute to the infinite variability that governs the game. Cusanus agrees, saying that all these factors must be taken into account "so that from them we may depart to the philosophical speculation that we propose to hunt. . . . For since art imitates nature we approach the powers of nature from these things which we find subtly in art" (translation, p. 57).

Using the "newly invented" game of the *ludus globi*, played with the spheroid created through the art of the turner as their central metaphor, Cusanus, Johannes, and Albertus proceed to discuss a number of interrelated themes. These include: the structure of the universe and the manner of its creation, the relationship of body and soul in man, man as microcosm, man as Christian *viator*, *Fortuna*, and, finally, the problem of value, which ties all the previous themes together. Cusanus', Johannes', and Albertus' conversations on these themes are not systematic or even logical, rather they skip from topic to topic, sometimes raising subjects, only to drop them almost immediately, sometimes later returning to them. There is moreover, a certain overlapping between the two parts of the dialogue. But this is all part of the game of thinking and it would be a mistake to try and "straighten it out." The challenge lies in the improvization; *Gyrans gyrando vadit spiritus*.

To begin, Cusanus argues that man can contemplate the universe and its origins through the *ludus globi*. The *globus* that man creates on the lathe is an imperfect, scooped-out, wooden spheroid. It is visible and material, with lateral spatial extension. In contrast to the man-made *globus*, the universe or world (*mundus*) possesses a kind of "ultimate spherical roundness." This roundness of the world has no spatial extension and so is invisible (translation, p. 59).

The true or ultimate roundness of the world is contained in a single "indivisible and unmultipliable point":

> Roundness cannot be composed out of points for since a point is indivisible and does not have quantity or parts or a front and back or other differences, it cannot be joined to another point. Therefore nothing is composed of points. For if you join a point to a point, the result is as if nothing is joined to nothing. Therefore the edge of the world is not composed of points, but its edge is roundness, which consists of one point (translation, p. 59).

The shapes, forms, and dimensions that man perceives in the world are all spatial extensions of this single point that is ultimate roundness:

> There is only one and the same point in a plurality of atoms, as there is only one whiteness in many white things. Hence a line is the evolution of a point, for a line's evolution is the unfolding of the point itself (translation, p. 59).

Cusanus' explanation leads Johannes to conclude that while he may see (and make) "round things," he can never see true roundness itself. This is indeed the point that Cusanus is making, for "nothing is seen except in matter. Moreover true roundness cannot exist in matter, but only the image of true roundness." Even the roundnesses that man perceives and shapes are not round but in fact are composed of lengths and widths:

> Although from the Platonic point of view you speak the truth, there is nevertheless a difference between roundness and other forms. If indeed it were possible for roundness to be in matter, it would nevertheless still not be visible. It is otherwise concerning the rest of the forms since they could be seen if they were in matter... But in roundness nothing is long or wide or straight. Roundness is a kind of circumference, a certain convexity led around from point to point whose top is everywhere. And its top is the atom, invisible because of its tinyness (translation, p. 59).

Cusanus here is referring to Plato's discussion of the being and knowledge of a circle in the *Seventh Letter*.

Cusanus was obviously fascinated by this passage. He included an important discussion of it in the *De beryllo*, where he used it as a basis for distinguishing his own theory of knowledge from that of Plato (and implicitly the Pythagoreans). Here in the *De ludo globi*, while he does not follow Plato's classification of levels of knowledge and being, he clearly follows Plato's implicit dichotomy between the "true" reality of the circle and the circle which is "drawn or turned on the lathe" and everywhere "touches the straight."[44]

The roundness of the world is therefore invisible; man sees only imperfect forms of roundness which are always subject to change and variation:

> Therefore the roundness that is attained by vision receives the greater and the lesser since one round thing is rounder than another. Invisible roundness is not of that nature, nor is it capable of being participated in through the body as is visible roundness. For that reason no body could be so round that it could not be rounder (translation, p. 61).

This argument of the *De ludo globi* clearly has its roots in the discussions of the universe found in Book II of the *De docta ignorantia*. These discussions were based upon the Hermetic dictum that "God is an infinite sphere whose center is everywhere, whose circumference is nowhere," and in fact Cusanus explicitly recalls Hermes' saying in support of his own discussion at this point.

And as he did in the *De docta ignorantia*, Cusanus here again emphasizes in the *De ludo globi* that although the roundness of the world would be "maximal" it is not however, absolute or true roundness:

> The round world is not that roundness itself than which no roundness can be greater, but that roundness than which nothing can be greater in act. Absolute roundness is not of the nature of the roundness of the world, but is its cause and exemplar, the absolute roundness of which the roundness of the world is the image (translation, p. 63).

Just as the world is not absolute roundness so it is not eternity itself though it is eternal. The world is not eternal in the sense that it has no beginning but because its duration "does not depend upon time":

> For if the motion of the heavens, and time, which is the measure of motion, were to cease, the world would not cease to exist. But if the world were to utterly cease, time would cease. Therefore it is more appropriate for the world to be called eternal than for time to be called eternal (translation, p. 63).

God is eternity; he is the truly infinite sphere whose center is everywhere and whose circumference is nowhere.

God creates freely and perfectly. So the world that he has created exists perfectly in the way that he intended it to be. However, God *could* have created another more (or less) perfect world than the one that he *actually* did had he so chosen. Cusanus here returns to an argument that he first presented in the *De docta ignorantia* and which must be read against the background of late scholastic discussions of the distinction between the *potentia absoluta* and the *potentia ordinata* of God. In the *De docta ignorantia* Cusanus distinguished between the absolute infinity (*infinitum absolutum*) that is God, and the privative or restricted infinity (*infinitum privatum*) that is the universe. Cusanus' *infinitum absolutum* parallels the late scholastic *potentia absoluta*; both designate the absolute unrestricted creative power of God. And Cusanus' *infinitum privatum* parallels the late scholastic *potentia ordinata*; both refer to God's selective or restricted use of his infinite power in order to create the universe in the way that he did. Both Cusanus and the late scholastics intend primarily to assure divine freedom and omnipotence in making these distinctions.

Here in the *De ludo globi*, Cusanus makes this same distinction in different terms; the world was created because of its *capacity to be made* (*posse fieri*), God on the other hand creates freely out of his *capacity to make* (*posse facere*):

> But this capacity to be made (*posse fieri*) that was made is not the absolute capacity to make (*posse facere*) of the omnipotent God itself. Although in God the capacity to be made and the capacity to make are the same thing, nevertheless something's capacity to be made is not the same thing as God's capacity to make. From this it appears that God created the world in the way that he wished to, which is truly why it is perfect because it is made according to the most free will of the best God (translation, p. 63).[45]

Cusanus first mentions the terms *posse facere* and *posse fieri* in the *Idiota de mente* but only fully develops them in late works such as the *De possest*, *De ludo globi* and, especially, the *De apice theoriae*. But the point that he wanted to make always remained the same. God could have chosen to create the universe differently than he did; that he created it in the mode that he did is proof of his transcendent freedom and omnipotence.

The world may be contemplated not only as an infinite sphere but also through the nine concentric circles upon which the *ludus globi* is played. Cusanus discusses this at some length with Albertus in the second part of the dialogue. The concentric circles of the *ludus globi* resemble standard medieval diagrams of the planetary spheres of the universe:

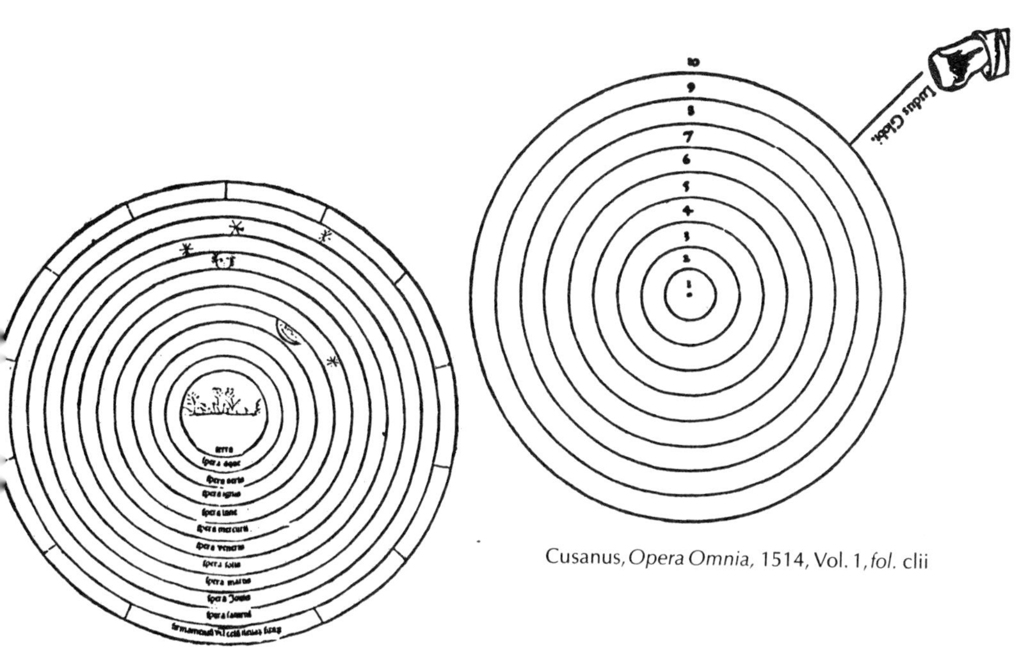

Cusanus, *Opera Omnia*, 1514, Vol. 1, *fol.* clii

S.K. Heninger, *The Cosmographical Glass*, p. 36
(reproduced by permission of The Huntington Library, San Marino, California)

But Cusanus does not interpret the concentricities of his *ludus globi* along traditional Aristotelian lines. He makes the *sun*, rather than the *earth*, the center of his universe. He does this as a result of a somewhat obscure integration of Dionysian angelic theophanies with his own cosmic numerology. In order to understand what he is saying here in the *De ludo globi*, it is necessary to refer back to the *De coniecturis*. There Cusanus argued that there is a certain natural "flux" of number which he diagrammed in this way:

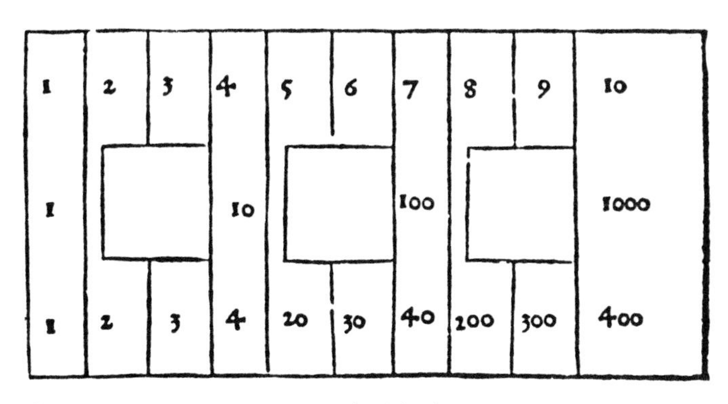

Cusanus, *Opera Omnia*, 1514, Vol. I *fol.* xliiv

The sum of one, two, three, four, is ten. Ten is a number with special status for Cusanus as it was for the Pythagoreans, representing what he calls "the numerical worth of simple unity." Centenary unity, the square of ten, is the sum of ten, twenty, thirty, and forty. Fourfold unity, the cube of ten, is the sum of one hundred, two hundred, three hundred and four hundred. From this Cusanus concludes that unity has four components. Cusanus then posits that each of these four numerical unities has an ontological correspondent. The ultimate unity, the unique exemplar is, of course, God. The first of the four subsumed unities is the angelic, the second the intelligences, the third order is rational and the fourth the sensible.[46] In the *De coniecturis*, Cusanus represents his ontology in this figure:

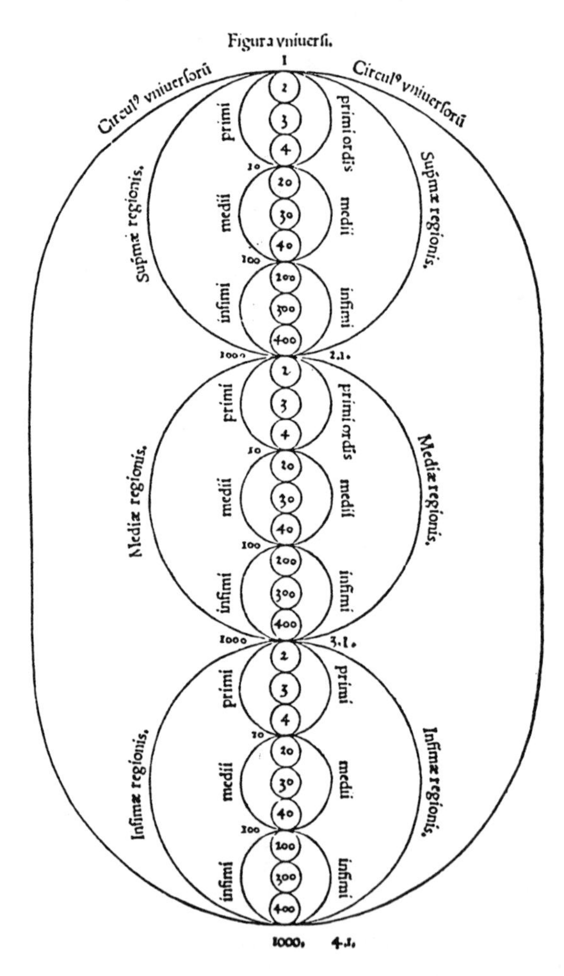

Cusanus, *Opera Omnia*, 1514 Vol. I, *fol.* xlix^{v}

In the *De ludo globi* Cusanus refers to this diagram to explain how unity unfolds into otherness in a fourfold progression. Echoing Dionysius the Areopagite, Cusanus says that God represents the all inclusive outermost circle, the three enclosed circles represent, respectively, the angels, the intelligencies, and the rational spirits. These unfold into nine orders (translation, p. 97).[47]

These same relationships are also represented in the concentric circles of the *ludus globi*. What Cusanus is doing here although it is not very explicit, is recalling the complicated diagrams of the *De coniecturis* and substituting for them the simpler pattern of the *ludus globi*. Both designate the same ontological and epistemological relationships but the concentric circles of the *ludus globi* now seem more appropriate, just as it now seems more appropriate to speak of God in terms of his *posse facere*.

The 'kingdom of life' can therefore be depicted through the concentricities of the *ludus globi*. But it is a kind of inversion of the Aristotelian elemental universe. Whereas the earth is the center of Aristotle's universe with the bands of water, air, and fire encircling it, Cusanus' 'kingdom' has the sun as its center with three circles of fire, three of air, and finally the three outermost circles of water descending into 'terrestrial blackness':

> And so there are ten diverse classes of distinction—namely the divine which is imagined in the center and is the cause of all things and the other nine in the nine choruses of angels. And there are no more in either number or in distinction. Hence it is evident why I have imagined the kingdom of life in this way and have conformed the center to the light of the sun and have depicted the three nearest circles as fire, the next three circles as aether, and the three outermost circles which descend into terrestrial blackness, as water (translation, p. 97).

Again here in the *De ludo globi*, it is Cusanus' creative, playful use of metaphor that leads him to speculate in what seem to be novel ways concerning the universe. The universe, he suggests, is not only an infinite sphere but one that is heliocentric.

This statement, like those in the second book of the *De docta ignorantia* mentioned above, invite discussion of Cusanus' place in the "scientific revolution" and his relationship to Copernicus. But at this juncture it is again important to note that in making these statements in the *De ludo globi* which suggest the heliocentricity of the universe, Cusanus may be associated with the long and rich Pythagorean tradition, or perhaps more aptly, undercurrent, of cosmological speculation. Ancient sources such as Aristotle and Plutarch mention that the Pythagoreans maintained that the sun or fire was at the center of the universe and that the earth was one of many stars that revolved around it. In a more general sense, the Pythagoreans believed that numbers and their proportions were the basis of the harmonious structure of the universe. This Pythagorean undercurrent persisted throughout the Middle Ages and Renaissance, and it can be argued, as S.K. Heninger has done, that figures such as Copernicus, Digges, and Kepler "saw themselves as latter day Pythagoreans." Surely such figures are "Pythagorean" in that they conceived of the universe as a mathematically harmonious system and believed that in their own work they were refining this system, not destroying it. And although it would be incorrect to argue that Cusanus was in any specific sense a forerunner of Copernicus' heliocentric system, he must be considered an important figure in the continuity of this Pythagorean cosmological speculation, a continuity broken, Heninger would argue, not by Copernicus, or even Galileo, but only by the advent of Newton's celestial mechanics.[48]

The *ludus globi* may be applied to the study of the human body and soul as well as to the contemplation of the cosmos. Indeed, these subjects are interrelated and the tracing of this interrelationship constitutes Cusanus' second major theme. According to Cusanus, God created the infinite sphere of the world and set it in motion "in likeness" of the way in which man creates the spheroid of the *ludus globi* and sets it in motion when playing the game. But although God initially sets the world in motion and man the *globus*, neither controls the movements of his projectile once the initial impetus has been given:

> JOHN: How did God create the ultimate sphere and its motion together?
> THE CARDINAL: In likeness of the way in which you create the motion of the ball. That sphere is not moved by God the creator or by the spirit of God just as the ball is not moved by you when you see it roll along. Nor is it moved by your spirit, although you have put it in motion by executing your will through the throw of the hand, making an impetus upon the ball, by which the ball is moved along as long as the impetus endures (translation, p. 65).

In this passage Cusanus, recalling the disjunctive metaphysic of the *De docta ignorantia*, emphasizes God as the *deus absconditus* who is hidden or absent from creation once he has set it in motion. In a certain parallel sense, he also emphasizes a man's estrangement from his own creations once he has brought them into being—he can no longer affect the movements of the ball once it has left his hand.

The world is an ultimate sphere but man also is a sphere—a sphere that is self-moving in a perpetual motion that is substantial and not accidental:

> So the motion which gives life to the animal never ceases to give life to the body as long as it is capable of life and sound because it is natural. And although the motion that gives life to the animal ceases with the declining health of the body, nevertheless the intellectual motion of the human soul, which exists and functions without the body, does not cease. For this reason that motion, which intellectually moves itself, is self-subsistent and substantial. That motion which is not self-moving is an accident, but that motion which is self-moving is a substance (translation, p. 65).

This self-moved motion of the sphere that is man contrasts with the spheroid of the *ludus globi* which moves only when thrown by one of the players. Cusanus here follows Aristotle's theory of natural and violent motion, modified by the 14th century conception of impetus:

> Notice that the movement of the ball declines and ceases, leaving the ball sound and whole, because the motion that is within the ball is not natural, but accidental and violent. Therefore when the impetus that is impressed upon it dies out, it stops. But if, as has already been said, that ball were perfectly round, its motion would be round. That motion would be natural and in no way violent and would never cease (translation, p. 65).[49]

Cusanus' description of the soul as a self-moving sphere invites comparison with Plato as well as with Aristotle.

In the *Timaeus*, Plato says that man was created in a spherical shape in imitation of the shape of the universe. And in the *Symposium*, Aristophanes presents his playful myth of creation, wherein he claims that in addition to males and females there was originally a creature that he called a man-woman, a hermaphrodite:

> each of these beings was globular in shape with rounded back and sides, four arms and four legs, and two faces, both the same, on a cylindrical neck, and one head, with one face one side and one the other, and four ears, and two lots of privates, and all the other parts to match. They walked erect, as we do ourselves, backward or forward whichever they pleased, but when they broke into a run they simply stuck their legs straight out and went whirling round and round like a clown turning cartwheels.[50]

For Cusanus, the soul moves itself not by any of Aristotle's six species of motion, but has its own "equivocal" motion. It moves through its powers to distinguish among and proportionally arrange its thoughts (translation, p. 69). Through its power to calculate the soul is able to recognize the immutability of certain mathematical truths. This is proof of the soul's own immutability.

The soul's immutability and unique capacity to be self-perpetuating is the source of its inventive power. This power of invention is a kind of self-generated motion through which the soul assimilates itself to all "knowable things":

> For this reason the soul is the inventive power of the arts and of new sciences. Therefore it cannot be moved in its inventive motion of the new except by itself. So when it makes itself the likeness of all knowable things it is moved by itself, so that when it is in the senses it makes itself the likeness of sensible things, in vision the likeness of visible things, in hearing the likeness of audible things, and so on for all the senses (translation, p. 69).

Though Cusanus does not explicitly say so here, he is referring back to the *De coniecturis* where he stated that the self-generating and self-perpetuating power of the soul stems from its creation in the image of God; so it enfolds and unfolds its conjectural world from itself in likeness of the way God unfolds the "real" world.

Cusanus points out that in fact the *ludus globi* itself is an example of the soul's inventive power which distinguishes it from the animals as he posited at the onset of the dialogue:

> I thought to invent a game of knowledge. I considered how it should be done. Next I decided to make it as you see. Cogitation, consideration, and determination are powers of our souls. No beast has such a thought of inventing a new game which is why the beast does not consider or determine anything about it (translation, p. 69).

When the soul thinks about its own action—thinks about thinking—it is self-reflexive, and its movement is circular:

> And when I seek the definition of the soul—what the soul is—do I not think and consider? And in this I find that the soul is self-moving in a circular motion because its motion turns back upon itself (translation, p. 71).

Each man thus freely creates and rules over his own kingdom. Animals, however, are not rational,

> Because they lack the free power that is in us...Therefore they are impelled to those things that they do by their nature so that all members of each species hunt and make nests in the same way (translation, p. 71).

Animals are moved by instinct or what Cusanus calls "the necessitating command of nature." Man is not:

> Our regal and imperial spirit is not bound by this stricture. Otherwise it would not invent anything but would only follow the impulse of its nature (translation, p. 71).

Man is ultimately for Cusanus, mind. In thinking and inventing, though man initially relies upon his senses for certain kinds of information, he actually later retreats from them: man's withdrawal from his body into his mind assures that he operates more freely:

> Everyone who observes that to think and also to consider and to determine is a certain kind of running about understands the movement of the rational spirit through that observation. The body offers no support in this operation. For this reason the soul withdraws as much as can from the body, so that it might better think, consider, and determine (translation, p. 69).

In the *Compendium* of 1463, Cusanus condenses his vision of the creative, operative power of mind into an image of man as maker and mapper of his own internal world. Again, withdrawal from the body is a necessity for this *homo cosmographicus*:

> He turns more towards this map, dismisses the messengers, closes the gates, and transfers his internal view to the creator of the world, who is none of all these things which are understood and noted by the

> messengers, but is the creator and cause of all things. He [man] thinks Him [the creator] to relate to the world in an anterior way, as he the cosmographer relates to the map, and from the relation of the map to the true world, the cosmographer speculates, he contemplates within himself with his mind the creator of the world, the truth in an image, the signified in the sign.[51]

In his creation of his own inner world of mind, over which he presides, man is god-like.

But man is, for Cusanus, not only a 'microtheus' but a 'microcosm' and this is the third of the central themes of the *De ludo globi*. In the *De ludo globi* Cusanus specifically calls him this or sometimes a 'little world' (*parvus mundus*). He compares man's body and soul to the larger cosmos. Some men say that the world, too, has a soul, called the *anima mundi* or sometimes 'fate in substance' (*fatum in substantia*):

> We cannot deny that man is called a microcosm: that is, a little world which has a soul. And likewise they say that the great world has a soul, which some men call nature and others the spirit of the universe. This world soul nourishes, unites, connects, warms, and moves all things from within...The entire corporeal world is related to the world soul just as the body of man is related to his soul (translation, pp. 73-75).[52]

Man is however, not entirely a self-contained kingdom, he is still part of the larger world as well. In fact man represents the perfection of the world:

> By all means man is the small world in such a way that he also is part of the large world. For the whole shines forth in all its parts since each part is part of the whole, and so the whole man shines forth in the hand proportionately to the whole. But still the whole perfection of man shines forth in a more perfect manner in the head. The universe shines forth in each of its parts in the same way, for all things maintain their status and proportion in relation to the universe. Yet it shines forth more in that part which is called man than in any other (translation, p. 75).[53]

Man may then be aptly compared to a smaller kingdom or territory that exists autonomously within a larger one – he is like the kingdom of Bohemia which exists as part of the Holy Roman Empire.

Just as God operates freely in the creation of the universe so man operates freely in the creation of his own, human world:

> For the mind, having the ability of freely conceiving, finds within itself the art of unfolding its conceptions, which now may be called the mastery of inventing. The potters, sculptors, painters, turners, metalworkers, weavers and similar artisans all possess this art (translation, p. 77).

The potter, for example, conceives of a pot in his head and invents tools, such as the potter's wheel "by whose motion he brings the preconceived form out of the possibility of matter."

Similarly, the turner makes a ball out of wood by inventing a lathe to help him give form to the idea of the ball that he has in his mind. Cusanus, following Aristotle's categories of possibility and act, argues that the ball exists archetypically in the mind of the potter, it exists in possibility in the wood and is led forth from this state of possibility into actuality in the wood through the motion of the lathe directed by the turner who desires to assimilate the ball in his mind to the matter of the wood (translation, p. 77).[54]

By understanding how the turner makes a ball out of wood man can understand how God himself creates, though he must always recall that these are speculations concerning divine creativity, not actual graspings of the process:

> You have therefore from this likeness of human art a way of conjecturing somehow concerning the nature of the divine creative art, although there is as much difference between the creativity of God and man's fabrication, as there is between creator and creature (translation, p. 77).

And, as he did in the dialogues of the *Idiota* where he discussed the art of spoonmaking, Cusanus here in the *De ludo globi* is quick to emphasize that man is not simply uncovering the form of the ball hidden in the wood, he is creating the ball out of the matter or possibility that is the wood according to the archetypal ball that is in his mind:

> For when the turner makes the ball by cutting off parts of the wood until he arrives at the form of a ball, the possibility which the turner saw in the wood when it conforms to the ball in his mind crosses over from the state of possible being to actual being. Its material cause is the wood and the efficient cause the artisan and the formal cause the exemplar in the mind of the artist and the final cause the artisan himself who brings it about for himself (translation, p. 79).

In this way the soul invents all the arts and disciplines and through these inventions, sees itself to be in effect, immortal:

> And the rational soul invents the disciplines such as arithmetic, geometry, music, and astronomy and discovers that they are enfolded in its power. For these disciplines are discovered and unfolded by men. And because these disciplines are incorruptible and remain always the same, the soul truly observes itself to be incorruptible, truly always permanent. These mathematical disciplines exist only in it and they are enfolded in its power and are unfolded through its power in such a way that if the rational soul itself did not exist they could not exist at all (translation, p. 105).

In this passage Cusanus suggests that the rational soul creates number from itself and that humanly created numbers have no extra-mental reality. In this statement Cusanus differs from Plato and the Pythagoreans who believed in number's innate existence in the universe and who thought that the mind understood number through participation in extra-mentally existent numerical forms or ideas. Cusanus, a Christian Platonist (and Pythagorean), instead sees number as divinely and humanly created and intra-mentally contained. Though he does not explicitly point out his differences with the Platonists on this important point here in the *De ludo globi*, he did do so in the *De beryllo*. In that work Cusanus argued that if Plato had understood that man was created in the image and likeness of God, he would have realized that humanly understood numbers and geometrical figures are human inventions and find their truest existence within the mind:

> But neither he [Plato] nor any other whom I have read, calls attention to that which I posited in the fourth proposition [that man is a second God]. But if he had considered this, he would doubtless have discovered that our mind, which fabricates mathematical things, has those things which are of its office more truly within itself than they are externally.
>
> For example, man has the mechanical art and the forms of art more truly in his mental conception than they would be if externally formed just as a house, which is made by art, has a truer figure in the mind than in the wood. Truly the figure which comes to be in the wood is a mental figure, the idea or exemplar. It is so for all such things. Thus it is so for the circle, line, triangle, and our number and all such things which have their origin from the concept of the mind and are lacking in nature.[55]

Man, then, creates and rules over his own human kingdom, though he remains part of the larger divinely created universe at the same time. Man is not only part of the natural universe but he is a member of the spiritual kingdom of Christianity as well.

The *ludus globi* also represents the spiritual pilgrimage of *homo viator*, the fourth theme that Cusanus treats. The center of the nine concentric circles upon which the *ludus globi* is played stands for Christ. Each circle carries a certain number. The player who first gets the number 34, the number of years Christ lived, wins. The closer his spheroid gets to the center, the higher his points:

> This game, I say, represents the movement of our soul from its kingdom to the kingdom of life in which is peace and eternal happiness. Jesus Christ, our king and the giver of life, resides in its center. Since he was similar to us, Christ moved the sphere of his person so that it came to rest in the middle of life, leaving us the example so that we would do just as he had done. And our sphere would follow him although it would be impossible that another sphere attain peace in the same center of life where the sphere of Christ rests. There is an infinity of places and mansions within the circle, for each person's sphere rests on its own point and atom which no other could ever attain. Nor can two spheres be equally distant from the center, but one is always more distant, the other less so (translation, p. 79).

It is necessary that all Christians "move their sphere in these terrestrial lands" if they hope to be saved in the next. Those who have faith will find it easy to "direct the curved sphere so that it follows the way of Christ in whom was the spirit of God, who himself leads to the center and font of life (translation, pp. 79-81)."

In the same way that a player practices in order to improve in his playing of the *ludus globi*, so must the Christian continually strive for spiritual perfection so that he might finally come to rest in the kingdom of life after his spiritual gyrations:

> This is the sum of the mysteries of this game: that we learn to rectify these inclinations and natural curvings by studious practice so that at last after many variations and unstable circlings and curvings we come to rest in the kingdom of life (translation, p. 81).

As always, Cusanus emphasizes that each gyrating inner pilgrimage is unique and involves the growth of each individual's self understanding:

> It is true, no one person can precisely follow another's path. But it is necessary that each person master the inclinations of his sphere and its tendencies through practice. The moderate person applies himself in precisely this way so that he at last finds the path which the curvature of the sphere does not impede, a path from which he may arrive at the circle of life. This is the mystical power of the game: through energetic practice, the curve of the sphere can actually be regulated, so that after unstable fluctuations, its motion comes to rest in the kingdom of life (translation, p. 81).

But however much a player may try to control his throw through practice, he does not always succeed. When, in spite of his intention, the ball does not approach the center of the circles, it seems that the ball is moved, not by the player but by fortune (translation, pp. 81-83).[56]

Cusanus calls fortune, the fifth of his themes, "that which happens outside of intention." Every player aims for the center so if he hits it, it is not by chance. But although each player intends to hit the center, he cannot necessarily effect the fulfillment of his intention:

> Fortune can be called that which happens outside of intention. And since each player aims for the center of the circle, if he hits it, it is not by fortune. Nor is it in our power that our will is carried out (translation, p. 83).

Once the ball leaves his hands the player can no longer influence its course, though he may try to through "body language":

> But since we did not initially put it on the right path and did not apply the impetus necessary for it to reach the center, we cannot modify its course by a later effort. It is just as if someone begins to run down a mountain; once he is in rapid motion he cannot stop even if he wishes to (translation, p. 83)

Those who play the game unsuccessfully are prone to blame their "bad luck," but it is only themselves that they have to blame (translation, p. 83).

All things human are under human control and fortune cannot be blamed for adversity, nor can the movement of the stars:

> You can well see that you put the ball in motion when and how you wish. Even if a heavenly constellation were able to make the ball remain in a fixed point, the influence of the heavens will not keep your hand from moving the ball if you wish, for the kingdom of each [man] is free and so is the kingdom of the universe in which the heavens and the stars are contained (translation, p. 83).

To be sure, Cusanus continues, there is a kind of "natural necessity" that prevails in that everything, including man, has been created in a certain way. In this sense fortune or what the Platonists call the *anima mundi* may be called omnipotent. But this natural disposition of things does not affect human actions or values:

> This fortune, which is called *anima mundi* above, does not determine those things in our kingdom which are man's...The noble kingdom is not in these extrinsic goods that are called fortuitous which man cannot influence no matter how much he would like to since they are not subject to the will as are the aforementioned good immortal things (translation, p. 83).[57]

Man cannot therefore totally control his destiny but he cannot on that account call himself subject to fortune. He must endeavor to approach the center of the kingdom of life through virtuous practice and finally, through faith in God:

> Human motion cannot persist in a straight line. It quickly declines, always fluctuating inconstantly and variously on account of its terrestrial nature. Man can nevertheless terminate the revolution in a circle through the exercise of his virtue. And God, who is sought in this motion and who perfects that good will, aids the good and perseverant intention (translation, p. 85).

Cusanus pulls together the several themes that we have presented above in a final vision of God and man based upon circles of yet another sort—*coins*. Punning on the word *valeo* which can mean "to bid farewell to" and "to be worth," Cusanus says that he can bring his thoughts to a close (bid farewell to them) in no better a way than through a summary of their worth. He will therefore pull together the worth of what he has been saying through an analysis of 'value' itself. For Cusanus, *God* is the ultimate value from which all values are unfolded; he lies hidden in the single center of all the circles of the *ludus globi*:

> Only the value that is the value of values which is in all things that have value and in which all things that have value exist, enfolds in itself all value and is unable to have value that is more or less. Conceive therefore that this absolute value, the cause of all value, is hidden in the center of all circles. And make the outermost circle the outermost value and close to nothing (translation, p. 115).

For Cusanus, all of creation can be seen as a kind of divinely created economy, an economy of being.

The activities of the marketplace, the world of the Idiot, are transposed into a cosmic commerce:

> Now consider how the value of all things is nothing but the being of these same things. And just as in the one greatest value which is simply and entirely incomposite and indivisible, every value of everything most truly exists, so the being of everything is in the most simple being. For just as in the value of a florin there is the value of a thousand little denarii and in the higher value of the double florin there is the value of two thousand denarii and so on ad infinitum so in the optimal florin than which none other could be higher there would necessarily be the value of an infinity of denarii (translation, p. 115).

As God, a kind of ultimate florin, is the source of the being or essence of value, so man through the "eye of the mind" discerns the value in things:

> When you observe this truth in yourself, what value has that eye of your mind, discerning in its power the value of all things? In its vision the value of all things and the values of singular things exist, but not as they exist in the value of values. Because the mind sees that which has the value of all things it does not on account of this itself have the value of all things. For values are not in it [the mind] in an essential way but rather in a notional way (translation, pp. 115-117).

To better understand this, God may be compared to the coiner of money, man to the mint-master. God creates the coins and he creates man, who interrelates the coins and so reveals their worth, and in this way discovers infinite uses for them:

> This metaphor is not absurd when you conceive of God as an omnipotent coiner of money who, from this high and omnipotent power can produce all money. And if some one would be of such a great power that he would produce from his hand whatever kind of money he wished and would establish a coin-broker having in his power the distinction of all monies and the knowledge of their numbering, while reserving to himself [the omnipotent money-maker] only the art of coinage, that coin-broker would disclose the nobility of the monies and he would reveal the value, number, weight, and measure which the money had from God, so that the price and value of his money and through it the power of the mint-master would be known. The similitude would be an apt one (translation, p. 117).

Cusanus' discussions of the interrelationships among the coiner, the coin-broker, and the monies themselves in this section can be related to late scholastic discussions of the covenantal nature of causality.

As William J. Courtenay has demonstrated, there was a theory of sacramental causality—known as *sine qua non* causality—that was popular in the middle of the fourteenth century. This theory of causality was often illustrated Thomas Aquinas (who incidentally opposed it) tells us, by an example drawn from the commercial world. Courtenay summarizes the *sine qua non* argument as follows:

> The sacraments effect grace not through an inherent, created virtue but rather through a pact, covenant, or ordination of God that guarantees grace to the person who receives the sacraments, if the latter are properly administered and the recipient places no obstacle in the way of their effectiveness. This type of sacramental causality, termed causality *sine qua non*, was usually illustrated, Thomas informs us, with the following example. A king might decree that any person possessing a certain leaden coin would receive 100 pounds. In such a case, it would not be the leaden coin that causes the reception of the 100 pounds, but rather the arbitrary acceptance of the token by the king. For Thomas, the leaden coin would only be the occasion for the reward, not its cause. Therefore Thomas rejected this solution which, it seemed to him, would make the sacraments nothing more than the occasion or accidental cause of grace.[58]

Courtenay points out that covenantal causality was "not a small point in sacramental theology but rather one of the fundamental principles of the nominalist world view." In a general sense then, for the nominalists,

> The covenantal theory of sacramental causality was based on a belief that certain causal relationships need depend for their efficacy on nothing more than a contract or a more general ordination, agreement, or understanding that is accepted by all persons concerned.[59]

Cusanus' whole discussion of value here in the final section of the *De ludo globi* parallels this nominalist conception of covenantal causality, though he arrives at it through his conception of the cosmic play that motivates both God and man. God creates the coins, but it is man, acting in the image of God, who determines their worth through agreements or "covenants" with other men. Such agreements or "covenants," such "legislations" (to borrow a term from F. Edward Cranz), give meaning not only to coinage systems, but to the entire range of human actions and inventions according to Cusanus.[60]

Man is not only the coin-broker, determining the value of the coins that God mints, he is himself a kind of living coin, bearing the image of his maker like a coin bears the likeness of the ruler of the country in which it was minted. It is as

> ...if a papal florin were to live the intellectual life, certainly it would know itself to be a florin and for this reason to be the money of him whose sign and image it would have. For it would know that it did not have the being of the florin from itself but from him who had impressed his image upon it. And through the fact that it would see a similar image in all living intellects it would know that all monies would be of the same person. Therefore, seeing one face in the signs of all coinages, it would see one equality through which all money would be constituted in act... (translation, p. 121).

There is, finally, but one form that shines forth in all things variously. The one form of being is God, the one form of knowing is God's image, man.

The *De ludo globi* can thus be said to be a cumulative statement of Cusanus' thinking on God, man, and the universe. Although he does not always explicitly say so, Cusanus continually refers to arguments made in previous works throughout his conversations with Johannes and Albertus, and attempts to draw them together into a synthetic vision. This vision is of an omnipotent creator God who has unfolded the richness and diversity of the universe from himself and created man to admire it. But God has also created man in his own image and in this, man is himself a "second god" who unfolds from his own mind an infinity of thoughts and objects. So while man lives in the divinely created universe he is not subject to fortune and the instincts that dominate the other creatures in it. Man transcends such vicissitudes and restraints in the "legislative" power of his mind which allows him to establish and live by commonly shared moral and cultural values. And finally man transcends the seemingly unbearable condition of his cosmic otherness through faith in the salvation promised to him by the god-man, Christ.

4.

The Historical Significance of the *De ludo globi*

The intellectual and religious history of the later Middle Ages and the Renaissance is a complicated one which involves the confluence of a number of important traditions. Each of these traditions, which include the scholastic, humanist, Platonist, and mystical, was at a different stage of its own internal development. And individual thinkers drew upon several or all of these traditions in different ways. Cusanus was familiar with all four and consciously strove to interrelate and reconcile them in his thinking; the originality and insight of his efforts to achieve a synthesis of these traditions makes him one of the most important fifteenth century thinkers.

The scholastic tradition which had flourished at Oxford and Paris in the earlier fourteenth century did not decline in the latter part of that century. However a greater number of important new centers of study appeared. The scholars and students of these newer universities were by and large migrants from the more established centers such as Paris. Their migrations were brought about by political uncertainties and coincidentally by the increasing pluralization of scholasticism itself. Beginning with William of Ockham's revolution of the study of logic towards the end of the second decade of the fourteenth century, *viae* other than the dominant Thomist, Albertist and

Augustinian ones began to gain ascendancy. The university curriculum became a hotly contested subject, with minority factions splitting off from centers such as Paris to form the nucleus of newer faculties such as those of Heidelberg and Cologne. In this sense, scholasticism can be said to have spread and diversified rather than declined in the later middle ages. Certainly it flourished in its various forms in Italian universities in the fifteenth and sixteenth centuries.[61]

Cusanus studied, albeit briefly, at both the universities of Heidelberg and Cologne. We do not know much about his stay at Heidelberg, then still under the intellectual influence of the important nominalist, Marsilius of Inghen. It is clear that he did study while at Cologne with Heimericus de Campo who had been trained in Paris and was the adherent of a particular brand of Albertism. Cusanus' library contains various writings of Heimericus, along with a number of scholastic sentence commentaries and other related works, and there can be no doubt that he was more than cursorily acquainted with the late scholastic *viae*. This is borne out by the *De docta ignorantia* itself, which proposes to replace such *viae* with a new method of philosophizing and theologizing. But at the same time that Cusanus wants to go beyond the logical discourse of scholasticism, he remains influenced by some aspects of both its epistemology and its theology. It is no accident that Johannes Wenck, the realist rector of the University of Heidelberg, felt called upon to defend vehemently the traditional realist position against the *De docta ignorantia*, whose premise, "there is no proportion between the finite and the infinite" corresponds exactly to the basis of nominalist metaphysics as described by Heiko Oberman. And in fact, Cusanus' disjunctive metaphysic is one of his important links with the nominalists.[62]

Cusanus' connections with the second of these four important fifteenth century traditions, that of humanism, are very strong and date also from his student years, those he spent taking his degree in canon law at Padua. There he formed friendships with Giuliano Cesarini and Paolo Toscanelli, both of whom had strong humanist connections. But it was at the Council of Basel that Cusanus first came to be known by a wider circle of humanists and he maintained these contacts throughout his lifetime, avidly collecting the humanists' translations of classical texts as they appeared. As he can be compared to the nominalists, so can Cusanus be compared to the humanists in certain basic premises of his thought. The humanist connection is perhaps most obvious first in the *De coniecturis* where he presents a philosophy of mind based upon the belief that the human mind is created in the image of the divine mind. In this he parallels a number of important humanist and later, Florentine Platonist, discussions of man, centered around *Genesis 1:26*. In subsequent writings, he elaborates, always through his explorations of the image/likeness relationship between man and God, a vision of the communality and historicity of human thought and action. In this too he may be compared to the humanists, and to a figure such as Leon Battista Alberti, like Cusanus, an intimate friend of Toscanelli.[63]

Cusanus has been called by Paul Oskar Kristeller one of the three great Platonists of the fifteenth century, an encomium shared by contemporaries of Cusanus such as Vespasiano da Bisticci and Andrea da Bussi, who both recognized that he played an important part in the fifteenth century "renaissance" of Plato. Cusanus was familiar as well with the medieval Platonic tradition and although there is no evidence that he actually owned copies of any of the commentaries of the twelfth-century Platonists, he certainly must have known of Thierry of Chartres at least. As Pierre Duhem and, more recently, Raymond Klibansky have demonstrated, in places in the *De docta ignorantia*, he seems to be following Thierry closely and certain key Chartrain discussions such as those of the *anima mundi* surface throughout Cusanus' writings, even in late works such as the *De ludo globi*. Cusanus' knowledge and understanding of Plato expanded during his own lifetime as he became acquainted with the humanists' translations of Plato and ancient Platonists. The ideal of wisdom personified in Socrates (which Cusanus knew through the Florentine chancellor Leonardo Bruni's early fifteenth century translations of the *Phaedo*, *Apology*, and *Crito*) and the dialectics of unity and plurality set forth in the *Parmenides* (translated for Cusanus by George of Trebizond) are basic Platonic principles to which Cusanus consistently returns.[64]

Cusanus grew up in the Moselle region of the Rhine Valley and so was undoubtedly familiar from an early age with the great tradition of Rhenish mysticism. This influence was subsumed under the stronger later influences of scholasticism, humanism and Platonism. However, it never entirely disappeared, but was transformed by these other influences. Cusanus was always a figure greatly admired by contemporary mystics; he was enthusiastically received by the Brethren of the Common Life when he visited Deventer during one of his papal legations and the Benedictine monks of Tegernsee, who regarded Cusanus as their spiritual guide, engaged him in a lengthy correspondence concerning the nature of the true mystical experience in the early 1450s. This correspondence led to Cusanus' composition of the *De visione* and the *De beryllo*, in which he sets forth his novel conceptions of the relationship of humanity and divinity in a brilliant adaptation of the traditional language of mysticism, creating a new conception of 'vision.'[65]

As was pointed out at the beginning of this introduction, scholars have spent a great deal of time tracing out the sources of Cusanus' thought and searching for the formal or orthodox "positions" in his writing. But seeking to identify him with a specific tradition, they have tended to overlook his real intention, and that is to work out a synthesis of those traditions to which he found himself heir. In his late works he makes it clear that this has been his purpose as he tries in various ways to present a summation of his lifetime of speculation. This is why these works are so important and deserve much more attention than they have heretofore received. The *De ludo globi* lies at the heart of Cusanus' last efforts to synthesize these intellectual traditions and through this to provide a new vision of man for his contemporaries. If we can grasp this vision, we will progress greatly in our attempts to understand the anthropology of the Renaissance and its historical implications.

Cusanus' thought, as he recalled it in the *De ludo globi*, began with the disjunctive metaphysic that led him to believe that reality could be best represented metaphorically. The universe became an infinite sphere, a globe that God created and threw, setting it forever in motion. In his adaptation of Hermes Trismegistus' aphorism: "God is an infinite sphere of which the center is everywhere and the circumference is nowhere," Cusanus had already upset the hierarchies of Neoplatonism which Ficino was to rediscover and elaborate. For Ficino, man was the bond of the emanative universe—the link between the material and the spiritual in the great chain of being. For Cusanus, God, whose center is everywhere and nowhere is the bond of the universe. In Cusanus' cosmic games, the Aristotelian elemental universe was turned inside out, and man's sense of being at its center became a trick of perspective—a *trompe d'oeil*.

Cusanus strove for a new kind of "vision," one that would free man from limitations of the "from what to which." He wanted to construct towers from which the "eye of the mind" could speculate transcendently. Early on in his intellectual and spiritual development, Cusanus stopped searching for man's place in a hierarchical universe (if indeed he ever seriously did). Instead he came to see man as a "second god," the creator of his own microcosmic, human world. Cusanus' thinking underwent a radical shift in perspective, from a direct interest in the ontology of the cosmos to a vision of the projected universe of human invention. In this he moved closer to the humanists and to the nominalist schools of scholasticism. Though man, as Cusanus saw him, also participated in the macrocosm of the created universe, especially in his bodily aspect, he was essentially free of the instinctual restraints that conditioned the lives of animals.

Man lives, according to Cusanus, mainly in the human world that he creates, pouring forth conjectures in likeness of the way in which God unfolded from his unity the endless diversity of the real world. Man creates not only thoughts but objects, he trades his thoughts and objects for those of other men and in this way the bonds of civilization are formed. These activities of men are voluntary, stemming from man's innate desire to know and make. Animals move only to feed their bodies, man moves essentially to satisfy the yearnings of his soul. Cusanus' emphasis upon the dominance of the human mind and spirit is equalled perhaps only by that of his friend Lorenzo Valla amongst early fifteenth-century thinkers.

These activities and yearnings are common to all men, not confined to isolated geniuses. The commercial transactions of the marketplace, the craftsmens' concoctions of spoons, jars, bowls, and balls are all proofs of man's godlike nature—his *deiformitas*. The secular becomes sacred; for Cusanus the *viator* feels his way towards his maker out of his communal and personal experiences as a man, not by leaving the human world behind.

Man, the creator and ruler of his own "little world," need therefore not fear the vagaries of *fortuna*. Through his mind he receives and communicates the value inherent in creation, he legislates it. In his communications with and exchanges with other men he creates moral and legal systems that perpetuate and improve his "little world" and protect it from the blind forces that dominate nature. Culture and acculturation are processes that will continue only as long as men privately and collectively engage in the serious play of introspection and communion which leads them back to their maker, with whose image they are stamped. Plato put this most beautifully in the *Laws* (in a passage quoted by Johan Huizinga in his *Homo Ludens*):

> Though human affairs are not worthy of great seriousness it is yet necessary to be serious; happiness is another thing. . . I say that a man must be serious with the serious, and not the other way about. God alone is worthy of supreme seriousness, but man is made God's plaything and that is the best part of him. Therefore every man and woman should live life accordingly, and play the noblest games, and be of another mind from what they are at present. For they deem war a serious thing, though in war there is neither play nor culture worthy the name, which are the things *we* deem most serious. Hence all must live in peace as well as they possibly can. What, then, is the right way of living? Life must be lived as play, playing certain games, making sacrifices, singing and dancing, and then a man will be able to propitiate the gods, and defend himself against his enemies, and win the contest."[66]

By engaging in the art of playful introspection through the *ludus globi*, Cusanus invites each reader to do the same for himself. Indeed the proper fulfillment of his humanity requires it. This vision and this invitation earn Cusanus his place amongst the seminal thinkers of the Renaissance.

NOTES

1. Nikolaus von Kues, *Philosophisch-Theologische Schriften*, Vol. I, p. 2: "Propositum est meas sapientiae venationes, quas usque ad hanc senectam mentis intuitu veriores putavi, summarie notatas posteris relinquere, cum nesciam, si forte longius et melius cogitandi tempus concedatur; sexagesium enim primum transegi annum."

2. The literature on Cusanus is vast. The best single biography remains E. Vansteenberghe, *Le Cardinal Nicholas de Cues (1401-1464): L'Action—La Pensée*, Paris, 1920. But Vansteenberghe's biography needs to be used in conjunction with E. Meuthen's important studies of specific periods in Cusanus' life. See in particular Meuthen's study of Cusanus' last years, *Die letzen Jahren des Nikolaus von Kues: Biographische Untersuchungen nach neuen Quellen, Wissenschaftliche Abhandlungen der Arbeitsgemeinschaft für Forschung des Landes Nordrhein-Westfalen* 3, Köln-Opladen, 1958. Cassirer's classic study of Cusanus' thought appears in English as *The Individual and The Cosmos in Renaissance Philosophy*, translated by Mario Domandi, Oxford: Basil Blackwell, 1963. There are numerous studies devoted to Cusanus' sources and to various specific aspects of his thought.

   For a study of the early sources of Cusanus' thought which emphasizes his scholastic background see H.G. Senger, *Die Philosophie des Nikolaus von Kues vor dem Jahre 1440:*

Untersuchungen zur Entwicklung einer Philosophie in der Frühzeit des Nikolaus (1430-1440), Beiträge zur Geschichte der Philosophe und Theologie des Mittelalters, Neue Folge 3, Münster: Aschendorff, 1971. On the influence of Lull and Lullism upon Cusanus, see E. Colomer, *Nikolaus von Kues und Raymund Lull aus Handschriften der Kueser Bibliothek,* Berlin: Walter De Gruyter & Co., 1961.

The important problem of the influence of twelfth-century Platonism upon Cusanus has yet to be systematically studied. For now, see P. Duhem, "Thierry de Chartres et Nicolaus de Cues," *Revue des Sciences philosophiques et théologiques,* Vol. 3, Paris, 1909. The connections between Thierry and Cusanus first pointed out by Duhem have been further documented by R. Klibansky and E. Hoffmann in their notes to the modern Heidelberg edition of the *De docta ignorantia*.

Cusanus' early humanist connections and his manuscript hunts during the Council of Basel can be traced through R. Sabbadini's "Niccolò da Cusa e i conciliari di Basilea alla scoperta dei codici," *Rendiconti della R. Accademia dei Lincei, Scienze morali, Ser.* 5, *Vol*. 20, 1911, pp. 3-40; on his later humanist associations see P.O. Kristeller's "A Latin Translation of Gemistos Plethon's *de fato* by Johannes Sophianos dedicated to Nicholas of Cusa," *Nicolò Cusano agli Inizi del Mondo Moderno, Atti del Congresso internazionale in occasione del V centenario della morte di Nicolo Cusanò, Bressanone, 6-10 settembre, 1964*, Florence: Sansoni, 1970, pp. 175-193.

Though the mystical strain in Cusanus' thought is often referred to by scholars, there is no thoroughgoing analysis of his mysticism. On the influence of Dionysius the Areopagite upon Cusanus, see L. Baur's "Cusanus Texte III, Marginalien 1. Nicolaus Cusanus und Ps. Dionysius im Lichte der Zitate und Randbemerkungen des Cusanus," *Sitzungsberichte der Heidelberger Akademie der Wissenschaften, Philosophisch-historische Klasse*, Heidelberg: Carl Winter, 1941. The influence of Meister Eckhart on Cusanus' early thought is studied by H. Wackerzapp in his *Der Einfluss Meister Eckharts auf die ersten philosophischen Schriften des Nikolaus von Kues*, Münster-Westfalen: Aschendorff, 1962.

On Cusanus' trinitarianism and his Christology, see R. Haubst's *Das Bild des Einen und Dreienen Gottes in der Welt nach Nikolaus von Kues, Trierer Theologische Studien* 4, Trier: Paulinus, 1952 and his *Die Christologie des Nikolaus von Kues,* Freiburg: Herder, 1956. A very useful general study of Cusanus' spirituality is J. Biechler's *The Religious Language of Nicholas of Cusa*, The American Academy of Religion Dissertation Series No. 8, Missoula, Montana: Scholars Press, 1975. On Cusanus' epistemology see the older work of R. Falckenberg, *Grundzüge der Philosophie des Nikolaus Cusanus mit besonderer Berucksichtigung der Lehre von Erkennen*, Breslau: Koebner, 1880 (anastatic reprint Frankfurt: Minerva, 1968) and, especially, the important study of Cassirer mentioned above. A more recent study is Clyde Lee Miller's introduction to his translation of Cusanus' *Idiota de mente*, *Nicholas de Cusa: Idiota de Mente*, New York: Abaris Books, 1979. On Cusanus' conciliarism, see Paul Sigmund's *Nicholas of Cusa and Medieval Political Thought*, Cambridge, Mass.: Harvard University Press, 1963 and M. Watanabe's *The Political Ideas of Nicholas of Çusa with special reference to his De concordantia catholica*, Geneva: Librairie Droz, 1963. On Cusanus' philosophical and theological anthropology, see my *Nicolaus Cusanus: A Fifteenth Century Vision of Man*, Leiden: E.J. Brill, 1982.

Comprehensive bibliographical articles on Cusanus appear periodically in *Mitteilungen und Forschungsbeiträge der Cusanus-Gesellschaft*, edited by R. Haubst. Those of H. Kleinen and R. Danzer (*MFCG* 1, 1968, 2nd edition), R. Danzer (*MFCG* 3, 1963), W. Traut and M. Zacher (*MFCG* 6, 1967), and M. Vazquez (*MFCG* 10, 1973) together provide an exhaustive list of works on Çusanus for the period 1920-1973. An excellent general bibliography is to be found in Jasper Hopkins' *A Concise Introduction to The Philosophy of Nicholas of Cusa*, Minneapolis: University of Minnesota Press, 1978, pp. 47-57.

"Accept now, reverend father, that which I have striven to attain for a long time by various doctrinal roads. I was unable to achieve it until, while at sea returning from Greece, I believe that I was led, through the supernatural generosity of the Father of lights from whom every excellent gift comes, so that I grasped the incomprehensible incomprehensibly in learned ignorance, through the transcendance of humanly knowable, incorruptible truths. Now I have set forth learned ignorance, this gift of Him

Who is Truth, in these books which can be limited or expanded from this same principle." For the Latin text, see *Nicolai De Cusa Opera Omnia*, Iussu et auctoritate Academiae Literarum Heidelbergensis ad codicum fidem edita, Vol. I, edited by E. Hoffmann and R. Klibansky, Leipzig: Felix Meiner, 1932 (hereafter cited as *DDI*), p. 163, *Epistola auctoris ad dominum Iulianum cardinalem*. Unless otherwise indicated, all translations from Cusanus' writings are mine.

4. *DDI* 1.1, p. 6: "...profecto, cum appetitus in nobis frustra non sit, desideramus scire nos ignorare. Hoc si ad plenum assequi poterimus, doctam ignorantiam assequemur. Nihil enim homini etiam studiosissimo in doctrina perfectius adveniet quam in ipsa ignorantia, quae sibi propria est, doctissimum reperiri; et tanto quis doctior erit, quanto se sciverit magis ignorantem."

5. On Wenck, see E. Vansteenberghe, "Le 'de Ignota Litteratura' de Jean Wenck de Herrenberg," *Beiträge zur Geschichte der Philosophie des Mittelalters*, Vol. 8, No. 6, Münster-Westfalen: Aschendorff, 1910. This piece includes a Latin text of the *De ignota litteratura* based upon a manuscript located in the municipal library of Mainz. Jasper Hopkins has recently published translations of Wenck's *De ignota litteratura* and Cusanus' reply, the *Apologia doctae ignorantiae*, along with an edition of the Latin text of the *De ignota litteratura* based upon a second manuscript located in the municipal library of Trier. See Hopkins' *Nicholas of Cusa's Debate with John Wenck: A Translation and an Appraisal of De Ignota Litteratura and Apologia Doctae Ignorantiae*, Minneapolis: The Arthur J. Banning Press, 1981. For further background on the Cusanus-Wenck debate, see R. Haubst's "Studien zu Nikolaus von Kues und Johannes Wenck aus Handschriften der Vatikanischen Bibliothek," *Beiträge zur Geschichte der Philosophie und Theologie des Mittelalters*, Vol. 38, No. 1, Münster-Westfalen: Aschendorff, 1955; Chapter II of my *Nicolaus Cusanus: A Fifteenth-Century Vision of Man*.

6. Nicolai De Cusa, *Opera Omnia*, Vol. II, *Apologia doctae ignorantiae*, edited by R. Klibansky, Leipzig, 1932 (hereafter referred to as *Apologia*), pp. 7-8: "Nam mystica theologia ducit ad vacationem et silentium, ubi est visio, quae nobis conceditur, invisibilis Dei; scientia autem, quae est in exercitio ad confligendum, illa est, quae victoriam verborum exspectat et inflatur, et longe abest ab illa, quae ad Deum, qui est pax nostra, properat."

7. *Apologia*, pp. 20-21: "Sed si se gratiam assequi sperat, ut de caecitate ad lumen transferatur, legat cum intellectu Mysticam theologiam iam dictam, Maximum monachum, Hugonem de Sancto Victore, Robertum Lincolniensem, Johannem Scotigenam, abbatem Vercellensem et ceteros moderniores commentatores illius libelli; et indubie se hactenus caecum fuisse reperiet."

8. *Apologia*, pp. 14-15: "Logica igitur atque omnis philosophica inquisitio nondum ad visionem venit. Hinc, uti venaticus canis utitur in vestigiis per sensibile experimentum discursu sibi indito, ut demum ea via ad quaesitum attingat...sic homo logica."

9. *Apologia*, p. 15: "Ratiocinatio quaerit et discurrit. Discursus est necessario terminatus inter terminos a quo et ad quem, et illa adversa sibi dicimus contradictoria."

10. *Apologia*, p. 16: "...doctam ignorantiam sic aliquem ad visum elevare quasi alta turris. Videt enim ibi constitutus id, quod discursu vario vestigialiter quaeritur per in agro vagantem; et quantum quaerens accedit et elongatur a quaesito, ipse intuetur. Docta enim ignorantia de alta regione intellectus existens sic iudicat de ratiocinativo discursu."

11. *DDI*, 1.11, p. 22: "Consensere omnes sapientissimi nostri et divinissimi doctores visibilia veraciter invisibilium imagines esse atque creatorem ita cognoscibiliter a creaturis videri posse quasi in speculo et in aenigmate. Hoc autem, quod spiritualia—per se a nobis inattingibilia—symbolice investigentur, radicem habet ex hiis, quae superius dicta sunt, quoniam omnia ad se invicem quandam—nobis tamen occultam et incomprehensibilem—habent proportionem, ut ex omnibus unum exsurgat universum et omnia in uno maximo sint ipsum unum. Et quamvis omnis imago accedere videatur ad similitudinem exemplaris: tamen praeter maximam imaginem, quae est hoc ipsum quod exemplar in unitate naturae, non est imago adeo similis aut aequalis exemplari, quin per infinitum similior et aequalior esse possit, uti iam ista ex superioribus nota facta sunt."

12. Proclus, *In Platonis Rem Publicam Commentarii*, 2 Vols., edited by W. Kroll, Leipzig, 1899-1901, reprinted Amsterdam, 1954, p. 158, lines 15-19. The English translation is that of James A. Coulter, *The Literary Microcosm: Theories of Interpretation of the Later Neoplatonists*, Leiden: E.J. Brill, 1976, pp. 50-51.

13. Pseudo-Dionysius the Areopagite, *De caelesti hierarchia*, II, 3, *Dionysiaca*, 2 Vols., ed. P. Chevalier et al., Paris-Bruges, 1937-1949, Vol. II, pp. 753-754: "Quod si quis absonas et absurdas imagines in jus vocet, vererique dicat divinis illis sanctissimisque spiritibus formas adeo foedas imponere, illum ita admonuisse sufficiet duplicem in sacris litteris tradi significandi modum: ex his, alterum per similes imagines figurasque procedere nihilque a sua natura deviare, alterum per dissimiles formas promovere ita effictum ut diversa prorsus et alia quam videatur insinuet... (pp. 756-757). Enim vero hujusmodi sacra figmenta honestiora quidem sunt et terrenis ac materialibus formes eminere videntur, ceterum ne sic quidem ad divinae similitudinis veritatem prope accederunt. Excedit enim illa substantiam omnem vitamque transcendit, nulla hanc exprimit lux, omnisque sermo, omnis mens atque ratio absque ulla comparatione illius similitudine inferior est. Aliquando item ab eisdem laudatur scripturis honestissime ac pene divine, dum in ejus laude dissimilibus utuntur signis, eamque invisibilem et infinitam, incomprehensibilem praedicant, his eam appellantes nominibus, quibus non quid sit sed quid non sit dicitur. Hoc enim verius (ut arbitror) in ipsa est et de illa proprie magis asseritur." The Latin version quoted above is that of Ambrogio Traversari; this is the translation that Cusanus knew.

14. *Apologia*, p. 24: "Sunt enim omnes similitudines, quas sancti ponunt, etiam divinissimus Dionysius, penitus improportionales et omnibus non habentibus doctam ignorantiam—huius scilicet scientiam, quod sunt penitus improportionales,—potius inutiles quam utiles."

15. *DDI*, I: 11, pp. 23-24: "Hac veterum via incedentes, cum ipsis concurrentes dicimus, cum ad divina non nisi per symbola accedendi nobis via pateat, quod tunc mathematicalibus signis propter ipsorum incorruptibilem certitudinem convenientius uti poterimus."

16. *DDI*, I: 12, p. 25: "Alii, qui unitatem infinitam figurare nisi sunt, Deum circulum dixerunt infinitum. Illi vero, qui actualissimam Dei existentiam considerarunt, Deum quasi sphaeram infinitam affirmarunt." Cf. Clemens Baeumker's edition of the *Liber XXIV philosophorum* in *Beiträge zur Geschichte der Philosophie des Mittelalters 25, 1928, proposition 2; Meister Eckhardt, Comment. in Ecclesiasticum*, quoted by H. Denifle in his "Meister Eckharts lateinische Schriften und die Grundanschauung seiner Lehre," *Archiv für Literatur und Kirchengeschichte des Mittelalters II*, 1886, pp. 417-615; p. 571. Cusanus noted Eckhart's reference to this Hermetic dictum in his manuscript of Eckhart's commentary. For a general history of the philosophical applications of the metaphor of the infinite sphere see D. Mahnke's *Unendliche Sphäre und Allmittelpunkt, Beiträge zur Genealogie der mathematischen Mystik* 8, Halle: Niemeyer, 1937; on Cusanus' use of this metaphor see also Karsten Harries' "The Infinite Sphere: Comments on the History of a Metaphor," *Journal of The History of Philosophy* 13, 1975, pp. 5-15; on Eckhart's role as a conduit for this image and its use by Cusanus, see H. Wackerzapp's *Der Einfluss Meister Eckharts auf die ersten philosophischen Schriften des Nikolaus von Kues, op. cit.*, pp. 140-151.

17. *DDI*, 2:11 and 12.

18. *DDI*, 1:3, p. 9: "Intellectus igitur, qui non est veritas, numquam veritatem adeo praecise comprehendit, quin per infinitum praecisius comprehendi possit, habens se ad veritatem sicut polygonia ad circulum, quae quanto inscripta plurium angulorum fuerit, tanto similior circulo, numquam tamen efficitur aequalis, etiam si angulos in infinitum multiplicaverit, nisi in identitatem cum circulo se resolvat."

19. *DDI* 2:12, p. 103: "Non enim apprehendimus motum nisi per quandam comparationem ad fixum. Si enim quis ignoraret aquam fluere et ripas non videret existendo in navi in medio aquae, navem quomodo apprehenderet moveri? Et propter hoc, cum semper cuilibet videatur, quod sive ipse fuerit in terra sive sole aut alia stella, quod ipse sit in centro quasi immobili et quod alia omnia moveantur, ille certe semper alios et alios polos sibi constitueret existens in sole et alios in terra et alios in luna et Marte, et ita de reliquis."

20. *DDI* 2.11, pp. 100-101: "Terra igitur, quae centrum esse nequit, motu omni carere non potest. Nam eam moveri taliter etiam necesse est, quod per infinitum minus moveri posset. Sicut igitur terra non est centrum mundi, ita nec sphaera fixarum stellarum eius circumferentia, quamvis etiam, comparando terram ad caelum, ipsa terra videatur centro propinquior et caelum circumferentiae. Non est igitur centrum terra neque octavae aut alterius sphaerae, neque apparentia super horizontem sex signorum terram concludit in centro esse octavae sphaerae." Lynn Thorndike denies that Cusanus had any influence upon Copernicus in Chapter VII, "Nicholas of Cusa and the Triple Motion of the Earth," of his *Science and Thought in the Fifteenth Century*, New York: Hafner, 1963. A. Koyré reaches the same conclusion in his *From The Closed World to The Infinite Universe*, New York: Harper & Row Torchbooks, 1958. However R. Klibansky has shown that the second book of the *De docta ignorantia* was in fact known to Copernicus in his piece "Copernic et Nicolas de Cues," in *Leonard de Vinci et l'expérience scientifique au 16è siècle*, Paris: Presses Universitaires de France, 1953, pp. 225-235. Two scholars, Thomas McTighe and Angelo Crescini, who consider Cusanus' contributions from the perspective of the problem of method, give him more due than Thorndike or Koyré. In his "Nicholas of Cusa's Theory of Science and Its Metaphysical Background," published in *Nicolò Cusano agli Inizi del Mondo Moderno, op. cit.*, pp. 317-339, McTighe concludes: "Nonetheless it is true that science is not a direct intelligible transcription of the ontological structures in the domain of sensible being, but rather a schematization whose trajectory to the sensible order is indirect and constructural. Then in this respect Cusa's philosophy of science is much closer than that of the great Galileo to the actual conditions of the scientific enterprise." In his *Il Problema Metodologico Alle Origini Della Scienza Moderna*, Rome: Edizioni Dell'Ateneo, 1972, Crescini pays a good deal of attention to what he sees to be the essentially mathematical foundations of Cusanus' thought, though he recognizes that its' goals are philosophical and theological. See Chapter II, Part I of his study: "'Precisione' e 'Passagio al limite' nel Cusano," pp. 60-78.

21. Grant's discussion of Bradwardine's position is in his article, "Medieval and Seventeenth-Century Conceptions of an Infinite Void Space beyond the Cosmos," *Isis*, 68, 1969, pp. 39-60. The passage from Bradwardine which Grant quotes is on page 46. The Latin text is in *Thomae Bradwardini Archepiscopi olim Cantuariensis De causa Dei contra Pelagium et de virtute causarum libri tres*, London: Henry Savile, 1618. Cusanus' abbreviated version of the *De causa Dei* remains in his library at Cues, catalogued by Marx as *cod. cusan. 93.* Note 16 contains further references to the literature on the metaphor of God as an infinite sphere.

22. Grant, *op. cit.*, p. 51. On the impact of the Condemnation of 1277 on philosophy and theology, see E. Grant, "The Condemnation of 1277, God's Absolute Power, and Physical Thought in the Late Middle Ages," *Viator* 10, Los Angeles: University of California Press, 1979. But now see his very important study, *Much Ado About Nothing: Theories of Space and Vacuum from the Middle Ages to the Scientific Revolution*, Cambridge, England: Cambridge University Press, 1981, pp. 138-141. In these pages (which I read only as my study was in press) Grant explicitly compares Bradwardine and Cusanus, which he had not done in the earlier articles cited above. My comparison of Bradwardine and Cusanus was written independently of Professor Grant's; I find no basic inconsistencies in our analyses, but there are different emphases. Certainly my indebtedness to his work is manifest throughout this section of my Introduction.

23. *Nicolai De Cusa Opera Omnia*, Vol. 3, *De coniecturis*, edited by Josef Koch, C. Bormann, and I.G. Senger, Hamburg: Felix Meiner, 1972, p. 4 (this volume is hereafter referred to as *DC*): "...in prioribus Doctae ignorantiae libellis multo quidem altius limpidiusque quam ego ipse nisu meo praecisionem veritatis inattingibilem intuitus es, consequens est omnem humanam veri positivam assertionem esse coniecturam. Non enim exhauribilis est adauctio apprehensionis veri. Hinc ipsam maximam humanitus inattingibilem scientiam dum actualis nostra nulla proportione respectet, infirmae apprehensionis incertus casus a veritatis puritate positiones nostras veri subinfert coniecturas. Cognoscitur igitur inattingibilis veritatis unitas alteritate coniecturali atque ipsa alteritatis coniectura in simplicissima veritatis unitate."

24. *DC*, pp. 7-8: "Coniecturas a mente nostra, uti realis mundus a divina infinita ratione, prodire oportet. Dum enim humana mens, alta dei similitudo, fecunditatem creatricis naturae, ut potest, participat, ex se ipsa, ut imagine omnipotentis formae, in realium entium similitudine rationalia exserit. Coniecturalis itaque mundi humana mens forma exstitit uti realis divina. Quapropter ut absoluta illa divina entitas est omne id quod est in quolibet quod est, ita et mentis humanae unitas est coniecturarum suarum entitas."

25. See Charles Trinkaus' *In Our Image and Likness: Humanity and Divinity in Italian Humanist Thought*, 2 Vols., Chicago: The University of Chicago Press, 1970, for a comprehensive discussion of humanist explorations and interpretations of *Genesis* I:26.

26. *DC*, pp. 143-144: "Homo enim deus est, sed non absolute, quoniam homo; humanus est igitur deus. Homo etiam mundus est, sed non contracte omnia, quoniam homo. Est igitur homo microcosmos aut humanus quidem mundus. Regio igitur ipsa humanitatis deum atque universum mundum humanali sua potentia ambit. Potest igitur homo esse humanus deus atque, ut deus, humaniter potest esse humanus angelus, humana bestia, humanus leo aut ursus aut aliud quodcumque. Intra enim humanitatis potentiam omnia suo existunt modo."

27. Pico Della Mirandola, *On The Dignity of Man, On Being and the One, Heptaplus*, introduction by Paul J.W. Miller, Indianapolis/New York/Kansas City: Bobbs-Merrill Co., Inc., 1965, p. 5.

28. See Trinkaus, *In Our Image and Likeness*, *op. cit.*, Vol. I, Part 2. for discussions of da Barga's, Facio's, and Manetti's treatises.

29. *DC*, p. 144: "Non ergo activae creationis humanitatis alius exstat finis quam humanitas. Non enim pergit extra se, dum creat, sed dum eius explicat virtutem, ad se ipsam pertingit. Neque quidquam novi efficit, sed cuncta, quae explicando creat, in ipsa fuisse comperit. Universa enim in ipsa humaniter exsistere diximus. Sicut enim humanitatis virtus potens est humaniter ad cuncta progredi, ita universa in ipsam, nec est aliud ipsam admirabilem virtutem ad cuncta lustranda pergere quam universa in ipsa humaniter complicare."

30. *DC*, p. 149: "Adverte etiam quod, etsi aut religio aut regimen aliquamdiu stabile videatur in aliqua mundi huius natione, non tamen in ipsa sua praecisione. Fluvius enim Rhenus stabiliter diu fluere visus est, sed numquam in eodem statu permanens, iam turbulentior, iam clarior, iam in augmento, iam in diminutione."

31. On the Renaissance dialogue, see Francesco Tateo's *Tradizione e realtà nell'Umanesimo italiano*, Bari: Dedalo Libri, 1967. "Parte seconda – Il dialogo morale"; David Marsh, *The Quattrocento Dialogue: Classical Tradition and Humanist Innovation*, Cambridge, Mass. – London: Harvard University Press, 1980.

32. Nicolai de Cusa, *Opera Omnia*, Vol. 5, edited by L. Baur, Leipzig: Felix Meiner, 1937 (hereafter referred to by the title of the dialogue in question: *Idiota de sapientia* or *Idiota de mente*). *Idiota de sapientia*, pp. 4-5: "Hoc est quod aiebam, scilicet te duci auctoritate et decipi: Scripsit aliquis verbum illud, cui credis. Ego autem tibi dico, quod sapientia foris clamat in plateis, et est clamor eius, quoniam ipsa habitat in altissimis." Cf. *Prov*. 1:20-21.

33. *Idiota de sapientia*, p. 22: "Identitas enim infinita non potest in alio recipi, cum in alio aliter recipiatur. Et cum non possit in aliquo nisi aliter recipi, tunc recipitur meliori modo quo potest, sed immultiplicabilis infinitas in varia receptione melius explicatur; magna enim diversitas immultiplicabilitatem melius exprimit."

34. *Idiota de mente*, p. 51: "Coclear extra mentis nostrae ideam aliud non habet exemplar. Nam etsi statuarius aut pictor trahat exemplaria a rebus, quas figurare satagit, non tamen ego, qui ex lignis coclearia et scutellas et ollas ex luto educo. Non enim in hoc imitor figuram cuiuscumque rei naturalis. Tales enim formae cocleares, scutellares et ollares sola human arte oerficiuntur. Unde ars mea est magis perfectiora quam imitatoria figurarum creatarum, et in hoc infinitae arti similior."

35. *Idiota de mente*, p. 105: "Nam velle cum exequi in omnipotentia coincidunt, quasi ut dum vitrificator vitrum facit; nam insufflat spiritum, qui exequitur voluntatem eius, in quo

spiritu est verbum seu conceptus et potentia; nisi enim potentia et conceptus vitrificatoris forent in spiritu, quem emittit, non oriretur vitrum tale."

36. Nikolaus von Kues, *Philosophisch-Theologische Schriften*, Vol. 3, p. 114: "Sicut enim oculus iste carneus per vitrum rubeum intuens omnia, quae videt rubea iudicat et si per vitrum viride omnia viridia; sic quisque oculus mentis obvolutus contractione et passione iudicat te qui es mentis obiectum secundum naturam contractionis et passionis."

37. *Nicolai De Cusa Opera Omnia*, Vol. 11/1, edited by L. Baur, Leipzig: Felix Meiner, 1940, p. 7: "Unde mensurat suam intellectum per potentiam operum suorum et ex hoc mensurat divinum intellectum, sicut veritas mensuratur per imaginem. Et haec est aenigmatica scientia. Habet autem visum subtilissimum, per quem videt aenigma esse veritatis aenigma, ut sciat hanc esse veritatem, quae non est figurabilis in aliquo aenigmate."

38. Edgar Wind, *Pagan Mysteries in the Renaissance*, New York: W.W. Norton & Co., Inc., 1968, p. 191.

39. The English translation of this passage is taken from Jasper Hopkins' *A Concise Introduction to the Philosophy of Nicholas of Cusa, op. cit.*, p. 83. Hopkins' book contains a Latin text and an English translation of the *De possest*.

40. Nikolaus von Kues, *Philosophisch-Theologische Schriften*, Vol. I, p. 10: "Nihil enim sunt philosophi nisi venatores sapientiae quam quisque in lumine logicae sibi cognatae suo modo investigat." See also pp. 48-50, where Cusanus describes the "fields" through which the hunter passes in his search for wisdom.

41. *Laws* 643b-d, translated by A.E. Taylor in *The Collected Dialogues of Plato*, edited by E. Hamilton and H. Cairns, Bollingen Series LXXI, Princeton: Princeton University Press, 1961, p. 1243.

42. Plotinus, *The Enneads*, 6 Vols., translated by A.H. Armstrong, Cambridge, Mass.: Harvard University Press, 1967; Vol. 3, pp. 361-363 (Third Ennead, Eighth Tractate).

43. See *The Shorter Oxford English Dictionary*, 3rd edition, Oxford: The Clarendon Press, 1973, entry for "bowl." For a further discussion of Cusanus' game, see Gerda von Bredow, *Vom Globusspiel*, *op. cit.*, Introduction and notes 1-17.

44. *The Seventh Letter* 342b-343c. I am not here concerned with the problem of the authenticity of *The Seventh Letter*; for the purposes of this analysis it suffices that Cusanus took it to be a genuine work of Plato.

45. Cf. *DDI* 2.1, pp. 64-65. In the *De possest* Cusanus extensively explores the interrelationship of God and the universe through the terms *posse facere* and *posse fieri*. See Hopkins' introduction to his translation of this work for some discussion of these terms and their applications. Hopkins does not discuss what seems to me to be a fundamental context for the understanding of Cusanus' use of these terms. Briefly put, Cusanus' analyses here in the *De ludo globi*, and also in the *De docta ignorantia*, *De possest*, and in the *De apice theoriae* must be seen as part of the late scholastic debate concerning the *potentia absoluta* and *potentia ordinata* of God. God, according to his *potentia absoluta* could have created things in a manner other than the way in which he did. But He did create the world in the way that it exists according to his *potentia ordinata*. Interestingly the important fifteenth century nominalist Gabriel Biel uses language similar to Cusanus' in his own discussion of God's *potentia absoluta* and the inviolability of the law of contradiction: "...posse aliquid aliquando accipitur secundum leges ordinatas et institutas a deo. Et illam sic deus dicitur posse facere de potentia ordinata. Aliter accipitur posse pro posse facere omne illud quod non includit contradictionem fieri, sive deus ordinavit se hoc facturum sive non, quia deus multa facere potest quod non vult facere secundum magistrum [I *Sent* d 43]. Et illa dicitur posse de potentia absoluta." This passage is quoted by Heiko Oberman in his fundamental study of late medieval thought, *The Harvest of Medieval Theology: Gabriel Biel and Late Medieval Nominalism*, Grand Rapids: William B. Eerdmans, 1967, p. 37. I have established some links between Cusanus' discussions and those of some nominalists on the subject of God's *potentia absoluta* and *potentia ordinata* in my *Nicolaus Cusanus: A Fifteenth Century Vision of Man*. But there is much

more to be done, not only on Cusanus' relationship to the nominalists on this particular point but also on other theological and epistemological questions.

46. *DC*, pp. 15-17.

47. Here Cusanus sees the universe as a kind of hierarchy or emanation which he conceives of along Dionysian lines as set forth in the *De caelesti hierarchia*. In this conception he apparently controverts the disjunctive metaphysic established in the *De docta ignorantia*. Cusanus does not squarely face this apparent dichotomy in his thinking; perhaps he did not find it inconsistent. While there can be little doubt that from the *De docta ignorantia* on he took as the basis of his metaphysics the premise *infiniti ad finitum proportionem non esse*, he seems also to have retained to a certain extent the language, if not actual belief in the hierarchical, emanative universe of Neoplatonism. For example, Cusanus was fascinated throughout his life by the idea of a world-soul—the *anima mundi*, but his thoughts about it are not always consistent. At some points in the *De docta ignorantia* and certainly in the *De beryllo* he outrightly rejects the idea of the actual existence of the *anima mundi*. In works such as the *De ludo globi* and at other points in the *De docta ignorantia* he writes as though the existence of the *anima mundi* were plausible. But even when he inclines towards the idea of a Neoplatonic hierarchical, emanative universe, he seems to be attracted mainly by its figurative powers as an image or metaphor, and does not explicitly accept its ontological reality (see footnote 52 for a further discussion of Cusanus' idea of the *anima mundi*).

48. S.K. Heninger, Jr., "Pythagorean Cosmology and The Triumph of Heliocentrism," *Le Soleil à la Renaissance: Sciences et Mythes*, Colloqué International 1963, Université Libre de Bruxelles, Travaux de L'Institut pour L'Étude de la Renaissance et de L'Humanisme, II, Brussels/Paris: Presses Universitaires, 1965, pp. 35-53, see especially pp. 52-53. A balanced discussion of Copernicus' "Pythagoreanism" is found in Paul Lawrence Rose, *The Italian Renaissance of Mathematics: Studies on Humanists and Mathematicians from Petrarch to Galileo*, Geneva: Librairie Droz, 1957, pp. 122-129. Rose raises some of the important issues involved in identifying a "Pythagorean" or the "Pythagorean tradition." In his accompanying notes Rose surveys the recent debate regarding Copernicus, Pythagoreanism, and the Scientific Revolution. Though Koyré's statements regarding Copernicus' Pythagoreanism have been challenged by Rosen and others, the points Heninger raises cannot be dismissed until a fuller understanding of medieval and Renaissance Pythagoreanism, based on the historical development of the four mathematically based disciplines of the *quadrivium*—music, arithmetic, geometry, and astronomy, has been achieved. Establishing the *Problematik* and its context is the key here, not lineages of individual figures.

49. Cusanus' analysis of the motion of the ball is a synthesis of Aristotle's theory of natural and violent motion, Plato's theory of the self-moving substance or soul, and the impetus theory of fourteenth-century nominalists such as Nicolas Oresme, Thomas Bradwardine, Albert of Saxony, and Jean Buridan. On fourteenth-century theories of motion see *A Source Book in Medieval Science*, edited by Edward Grant, Cambridge, Mass.: Harvard University Press, 1974, "Dynamics;" H.G. Senger's *Die Philosophie des Nikolaus von Kues vor dem Jahre 1440*, "Ideen-und Quellengeschichtliche Untersuchungen (Exkurs II)," pp. 130-154.

50. *Timaeus* 44d; *Symposium* 190 sqq., translated by Michael Joyce in *The Collected Dialogues of Plato*, pp. 542-543.

51. Nicolai de Cusa, *Opera Omnia*, Vol. 11/3, *Compendium*, edited by B. Decker and K. Bormann, pp. 18-19: "Demum quando in sua civitate omnem sensibilis mundi fecit designationem, ne perdat eam, in mappam redigit bene ordinatum et proportionabiliter mensuratam convertitque se ad ipsam nuntiosque amplius licentiat clauditque portas et ad conditorem mundi internum transfert intuitum, qui nihil eorum est omnium, quae a nuntiis intellexit et notavit, sed omnium est artifex et causa. Quem cogitat sic se habere ad universum mundum anterioriter, sicut ipse ut cosmographus ad mappam, atque ex habitudine mappae ad verum mundum speculatur in se ipso ut cosmographo mundi creatorem, in imagine veritatem, in signo signatum mente contemplando."

52. Cusanus discussed the *anima mundi* in a number of his works and adopted various positions regarding it. In the *De docta ignorantia* (II: 9 "De anima sive forma universi") Cusanus points out that all wise men have believed that some kind of intermediary agent is necessary to effect actuality out of possibility. Men have called this "high nature" by various names; the "Platonists" have often designated it by the concept of a "world soul" or *anima mundi*. Cusanus here seems to accept at least the historical validity of this concept which he understood through the *Timaeus* and Calcidius' commentary on it as well as through certain twelfth century Platonist commentaries (particularly those of Thierry of Chartres) with which he was undoubtedly familiar. In the *De beryllo*, Cusanus returned to the problem of the *anima mundi* and other intermediary creating agents. After recalling his own statements in the *De docta ignorantia* concerning the history of these concepts, he strongly refutes them. According to Cusanus, Plato and Aristotle (whom Cusanus considered to have accepted the notion of the *anima mundi* though Aristotle never explicitly said so) were wrong in believing that a kind of agent intellect was involved in the process of creation. They were also incorrect in believing that God created out of necessity. For Cusanus, God is the single source of creation and He created freely and knowingly. On these grounds then he rejects the *anima mundi* of the Platonists, which in the *De docta ignorantia* he seemed implicitly to accept. See *De beryllo*, Chapter XXIII. The key summary passage occurs on p. 29: "Solum autem notes non esse necessarium universalem esse creatum intellectum aut universalem mundi animam propter participationem, quae Platonem movit. Sed ad omnem essendi modum sufficit habunde primum principium unitrinum; licet sit absolutum et superexaltatum, cum non sit principium contractum ut natura, quae ex necessitate operatur, sed sit principium ipsius naturae et ita supernaturale, liberum, quod voluntate creat omnia. Illa vero, quae voluntate fiunt, in tantum sunt, in quantum voluntati conformantur, et ita eorum forma est intentio imperantis. Intentio autem est similitudo intendentis, quae est communicabilis et receptibilis in alio. Omnis igitur creatura est intentio voluntatis omnipotentis." Interestingly, in the *De ludo globi*, Cusanus appears to return to the earlier, more tolerant position of the *De docta ignorantia*, though he certainly would not have denied the position that he takes here in the *De beryllo*. It is really rather the microcosm-macrocosm relationship between man and the universe that he wishes to stress here. He is therefore interested in the *anima mundi* as an image that reinforces this relationship rather than as an ontological reality.

53. Cf. *De beryllo*, pp. 20-21.

54. Cf. the discussions of spoonmaking and glass blowing in the *Idiota de mente*, through which Cusanus also emphasizes that man creates by acting in the divine image.

55. *De beryllo*, p. 41: "Sed nec ipse nec alius, quem legerim, advertit ad ea, quae in quarto notabili praemisi. Nam si considerasset hoc, reperisset utique mentem nostram, quae mathematicalia fabricat, ea, quae sui sunt officii, verius apud se habere quam sint extra ipsam.

    "Puta homo habet artem mechanicam et figuras artis verius habet in suo mentali conceptu quam ad extra sint figurabiles: ut domus, quae ab arte fit, habet veriorem figuram in mente quam in lignis. Figura enim, quae in lignis fit, est mentalis figura, idea seu exemplar. Ita de omnibus talibus. Sic de circulo, linea, triangulo atque de nostro numero et omnibus talibus, quae ex mentis conceptu initium habent et natura carent."

56. Cusanus' interest in the autonomy and intent of human thought and action in the face of fortune was shared by many of his humanist contemporaries. The humanists' preoccupation with this problem began with Petrarch and was very much related to their emphases upon the volitional and operative nature of man. Cusanus shares these emphases as well.

57. Cf. translation, pp. 73-75.

58. William J. Courtenay, "The King and the Leaden Coin: The Background of *Sine Qua Non* Causality," *Traditio* 28, 1972, pp. 185-209, p. 185. According to the *sine qua non* theory, value is something that is based upon common agreement and a mode of exchange established by man, not on any inherent value in the coins themselves. Cusanus'

conception of value comes very close to this theory although he is speaking within a more general epistemological context. But so did many of the late scholastics, who applied the notions of legislation and covenant to larger discussions of knowledge and being as well as to sacramental causality and monetary theory.

59. *Ibid*., p. 186, note 3. See also Courtenay's article, "Covenant and Causality in Pierre D'Ailly," *Speculum* 46, 1971, pp. 94-119 for a more general discussion of the late scholastic idea of causality.

60. F. Edward Cranz, "Cusanus, Luther, and the Mystical Tradition," in *The Pursuit of Holiness*, edited by Charles Trinkaus with Heiko A. Oberman, Leiden: E.J. Brill, 1974, pp. 93-103.

61. See the collection of pieces in *Antiqui und Moderni*, edited by A. Zimmerman in *Miscellanea Medievalia*, Vol. 9, Berlin: Walter De Gruyter, 1974. The contribution of Astrik Gabriel, "'Via antiqua' and 'via moderna' and the Migration of Paris Students and Masters to the German Universities in the Fifteenth Century," is especially useful for understanding Cusanus' background.

62. See Heiko A. Oberman, "Some Notes on the Theology of Nominalism with Attention to its relation to the Renaissance," *Harvard Theological Review* 53, 1960, pp. 47-76; Chapter II of my *Nicolaus Cusanus: A Fifteenth-Century Vision of Man*.

63. See especially Alberti's *I Libri della Famiglia*, translated by Renée Watkins in *The Family in Renaissance Florence*, Columbia, S.C.: University of South Carolina Press, 1969; Chapter III of my *Nicolaus Cusanus: A Fifteenth-Century Vision of Man*.

64. Sabbadini, "Niccoló da Cusa e i conciliari di Basilea alla scoperta dei condici," *op. cit.* and Kristeller, "A Latin Translation of Gemistos Plethon's *de fato* by Johannes Sophianos dedicated to Nicholas of Cusa, *op. cit.;* Chapter I of *Nicolaus Cusanus: A Fifteenth-Century Vision of Man.*

65. For a brief but brilliant assessment of Cusanus' mysticism, see F. Edward Cranz, "Cusanus, Luther, and the Mystical Tradition," *op. cit.*

66. *Laws* 803-804, quoted by J. Huizinga in his *Homo Ludens: A Study of The Play Element in Culture*, Boston: The Beacon Press, 1955, pp. 211-212.

4. TEXT AND TRANSLATION

Nicholas of Cusa – THE GAME OF SPHERES I

¶REVERENDISS. IN CHRISTO P.D.NICOLAI DE CVSA CARD. DIALOGORVM DE LVDO GLOBI LIBER PRIMVS.

Interlocutores IOANNES dux Baioariæ. Et NICOLAVS CARDINALIS.

Vm te videam ad ſedem retractum / forte fatigatum ex ludo globi: tecum (ſi gratū viderem) de hoc ludo cōferrem. CARDINALIS. Gratiſſimū. IOANNES. Admiramur omnes hunc nouū iocundūq; ludum: forte quia in ipſo eſt alicuius altæ ſpeculationis figuratio / quā rogamus explanari. CARDINALIS. Non male mouemini. habent enim aliquæ ſcientiæ inſtrumenta & ludos. Arithmetica rythmimachiam. Muſica: monochordū. Nec lud⁹ Latrūculorū ſeu ſchacorū: caret myſterio moraliū. Nullū enim puto honeſtū ludū: penitus diſciplina vacuum. Hoc vero tam iocūdum globi exercitiū: nobis non paruā puto repræſentare philoſophiā. IOANNES. Aliquid igit / rogamus: dicito. CARDI. Timeo ſubintrare laborē quē magnū video: & prius lōga meditatiōe depurandū. IOANNES. Nō cuncta ꝓfundari petimus: ſed paucis nobis ſatiſfacies.

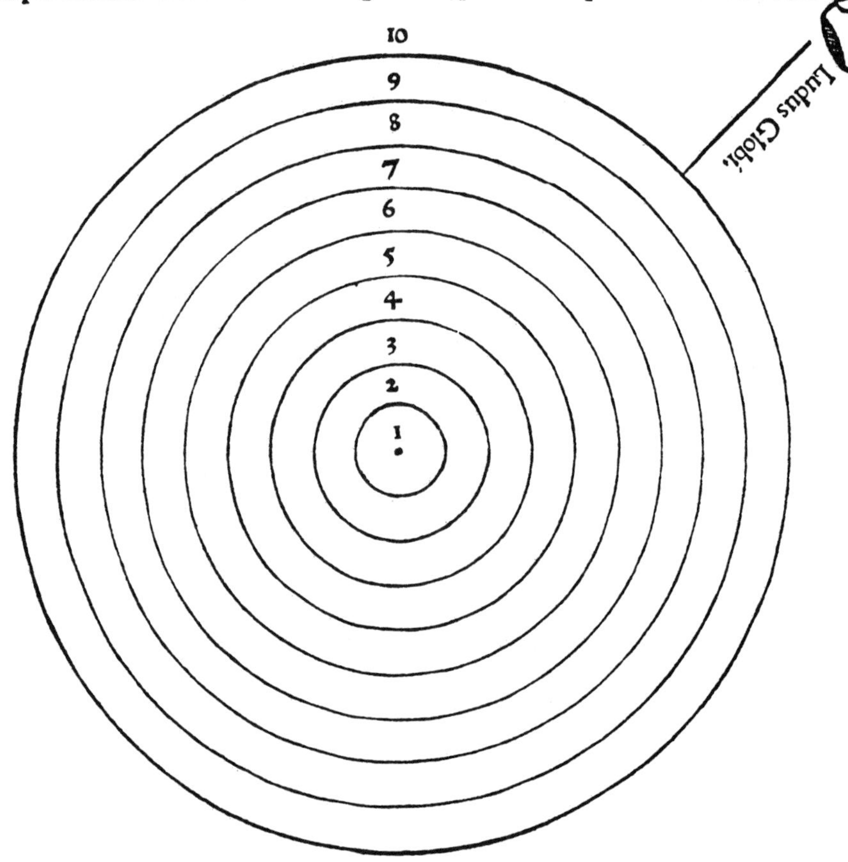

MOST REVEREND IN CHRIST LORD OUR FATHER, THE CARDINAL NICHOLAS OF CUSA'S DIALOGUES ON THE GAME OF SPHERES, BOOK ONE.

The Interlocutors are JOHN, Duke of Bavaria and THE CARDINAL NICHOLAS.

JOHN: Since I see that you have withdrawn to your seat, perhaps fatigued from the game of spheres, I would like to talk over this game with you if it is agreeable.
THE CARDINAL: It's most agreeable.
JOHN: We all admire this new and delightful game, perhaps because it represents for us some deep speculation which we are asking to be explained.
THE CARDINAL: You are not wrongly moved. In fact, some branches of knowledge have their instruments and games; arithmetic has its number games, music its monochord – nor is the game of chess or checkers lacking in the mystery of moral things. Indeed I think that no honest game is entirely lacking in the capacity to instruct. I think that this delightful exercise with the ball represents a significant philosophy for us.[1]
JOHN: Therefore we ask that you say something concerning this philosophy.
THE CARDINAL: I am afraid to venture upon a task which I see to be great and which must first be pruned through lengthy meditations.
JOHN: We don't demand that everything be explained, but you'll satisfy us with a few points.

CARDINALIS.Iuuẽtus q̃uis auida & feruẽs:cito tamẽ ſaturat̃. Faciam igit̃ & ſeminabo in nobilibus mentibus veſtris aliqua ſcientiarũ ſemina:quæ ſi intra vos receperitis & cuſtodieritis/magnæ diſcretiõis circa ſuiipſius deſideratiſſimã notitiã/lucis fructũ generabunt.Primũ igit̃ attente cõſiderabitis globũ & eius motũ: quoniam ex intelligentia ꝓcedunt.Nulla enim beſtia:globum & eius motũ ad terminũ producit. Hæc igitur opera hominis ex virtute ſuperãte cætera mundi huius animalia:fieri videtis.IOANNES.Vtiq; ſic eſſe ſcimus vt dicis.CARDI.Sed cur globus arte tornatili cepit illã mediæ ſpheræ figuram aliquãtulum cõcauam:non vos ignorare puto.Non enim faceret motum quẽ videtis:elicoidem/vertiginoſum/ſeu ſpiralẽ / aut curuæ inuolutũ: niſi talem teneret figurã.Pars enim globi qui eſt perfectus circulus/in rectum moueret̃:niſi pars ponderoſior & corpulenta motũ illum retardaret & cẽtraliter ad ſe retraheret.Ex qua diuerſitate: figura motui eſt apta/qui nec eſt penitus rectus/nec penitus curuus/vti eſt circuli/circũferẽtia ab eiꝰ centro æque diſtante.Vnde primo cauſam figurę globi attendite.in quo videtis ſuꝑficiem cõuexam medietatis maioris ſpheræ/ & ſuꝑficiem concauã medietatis minoris ſpheræ:& inter illas corpus globi cõtineri.Ac ꝙ globus infinitis modis ſecundũ variam habitudinẽ dictarũ ſuperficierũ poteſt variari:& ſemꝑ ad alium & aliũ motum adaptari.IOANNES.Sane hæc capimꝰ.Scimus enim ſi armilla poſſet eſſe circulus ſine omni latitudine circũferentiæ & volueret̃ ſuper æquali plana ſuperficie/puta ſuper glaciem:ipſa/nõ niſi rectã lineam deſcriberet . Ideo cum hic armillã globoſam videmus addita corpulentia:ideo recta linea nõ deſcribitur ſed curua/varia curuitate ſecundũ varium globum.CARDI.Recte.ſed oportet etiã cõſiderare:lineas deſcriptionis motus vnius & eiuſdem globi variari/& nunq̃ eandem deſcribi/ſiue per eundem ſiue per alium impellatur/quia ſemꝑ varie impellitur.& in maiori impulſu deſcripta linea videt̃ rectior: & ſecundũ minorem curuior.quare in principio motus qñ ĩpulſus eſt recẽtior: lineæ motus ſunt rectiores/q̃ quãdo motus tepeſcit.Non enim impellit̃ globus:niſi ad rectum motum. Vnde in maiori impulſu/globus a ſua natura magis violentatur : vt cõtra naturam/etiam quãtum fieri poteſt recte moueatur.In minore vero impulſu ad motũ naturalẽ minus violentatur:ſed aptitudinem naturalem formę ſuæ/motus ſequitur. IOANNES.Hæc clare ſic eſſe experimur. Nunq̃ enim globus mouetur vna vice ſicut alia. Oportet igitur ex alia & alia impulſione aut vario medio:hoc euenire.CARDINA.Dum quis globũ proiicit:nec vna vice ſicut alia ipſum ĩ manu tenet aut emittit/aut in plano ponit/aut æquali virtute pellit.nihil enim:bis æqualiter fieri poſſibile eſt.Implicat enĩ cõtradictionem eſſe duo:& per omnia æqualia ſine omni differentia.Quomodo enim plura poſſent eſſe plura:ſine differentia? Vnde q̃uis peritior ſemꝑ nitatur eodẽ modo ſe habere:non eſt tamẽ hoc pręciſe poſſibile/licet differentia non ſemꝑ videatur. IOANNES.Multa ſunt quæ varietatẽ inducũt:etiã pauimenti diuerſitas/& lapillorũ interceptio curſum impedientiũ & ſæpe ſuffocantiũ/ atq; globi fœculẽtia/immo fiſſura ſuꝑueniens/& talia multa. CARDINALIS. Hæc omnia cõſiderari neceſſe eſt:vt deueniamus ex iſtis ad ſpeculationẽ philoſophicã/quã venari ꝓponimꝰ. Deficit enim motio:aliquãdo ſubito cadente globo ſuꝑ planã ſuã ſuperficiem.Impeditur ob medii globi atq; circũſtantis variationẽ:naturaliterq; deficit dum ſuꝑ polo ſeu medio curuæ ſuperficiei ſucceſſiue in ipſo motus minuit̃. Hæc & multa alia puto ſubtiliter annotanda: propter ſimilitudinẽ artis & naturæ.Cũ enim ars naturam imitetur : ab iis quæ in arte ſubtiliter reperimus/ad naturæ vires accedimus.

THE CARDINAL: Although youth is avid and fervent, it is nevertheless speedily satiated. Therefore I will do what you ask and sow in your noble minds some seeds of knowledge. If you receive and protect these seeds within yourselves, each of them will produce the fruit of light which is of great importance for that most desired self-knowledge. First, therefore, consider the ball and its movement attentively. Both proceed from the intelligence, for no beast produces a ball and directs its motion to an end. Therefore you see that these works of man originate from a power which surpasses that of the other animals of this world.
JOHN: You're undoubtedly right.
THE CARDINAL: I think that you're not ignorant of why, through the art of the turner, the ball assumes a hemispherical shape that is somewhat concave. In fact, the ball would not make the helical/vertiginous, that is spiral or inwardly curving motion that you see, unless it had such a shape. For the part of the ball that is a perfect circle would be moved in a straight line unless its heavier and corpulent part retarded that motion and drew the ball centrally back towards itself. From its lack of symmetry the shape of the ball is predisposed towards a motion which is neither entirely straight nor entirely curved as it is in the circumference of a circle that is equidistant from its center. From this you will first observe the reason for the shape of the ball in which you see the convex surface of half of a greater sphere and the concave surface of half of a smaller sphere; the body of the ball is contained between the convex and concave surfaces. You will then observe that the ball can be varied in infinite ways according to the various conditions of the surfaces that have been described and can always be adapted to a variety of motions.[2]
JOHN: We grasp this very well, for we know that if an iron hoop could be a circle without any thickness of circumference and if it were rolled along upon a totally flat surface, for example, on a sheet of ice, it would describe only a straight line. For this reason, when we see a spherical corpulence added to the hoop, it does not describe a straight line but various curves according to the curvature of the various spheres.
THE CARDINAL: Correct. But it is also necessary to consider that the lines described by the motion of one and the same ball are varied and the same one is never described twice. This is so whether the ball is thrown by the same person or by someone else, because it is always thrown differently. And in a stronger throw the path of the described line appears straighter and following a weaker throw, more curved. This is why, in the beginning of the motion, when the impetus is more recent, the lines of the motion are straighter than when the motion decreases. The ball is thrown only in a straight motion. Hence in a stronger throw the ball is forced more out of its nature so that it is moved against its nature in a straight line to the extent that is possible. Yet in a weaker throw the ball is forced into a motion that is more natural and less violent, but its motion follows the natural aptitude of its form.
JOHN: Clearly, we have experienced this to be so, for the ball is never moved in the same way in one player's turn as it is in another's. Therefore this must occur because of the difference in the impetus [of the throw] or through a medium that varies.
THE CARDINAL: When someone throws the ball he does not hold it in his hand, release it, or place it on the ground in the same way twice, nor does he hurl it with the same power one time as he does another. It is not possible to do anything the same way twice, for it implies a contradiction that there be two things that are equal in all respects without any difference at all. How can many things be many without difference? Hence, however much the more skilled player always strives to exert himself in the same way, this is nevertheless not precisely possible although the difference might not always be apparent.
JOHN: There are many things that induce variety, certainly the uneveness of the pavement [does] and [so do] the obstruction of the stones which impede the course [of the ball] and often choke it, the dirtiness of the ball and even the unexpected occurrence of fissures in it and many other such things.
THE CARDINAL: It is necessary that all these things be considered so that from them we may arrive at the philosophical speculation that we propose to hunt. Motion sometimes suddenly ceases when the ball falls on the flat part of its surface. The motion is hindered because of the irregularities in the hemispherical ball and in what it encounters, and it [the ball] stops naturally when the motion successively lessens in itself above the pole or the middle of the curved surface. I believe that these and many other things must be subtly noted on account of the likeness of art and nature. For since art imitates nature we approach the powers of nature from these things which we find subtly in art.

IOANNES.Quid intendis dicere:per circunstantis variationẽ. CARDINALIS. Cæli/stellarum/& aeris/atq; temporis mutationẽ.hæc omnia immutata: immutãt illa quæ circũstant & cõtinent.IOANNES.Aiebas globum semisphericam habere superficiem.Posset ne habere minorẽ aut maiorem/siue integrę sphera rotũditatẽ? CARDINALIS. Globum posse habere superficiem maiorem aut minorem aut integræ spheræ nõ nego:si de visibili figura seu rotũditate loquimur/quæ nequaq̃ est vera aut perfecta.Nam rotũditas quæ rotundior esse non posset: nequaq̃ est visibilis.Cum enim superficies a cẽtro spheræ vndiq; æque distet: extremitas rotundi in indiuisibili puncto terminata/manet penitus nostris oculis inuisibilis. Nihil enim nisi diuisibile & quãtum:a nobis videtur.IOANNES.Vltima igitur mundi spherica rotunditas quã puto perfectissimã:nequaq̃ est visibilis. CARDINALIS. Nequaq̃.immo nec diuisibilis mundi rotunditas: cum in puncto cõsistat indiuisibili & immultiplicabili. Non enim rotũditas: ex punctis potest esse cõposita. pũctus enim cum sit indiuisibilis & non habeat aut quantitatẽ aut partes/siue ante/siue retro/& alias differentias:cum nullo alio puncto est cõponibilis. Ex punctis igitur nihil cõponitur.pũctum enim puncto addere perinde resultat:acsi nihil nihilo iungas. Nõ est igitur extremitas mundi ex punctis cõposita : sed eius extremitas est rotũditas/quæ in puncto consistit.Nam cum vna sit altitudo rotũditatis quæ vndiq; est æque distans a centro/& non possunt esse plures lineæ præcise æquales : erit vna tantum æque distans rotunditatis altitudo quæ in puncto terminatur. IOANNES. Mira dicis.Nam intelligo has omnes varias visibiles formas in mundo inclusas esse: & tamen si possibile esset aliquẽ extra mundum constitui/mũdus esset illi inuisibilis instar indiuisibilis puncti. CARDINALIS. Optime cepisti.& sic cõcipis mundũ quo nulla quantitas maior: in puncto quo nihil minus contineri/& centrum atq; circũferentiam eius non posse videri.Nec esse plura diuersa puncta:cum punctus non sit plurificabilis. in pluribus enim atomis:non est nisi vnus & idem punctus . Sicut in pluribus albis:vna albedo.vnde linea:est puncti euolutio.euoluere vero: est punctũ ipsum explicare.quod nihil aliud est: q̃ punctum in atomis pluribus ita q; in singulis coniunctis & continuatis esse. IOANNES.Nonne sic extremitas anguli cum sit punctus:est inuisibilis? CARDINALIS. Immo.Sed si angulus non esset nisi extremitas/sicut est rotunditas rotundi extremitas:certum esset totum angulũ non esse visibilem.IOANNES.Intelligo:& ita est vt ais. Ideo nec summũ nec imum rotundi videri potest:cum sit idem atomus . Quicquid autem in sphera vel rotundo est: est summum & imum.ideo nec rotunditas nec aliqua pars eius: videri potest.Non tamen dico q; res rotunda videri nequeat:sed ipsa rotũditas rei/est inuisibilis. Nec secundum veram rotũditatem:quicq̃ est visibile. Quare cum visus iudicat aliquid esse rotundum : in eo non est vera rotunditas . Hoc quidem videre videor te dicere velle:scilicet iudicium visus de rotundo/verum non esse. CARDINALIS. Hæc dicere intendo . Nihil enim videtur : nisi in materia. Vera autem rotunditas non potest esse in materia:sed veritatis tantũ imago.IOANNES.Sic nulla forma est vera in materia/sed veritatis tantũ imago veræ formæ: cum veritas formæ sit ab omni materia separata . CARDINALIS. Quis platonice verum dicas : tamen refert inter rotunditatem & aliam formam.Quoniã si etiam possibile esset rotunditatem esse in materia/tamen adhuc non esset visibilis. Secus de cæteris formis si in materia essent:quoniam videri possent.nõ tamen rotunditas : nec rotundum secundum eam videretur.Solum enim longum & latum videri potest.sed in rotunditate nihil

V

JOHN: What do you mean by the variation of circumstance?
THE CARDINAL: The mutation of heaven, the stars, and of the air and time. All these things when they change, change those things which they encompass and contain.
JOHN: You have said that the hemispherical ball has a hemispherical surface. Could it have a lesser or greater surface than that of the whole sphere or is its surface equivalent to that of the whole sphere?
THE CARDINAL: I do not deny that the ball can have a greater or lesser surface than that of the whole sphere or that its surface can be equivalent to that of the whole sphere if we are speaking of a visible figure or visible roundness, which is never true or perfect. The roundness which could not be rounder is never visible. Since the surface of the invisible sphere is everywhere equidistant from the center of the sphere, the outer edge of the roundness is terminated in an indivisible point that remains entirely invisible to our eyes. We can see only those things that are divisible and have size.
JOHN: Therefore the ultimate spherical roundness of the world which I believe is the most perfect roundness is never visible.
THE CARDINAL: Never. On the contrary, the roundness of the world is not divisible since it consists of an indivisible and unmultipliable point. Roundness cannot be composed out of points for since a point is indivisible and does not have quantity or parts or a front and back or other differences, it cannot be joined to another point. Therefore nothing is composed of points. For if you join a point to a point, the result is as if nothing is joined to nothing. Therefore the edge of the world is not composed of points, but its edge is roundness, which consists of one point. For since there is but one height of roundness which is everywhere equidistant from the center, and there could not be many precisely equal lines, there would be only one equally distant height of roundness, which is terminated in a point.
JOHN: You talk in an extraordinary way. I understand that all the various visible forms are included in the world. Nevertheless if it were possible for anybody to stand outside the world, the world would be invisible to him just as the indivisible point would be invisible to him.
THE CARDINAL: You have grasped what I'm saying very well. And in this way you conceive that the world, than which no quantity is greater, is contained in a point than which there is nothing smaller, and that its center and circumference cannot be seen. Nor can there be many diverse points, since the point is not capable of being made plural. There is only one and the same point in a plurality of atoms, as there is only one whiteness in many white things. Hence a line is the evolution of a point, for a line's evolution is the unfolding of the point itself. A line is nothing other than that a point is in a plurality of atoms in such a way that it is conjoined and continued in singular things.
JOHN: Since the edge of an angle would be a point, is it not invisible?
THE CARDINAL: Yes indeed. But if the angle were the only edge of a figure just as roundness is the only edge of roundness, it is certain that the whole angle would be invisible.
JOHN: I understand; it is as you have said. For this reason neither the top nor the bottom of roundness can be seen since it would be the same atom. Yet whatever is in a sphere or roundness is the top and bottom. Therefore neither roundness nor any of its parts can be seen. Nevertheless, I don't say that a round thing cannot be seen, but rather that the roundness itself of the thing is invisible. Nor is anything that is in accord with true roundness visible, therefore when the vision judges something to be round true roundness is not in it. In fact, it appears to me that you want to say this: that evidently the judgment of the vision concerning roundness is not true.
THE CARDINAL: This is what I mean; nothing is visible except in matter. Moreover, true roundness cannot exist in matter but only the image of true roundness.
JOHN: Since the truth of form is separated from all matter, no form is true in matter but only the image of the true form of truth is in matter.
THE CARDINAL: Although from the Platonic point of view you speak the truth, there is nevertheless a difference between roundness and other forms. If indeed it were possible for [true] roundness to be in matter, it would nevertheless still not be visible. It is otherwise concerning the rest of the forms since they could be seen if they were in matter. Nevertheless roundness or a round thing in accordance with roundness could not be seen, for only length and width can be seen. But in roundness nothing is long or wide or straight. Roundness is a kind of circumference, a certain convexity led around from point to point whose top is everywhere. And its top is the atom, invisible because of its tinyness.

longum aut latum seu directum:sed circũductio quædam / & circunducta quædam de puncto ad punctum conuexitas / cuius summum est vbiq₃.& est atomus / sua paruitate inuisibilis. IOANNES. Nonne plures atomi sunt plura rotunditatis summa / & facere possunt lineam quandam conuexam quæ videri potest & sic quædam pars rotunditatis videtur? CARDINALIS. Hoc esse non potest: cum quicquid est in rotunditate / sit summũ. Atomus autem summitatem rotunditatis cum teneat: vnde initium videndi rotunditatẽ sumeret oculus? non ab atomo: cum sit inuisibilis.nec ab alio q̃ a summo rotunditatis:oculus recipere posset initium videndi rotũditatem.Summũ enim est: quicquid in rotunditate est. summũ autem: atomus est. Nonne si poneretur ꝙ a summo rotunditatis inciperet visus:oporteret ipsum duci a summo ad summũ? IOANNES.Certum est hoc fieri oportere:cum nihil in ea sit nisi summũ.CARDINALIS.Summum autem atomus est:quæ non est visibilis.Patet igitur Mercurium recte dixisse: mundum ex se non esse visibilem / quia rotũdus est. & nihil de eo vel in eo videtur: nisi rerum formæ in eo contentæ. IOANNES. Mundi rotunditas cum sit in materia / & propter adiunctionem ad materiã sit imago rotunditatis:quare illa rotunditatis imago in materia videri non potest? CARDINALIS. Intantum illa rotunditatis imago ad veram rotunditatem accedit: ꝙ visum & omnem sensum subterfugit.IOANNES.Ideo mundum non videmus:nisi inquãtum per partes:rerum formas videmus. quibus subtractis: nec mundũ nec eius formam videremus. CARDINALIS. Bene dicis.Nam mundi forma:rotunditas est inuisibilis. Visibilibus igit̃ formis subtractis:vn⁹ manet in toto orbe vultus / scilicet essendi possibilitas / siue materia inuisibilis / in qua dicitur esse rerũ vniuersitas. & satis philosophice concedi potest: ꝙ propter perfectionem ibi sit rotunditas.IOANNES.Hæc meum excedunt conceptum.licet videam in mente te vera dicere:admiror tamen / ꝙ nec in mundo vera est rotunditas / sed tantum imago rotunditatis / veritati propinqua.CARDINALIS.Non mireris.Nam cum vnum rotundum sit perfectius alio in rotunditate: nunq̃ reperitur rotundũ quod sit ipsa rotunditas / seu quo non possit dari magis rotundũ.Et hæc regula est verisimiliter vera. quoniã in omnibus recipientibus maius aut minus: non deuenitur ad maximũ aut minimũ simpliciter quo maius aut minus esse non possit.Nam posse esse maius aut minus:nõ sunt de natura eorũ quæ nõ possunt esse maius aut minus. Sicut mutabile:non est de natura immutabilis. & diuisibile:de natura indiuisibilis. & visibile:de natura inuisibilis.& temporale:de natura intempoaalis.& corporale:de natura incorporalis.& ita de similibus. Rotũditas igitur quæ visu attingitur: magis & minus recipit / quoniã vnum rotundũ est alio rotundius.Igitur rotunditas inuisibilis non est de illa natura. non est igitur per corpus participabilis sicut visibilis. Ideo nullum corpus potest esse adeo rotundũ quin possit esse rotundius.Corporalis igitur mundus licet sit rotundus: tamẽ illa rotunditas est alterius naturæ q̃ sit rotunditas cuiuscũq₃ alterius rotundi corporis.Sed cũ nõ omne corpus sit visibile:requiritur certa magnitudo vt videatur.sic etiã rotunditas atomi non est visibilis:quãdo atomus non videtur. Mũdus igitur:in sua rotunditate est inuisibilis. quia id qđ se visui offert de rotunditate mundi: atomus est. IOANNES. Clare declarasti:& in paucis multa explanasti. Sed scire cupio quomodo intelligis perfecti mundi rotũditatem esse imaginem:quę videtur semp posse fieri pfectior? CARDINALIS.Scio rotunditatẽ vnius rotundi rotũdiorem alia.Et ideo in rotundis deueniri oportere ad rotundum maximæ rotunditatis: qua nulla maior esse potest,quoniam non po-

JOHN: Aren't there many atoms, many tops of roundness, and can't they form a certain kind of convex line which can be seen? Thus, can't a certain part of the roundness be seen?
THE CARDINAL: This cannot be, since whatever is in roundness would be the top. Moreover since the atom occupies the top of roundness, where would the eye commence seeing the roundness? The eye couldn't commence seeing roundness from the atom since it is invisible, nor from anything else, but only from the top of roundness. The top is whatever is in roundness. Moreover the top is the atom. Is it not true that if vision is considered to begin at the top of roundness, it is necessary that it [vision] be led from top to top?
JOHN: Certainly it is necessary that this be done since nothing except the top would be in roundness.
THE CARDINAL: Moreover the top is the atom, which is not visible. Therefore it is evident that Hermes Trismegistus spoke correctly when he said that the world is not visible from itself because it is round and that nothing is seen of it or in it except the forms of things contained in it.[3]
JOHN: Since the roundness of the world is in matter and is the image of roundness on account of its being conjoined to matter, why can't that image of roundness be seen in matter?
THE CARDINAL: That image of roundness so nearly approaches true roundness that it escapes vision and all the senses.
JOHN: Therefore we do not see the world except inasmuch as we see forms through the parts of things. If the things were subtracted, we would see neither the world nor its form.
THE CARDINAL: What you say is right. Roundness, the form of the world, is invisible. Therefore, if the visible forms were subtracted, one aspect in which the universe of things is said to exist would remain throughout the orb—namely the possiblity of being or invisible matter. And, philosophically speaking, it can be satisfactorily granted that, on account of its perfection, here would be roundness.
JOHN: I am incapable of conceiving of these things. Although I see in my mind that what you say is true, nevertheless I am astonished that true roundness is not in the world, but only the image of roundness resembling the truth.
THE CARDINAL: Don't be amazed. Since one round thing is more perfect than another in roundness, nothing round is ever discovered that is roundness itself or that than which nothing rounder can be posited. And this rule is universally true since in all things receiving the greater or lesser one does not arrive at the maximum that cannot be greater or minimum that cannot be lesser.[4] The possibility of being greater or lesser is not in the nature of things which cannot be greater or lesser just as mutability is not in the nature of an immutable thing, or divisibility in the nature of an indivisible thing, or visibility in the nature of an invisible thing, or temporality in the nature of an atemporal thing, or corporeality in the nature of an incorporeal thing, and so on for similar things.

Therefore the roundness that is attained by vision receives the greater and the lesser since one round thing is rounder than another. Invisible roundness is not of that nature, nor is it capable of being participated in through the body as is visible roundness. For that reason no body could be so round that it could not be rounder.

Therefore although the corporeal world is round, nevertheless its roundness is of another nature than is the roundness of any other round body. Since not every body is visible, but requires a certain magnitude in order to be seen, so also the roundness of an atom is not visible when the atom is not seen. Therefore the world is invisible in its roundness because that which offers itself to the vision concerning the roundness of the world is the atom.
JOHN: You have argued clearly and have explained many things in a few words. But, I want to know in what way you understand that the roundness of the perfect world is an image which appears to be capable of being always more perfect.
THE CARDINAL: I know that the roundness of one round thing is rounder than another and for this reason in round things it is necessary to arrive at the round thing of greatest roundness than which no roundness can be greater, since it is not possible to proceed into infinity.

test in infinitum procedi. & hæc est mundi rotunditas: participatione cuius omne rotundum est rotũdum. Hæc est participabilis rotunditas in omnibus mundi huius rotundis: quæ gerunt imaginem rotunditatis mundi. Sed mundi rotunditas licet sit maxima qua nulla maior est actu: non est tamen ipsa absoluta verissima rotũditas. Ideo est imago rotunditatis absolutę. Rotundus enim mundus nõ est ipsa rotunditas qua maior non est: sed qua maior non est a ctu. Absoluta vero rotunditas non est de natura rotunditatis mundi: sed eius causa & exemplar / cuius rotunditas mundi / est imago. in circulo enim vbi non est principium nec finis cum nullus punctus in eo sit qui potius sit principium q̃ finis: video imaginem trinitatis. quare & rotũditatem / imaginem assero æternitatis: cum sint idẽ. IOANNES. Placent hæc. Sed quæro. Nõne sicut mundus dicitur rotundus: potest etiam dici æternus? Videtur enim cum æternitas & rotunditas illa absoluta sint idem: ita & æternum sit idem cũ rotundo. CARDINALIS. Non puto intelligentẽ negare mundum esse æternum: licet non sit æternitas. Solus enim omniũ creator: sic est æternus ꝙ æternitas. si quid aliud dicitur æternum: hoc habet non quia ipsa est æternitas / sed quia eius participatiõe seu ab ipsa est. Aeternitas enim oĩa æterna præcedit: nisi sit æternum illud quod idem est cum æternitate. Aeternitas igitur mundi cum sit mundi æternitas: est ante mundũ etiã æternũ. Ab ea enim habet ꝙ est æternus: sicut albũ ab albedine ꝙ est albũ. Aeternitas igitur mũdi cũ habeat id q̃d est absoluta æternitas: constituit mundũ æternum / scilicet nunq̃ finibilem siue perpetuũ qui dicitur æternus. Quoniã nunq̃ verũ fuit dicere æternitas est: quin verũ fuit dicere mũdus est / licet mundus ab ipsa sit id quod est. IOANNES. Si recte intelligo: tunc non potest esse nisi vnus mũdus maxime rotundus & æternus. CARDINALIS. Bene cepisti. Nam cũ in rotũdis ad vnum maximũ actu necesse sit deuenire: sicut inter calida ad ignem qui est maxime calidus: erit igitur vnus tantũ mundus. & hic tantum habet rotunditatis: ꝙ ad ipsam rotunditatem æternam maxime accedit. & hinc etiam inuisibilis. quare etiam æternus dici potest. Dicente apostolo Paulo. quæ non videtur / æterna sunt. non ꝙ propterea æternus dicatur: quia sine initio. sed quia nunq̃ fuit verum dicere æternitas est: quinetiam fuerit verum dicere mundus est. Mũdus enĩ non incepit in tempore. Non enim tempus præcessit mundum: sed sola æternitas. Sic & tempus aliquãdo dicitur æternum: vt propheta ait de æterno tempore / cum tempus non habuerit initium in tẽpore. Tempus enim non præcessit tempus: sed æternitas. Dicitur igitur æternum tẽpus: quia ab æternitate fluit. Sic & mundus æternus: quia est ab æternitate & non a tempore. Sed mundo magis conuenit nomen vt dicatur æternus q̃ tempori: quia mundi duratio non dependet a tempore. Cessante enim motu cæli & tempore quod est mensura motus: non cessat esse mundus. Sed mundo penitus deficiente: deficeret tempus. Magis igitur conuenit mundo ꝙ dicatur æternus / q̃ tempori. Aeternitas igitur mundi creatrix / deus est: qui vt voluit cuncta fecit. Mundus enim non est sic perfecte creatus / ꝙ in eius creatione deus omne quod potuit facere fecerit: licet mundus factus sit ita perfectus sicuti fieri potuit. quare perfectiorem & rotundiorem mundum atq; etiam imperfectiorem & minus rotundum potuit facere deus: licet factus sit ita perfectus sicut esse potuit. Hoc enim est factus quod fieri potuit: & fieri posse ipsius / factum est. Sed hoc fieri posse eius quod factum est: non est ipsum facere posse absolutum omnipotentis dei. licet in deo posse fieri & posse facere sint idem: non tamen fieri posse cuiuscunq; est idem cum facere posse dei. Ex hoc videtur / deum / mundum vt

V ii

And this is the roundness of the world by participation in which every round thing is round. This is the participative roundness in which all the round things of this world which produce the image of the roundness of the world participate. But although the roundness of the world is the maximal roundness than which nothing is actually greater, it is nevertheless not the absolute, most true roundness itself. For that reason it is the image of absolute roundness.

The round world is not that roundness itself than which no roundness can be greater, but that roundness than which nothing can actually be greater. Absolute roundness is not of the nature of the roundness of the world, but is its cause and exemplar, the absolute roundness of which the roundness of the world is the image. I see the image of eternity in a circle, where there is neither a beginning nor an end since there is no point in it which would be the beginning rather than the end.[5] This is why I assert that roundness is the image of eternity since the circle and roundness are the same thing.

JOHN: These things are pleasing, but, I ask, just as the world is called round, can it not also be called eternal? For it seems that since eternity and absolute roundness are the same thing that therefore the eternal is the same as the round.

THE CARDINAL: I don't think that the intelligent person denies that the world is eternal although it is not eternity. The creator alone of all things is eternal in such a way that he is eternity. If something else is called eternal this obtains not because it is eternity itself but because it is eternal by participation in eternity or because it is derived from it [eternity]. Eternity precedes all eternal things except for that eternal thing that is identical with eternity. Therefore the eternity of the world since it is the eternity of the world also exists prior to the eternal world. For the eternal world has from eternity that it is eternal as a white thing has from whiteness that it is white. Therefore the eternity of the world, since it is that which it is from absolute eternity, makes the world eternal, namely that which is never terminable or is perpetual, which is called eternal. Therefore, it was never true to say that the eternity exists, indeed rather it was true to say that the world exists, although the world is made that which it is from eternity.

JOHN: If I understand correctly then there can be only one maximally round and eternal world.

THE CARDINAL: You have grasped this well. Since in round things it is necessary to arrive at one actually existent maximum, just as in hot things it is necessary to arrive at fire, which is the maximum in heat, there will therefore be only one world. And this one world is so round that it comes closest to maximally eternal roundness itself. And hence it is also invisible, which is why it can also be called eternal.

According to the saying of the Apostle Paul, those things that cannot be seen are eternal (II *Cor.* 4:18). The world is called eternal not because it is without beginning, but because it never was true to say that eternity is, without it also being true to say the world is. The world did not begin in time, time did not precede the world, but only eternity. Thus sometimes time is called eternal; so the prophet spoke of 'eternal time' since time did not have its beginning in time (*Baruch* 3:32). Time did not precede time, but eternity did.

Therefore time is called eternal because it flows from eternity. And so is the world called eternal, because it is from eternity and not from time. Therefore it is more appropriate for the world to be called eternal than temporal because the duration of the world does not depend upon time. For if the motion of the heavens, and time, which is the measure of motion, were to cease, the world would not cease to exist. But if the world were to utterly cease, time would cease. Therefore it is more appropriate for the world to be called eternal than for time to be called eternal.

Therefore God, who made all things as he wanted to, is the eternity that creates the world. For the world is not created so perfectly that God made everything which he could make in his creation although the world was made just as perfect as it could have been made. Hence God could make a more perfect and rounder and even a more imperfect and less round world although the world was made as perfect as it could be. For it was made in the way that it was able to be made and its capacity to be made was made.

But this its capacity to be made that was made is not the omnipotent God's absolute capacity to make itself. Although in God the capacity to be made and the capacity to make are the same thing, nevertheless something's capacity to be made is not the same thing as God's capacity to make. From this it appears that God created the world in the way he wished to, which is truly why it is perfect because it is made according to the most free will of the best God.

voluit creasse.quare perfectus valde:quia secundum dei optimi liberrimã factus est voluntatem.Quæ quia in aliis locis luculenter scripta legi possunt:nũc de hoc sufficiat. IOANNES. Reuertere igitur ad ludum nostrum: & de motu globi aliquid adiicias. CARDINALIS .Multa dicenda restant:si/quæ occurrunt/referrem.Primum noto dum de motu globi a puncto vbi statur ad signum medium signati circuli globum proiicio:quomodo per lineam rectam hoc fieri nequit. vt si punctus a: sit statio.& b d/circulus.cuius cẽtrum:c.& e:globus. Volo de a/proiicere ad c. hoc per lineam motus globi fieri necesse est/quæ non sit recta : cuiuscunq; etiam figuræ fuerit globus. IOANNES. Videtur ꝙ si sphericus fuerit:fieri posset motus per lineam rectam vt est a c/linea.Non enim video cur sphera per a c moueri non possit: & in c quiescere. CARDINALIS. Facile capies te errare:si attendis vnam lineam rectiorẽ esse alia.& ideo ad verissime & præcisissime rectam per supra datam doctrinam nequaq̃ perueniri. Ideo nõ est possibile etiam perfectissimã spheram de a in c/ per præcisam rectam pergere: esto etiam ꝙ pauimentum sit perfectissime planum/ & globus rotundissimus . Nam talis globus non tangeret planiciem nisi in atomo. Ex motu non nisi inuisibilem lineam describeret:& nequaq̃ rectissimam inter a & c puncta cadẽtem.neq; vnq̃ in c quiesceret. Quomodo enim super atomũ quiesceret? Perfectæ igitur rotundus cum eius summũ sit etiam imum & sit atomus:postq̃ incepit moueri/quantũ in se est nunq̃ cessabit/cum varie se habere nequeat.Nõ enim id quod moueť aliquãdo cessaret: nisi varie se haberet vno tẽpore & alio.Ideo sphera in plana & æquali superficie se semper æqualiter habens:semel mota semper moueretur. Forma igitur rotunditatis : ad perpetuitatem motus est aptissima. Cui si motus aduenit naturaliter:nunq̃ cessabit. Ideo si super se mouetur vt sit centrũ sui motus:perpetue mouetur.Et hic est motus naturalis:quo motu vltima sphera mouetur sine violentia & fatigatione.quem motũ:omnia naturalem motum habentia/ participant.IOANNES.Quomodo concreauit deus motũ vltimæ spheræ?CARDINALIS.In similitudine:quomodo tu creas motũ globi. Nõ enim mouetur sphera illa per deum creatorẽ aut spiritũ dei : sicut nec glob⁹ mouetur per te quãdo ipsum vides discurrere nec per spiritũ tuũ.licet posueris ipm in motu: exequẽdo per iactũ manus/volũtatẽ/impetũ in ipm faciendo/quo durante mouetur.IOANNES. Sic forte & de anima dici posset / quo existente in corpore homo moueť. CARDINALIS.Non est ꝓpinquius fortasse exemplũ intelligendi creationẽ animæ: quã sequitur motus in homine . Nõ enim deus est anima:aut spiritus dei mouet hominẽ. Sed creatus est in te motus seipsum mouẽs secundũ platonicos:qui est anima rationalis mouens se & cuncta tua.IOANNES. Viuificare:animæ cõuenit.Est igiť motus.CARDINALIS. Vtiq; viuere motus quidã est.IOANNES.Placet valde.Nũc enim video hoc sensibili exemplo:multos errasse circa animæ cõsiderationẽ.CARDINALIS. Attende motũ globi deficere & cessare manente globo sano & integro: quia non est motus qui globo inest/naturalis/sed accidẽtalis & violentus.Cessat igitur:impetu qui impressus est ei deficiente . Sed si globus ille esset perfecte rotundus (vt prædictũ est) quia illi globo rotundus motus esset naturalis ac nequaq̃ violentus/nunq̃ cessaret.Sic motus viuificans animal nunq̃ cessat corpus viuificare q̃diu viuificabile & sanum est:quia est naturalis . Et licet motus viuificandi/animali cesset deficiente sanitate corporis:tamẽ non cessat motus intellectualis animæ humanæ/quem sine corpore habet & exercet. Ideo motus ille seipsum intellectualiter mouens : est in se subsistens & substantialis . Motus enim qui non est seipsum mouens:

Because excellent writings can be read in other places concerning these things, enough has been said concerning this for now.[6]
JOHN: Return now to our game and add something concerning the motion of the ball.
THE CARDINAL: Many things remain to be said which I will refer to if they should come up. Concerning the motion of the ball, I first note that I cannot throw the ball from the point where it is fixed toward the middle of the circle that has been marked out in a straight line. Thus, if point A were fixed and BD a circle whose center was C, and E the ball, and if I want to throw from A to C, it is necessary that this be done through the line of the motion of the ball which would not be straight, regardless of the shape of the ball.
JOHN: It seems that if the ball were spherical, the motion could be made in a straight line, that is, the line AC. I do not see why the sphere cannot be moved in the line AC and come to rest in point C.
THE CARDINAL: You will easily grasp your error if you consider that one line is straighter than another. And for that reason the most truly and precisely straight line will never be arrived at by the instruction given above. And also for this reason it is not possible that the most perfect sphere proceed from point A to point C in a straight line, even if the pavement were most perfectly flat and the ball most round. For such a ball would not touch the level ground except in an atom. The ball would describe only an invisible line in its motion and not the straightest line between points A and C and it would never come to rest in point C. For how would it come to rest upon an atom?

Therefore since the top of the perfectly round object would also be its bottom and since it would be an atom after it was set in motion, its motion will never cease by itself since it cannot vary. But that which is moved stops whenever it is set in motion because its movement varies from one time to another. For this reason the sphere, which always exists evenly on a flat and even surface, would be in perpetual motion once it is set in motion. Therefore the form of roundness is most suited for perpetual motion. If it arrives at such a motion naturally, it will never cease. For this reason if it is moved upon itself so that it is the center of its motion, it is in perpetual motion and this is natural motion by which the ultimate sphere is moved without violence and fatigue. All things having natural motion participate in this motion.[7]
JOHN: How did God create the ultimate sphere and its motion together?
THE CARDINAL: In likeness of the way in which you create the motion of the ball. That sphere is not moved by God the creator or by the spirit of God just as the ball is not moved by you when you see it roll along. Nor is it moved by your spirit, although you have put it in motion by executing your will through the throw of the hand, making an impetus upon the ball, by which the ball is moved as long as the impetus endures.
JOHN: And perhaps the same thing could be said of the soul, for man is moved through its existence in the body.
THE CARDINAL: It is probably not the closest example for understanding the creation of the soul, which is followed by motion in man. For God is not the soul nor does the spirit of God move man. But, according to the Platonists, self-moving motion which is the rational soul moving itself and your entirety, is created within you.
JOHN: It is for the soul to give life. Therefore life is motion.
THE CARDINAL: Certainly life is a kind of motion.
JOHN: This is greatly pleasing, for now I see by this sensible example that many have been in error in their considerations about the soul.
THE CARDINAL: Notice that the movement of the ball declines and ceases, leaving the ball sound and whole, because the motion that is within the ball is not natural, but accidental and violent. Therefore when the impetus that is impressed upon it dies out, it stops. But if, as has already been said, that ball were perfectly round, its motion would be round. That motion would be natural and in no way violent and would never cease.

So the motion which gives life to the animal never ceases to give life to the body as long as it is healthy and capable of life, because it is natural. And although the motion that gives life to the animal ceases with the declining health of the body, nevertheless the intellectual motion of the human soul, which exists and functions without the body, does not cease. For this reason that motion, which intellectually moves itself, is self-subsistent and substantial. That motion which is not self-moving is an accident, but that motion which is self-moving is a substance.

accidens est. sed seipsum mouens: substantia est. non enim illi accidit motus: cuius natura est motus. vti de natura intellectus: qui non potest esse intellectus sine motu intellectuali per quē est actu. Ideo intellectualis motus: est substantialis seipsum mouens. Nunq̄ igitur deficit. Viuificatio vero est motus vitæ qui accidit corpori: qđ de sua natura non est viuum. sine vita enim corpus: verum corpus est. Potest igitur ille motus qui corpori accidit: cessare. sed propter hoc non cessat motus substantialis seipsum mouens. Nam virtus illa quæ & mens dicitur: corpus deserit / quando cessat in ipso viuificare / sentire / & imaginari. Has enim habet operationes virtus in corpore: quas etiam dum non exercet nihilominus manet in perpetuum: licet etiam localiter separaretur a corpore. Virtus enim illa / licet in loco circunscribatur vt non sit nisi ibi: non tamen occupat locum cum sit spiritus. Propter eius enim præsentiam non distenditur aer aut locus occupatur: vt minus capiat de corpore q̄ prius. IOANNES. Valde placet similitudo globi ad corpus: & motus eius ad animam. homo facit globum & eius motum / quem impetu ei imprimit: & est inuisibilis / indiuisibilis / non occupans locum / sicut anima nostra. Sed ꝙ anima nostra sit motus substantialis: libenter melius intelligerem. CARDINALIS. Deus dator est substantiæ: homo accidentis seu similitudinis substantiæ. forma globi data ligno per hominem: addita est substantiæ ligni. sic & motus: additus est formæ substantiali. deus autem: creator substantiæ. Multa motum participant: vt moueantur ex participatione motus. Deuenitur igitur ad vnum: quod per se mouetur. & illi non accidit ex participatione motus vt moueatur: sed ex sua essentia. & est anima intellectiua. Intellectus enim: seipsum mouet. Et vt clarius hoc capias: attende quomodo in rotunditate est aptitudo ad motum. Facilius enim mouetur magis rotundum. Quare si rotunditas esset maxima qua etiam maior esse non posset: vtiq̧ per seipsam moueretur / & esset mouēs pariter & mobile. Motus igitur qui anima dicitur / est concreatus corpori & nō impressus ei vt in globo / sed per se motus / corpori adiunctus. & taliter: ꝙ separabilis ab ipso. ideo substantia. IOANNES. Igitur bene dicitur ꝙ virtus illa quam animā dicis intellectiuam: patiatur aut præmietur. CARDINALIS. Certissime hoc verū credas. Sicut enim in corpore affligitur affectionibus corporis: ita etiā extra corpus affligit̄ ira / inuidia / & cæteris afflictionibꝰ / grauata adhuc sorde corporea / nec corporis oblita. Etiam affligitur igne materiali ad hoc præparato: ita vt ardoris lęsionem sentiat. Nostro enim igne non posset affligi. Similiter etiam virtus illa hoc est anima: saluatur / hoc est in quiete est / & nullis tormentis affligitur. IOANNES. Intelligo te nūc dicere / ꝙ anima est substantia incorporea: & virtus diuersarum virtutum. Nam ipsa est sensualitas. Est etiam ipsa imaginatio. Eadem etiam est ratio / & intelligentia. Sensualitatem & imaginationem exercet in corpore. Rationē & intelligentiam extra corpus exercet. Vna est substantia sensualitatis / imaginationis / rationis / & intelligentiæ: licet sensus non sit imaginatio / nec ratio / nec intellectus. Ita nec imaginatio / aut ratio / aut intellectus aliquid aliorum. Sunt enim diuersi modi appræhendendi in anima: quorum vnus / alius esse non potest. Sic puto te dicere velle. CARDINALIS. Vtiq̧ sic dicere volo. IOANNES. Tu etiam videris dicere: animam in corpore esse simul in diuersis locis. CARDINALIS. Sic dico. Nam cū sit virtus / & quælibet pars virtutis de toto verificetur secundum veram philosophiam: tunc viuificatio animæ anima est. Ipsa autem anima: diuersa corporis membra quæ in diuersis locis sunt / viuificat. Igitur ibi est vbi viuificat. Tota igitur animæ substantia dum est in corpore in diuer-

Motion does not happen to that whose nature is motion, as in the case of the nature of the intellect which cannot be intellect without the intellectual motion through which it is in act. For this reason intellectual motion is substantial and self-moving. Therefore it never ceases.

However, vivification is the motion of life which happens to the body which is not alive from its own nature. Without life the body is a true body. Therefore that motion which happens to the body can cease, but the substantial self-moving motion does not cease because of this cessation of bodily motion. That power, the substantial self-moving motion, which is also called the mind, deserts the body when it ceases to give life, to sense, and to imagine in it [the body], for this power [the mind] has these operations in the body. When it does not practice them, the mind nevertheless remains in perpetuity although it is also locally separated from the body. For although that power [the mind] is circumscribed within a place, so that it would not be unless it were here, it nevertheless does not occupy a place since it is a spirit. For the air is not distended nor a place occupied on account of the soul's presence, as it occupies less space outside of the body than it did before.

JOHN: The likeness of the ball to the body and of its motion to the soul is deeply pleasing. Man makes the ball and its motion which he imprints upon it by impetus and it is invisible, indivisible, not occupying a place, just like our soul. But I very much want to understand better the way in which our soul might be substantial motion.

THE CARDINAL: God is the giver of substance, man the giver of accidents or the likeness of substance. The form of the ball is given to the wood through man having added to the substance of the wood just as motion is added to the substantial form. Moreover God is the creator of substance. Many things participate in motion so that they may be moved out of participation in motion. Therefore one thing is arrived at that is self-moving and it does not happen that it is moved from participation in motion, but [it is moved] from its essence. And it is the intellective soul.

The intellect is self-moving. And in order that you may grasp this more clearly, observe how there is an aptitude towards motion in roundness. For the rounder a thing is, the more easily it is moved. This is why if the roundness were maximal, so that it could not be greater, it [the maximally round thing], would undoubtedly be moved through itself and it would move evenly and quickly. Therefore the motion that is called the soul is created together with the body and not impressed upon it as in the ball, but the motion is joined to the body through itself and in such a way that it is separable from it and for this reason the soul is a substance.

JOHN: Therefore it is right that that power which you call the intellective soul may suffer or be rewarded.

THE CARDINAL: Certainly you may believe this to be true. For just as the intellective soul is afflicted in the body by the affections of the body, so also outside the body it is afflicted by anger, envy, and by other afflictions, being still burdened by the squalor of the body and not oblivious to it. And also the soul is afflicted with a material fire prepared to this end; that it may feel the burning of the flame. Our fire could not afflict it. In like manner also that power that is the soul is saved—that is, it is at peace and is afflicted by no torments.

JOHN: Now I understand you to say that the soul is an incorporeal substance and the power of diverse powers. For it is sensuality itself, it is also imagination itself, and the same soul is also reason and intelligence. It practices sensuality and imagination in the body, reason and intelligence outside the body. It is the one substance of sensuality, imagination, reason, and intelligence, although sense is not imagination, reason or intellect. And in the same way neither imagination nor reason, nor intellect is any of the others. They are diverse modes of apprehending in the soul, and one mode cannot be another. I think that this is what you mean.

THE CARDINAL: It certainly is what I mean.

JOHN: You also seem to be saying that the soul exists simultaneously in different places in the body.

THE CARDINAL: That's it. For since it [the soul] is a power and each part of the power is, according to the true philosophy, verified concerning the whole, then the vivification of the soul is the soul. Moreover the soul itself gives life to different parts of the body that are in different places. The soul is in that place where it gives life, therefore the whole substance of the soul exists in diverse places where it is in the body.

sis locis est. Sed dum est extra corpus: nō est in diuersis locis. Sicut nec angelus: qui non viuificat. In corpore igitur est tota anima in qualibet parte corporis: sicut eius creator in qualibet parte mundi. IOANNES. Retrahit ne se anima: dum digitus abscinditur? CARDINALIS. Nequaq̄: sed desinit digitum viuificare. Non enim retrahit se: quia non transit de vna corporis particula ad aliam/cū sit simul in omnibus & singulis. IOANNES. Adhuc vnum rogo: iterum circa animæ motum declares/ quādo ais animam seipsam mouere/dicito qua specie motus se perpetuo mouet? CARDINALIS. Nulla specie ex omnibus sex speciebus motus se mouet anima: sed æquiuoce. Mouet enim seipsam anima: id est discernit/abstrahit/diuidit & colligit. Ratiocinari: virtus est animæ. igitur & anima. Aliqua est ratio perpetua & immutabilis: vt q̄ quatuor non sint duo/ quia quatuor in se habēt tria quæ non habēt duo/igitur quatuor non sunt duo. Hæc ratio est immutabilis. Anima igitur est immutabilis. dū autē ratio sic discurrit ratiocinādo: vtiq̄ ille discursus rationalis est. A se igitur rationalis anima: ratiocinando mouetur. Adhuc anima est vis inuentiua artium & scientiarum nouarum. In motu igitur illo inuentiuo noui: non nisi a seip̄a moueri potest. Sic dum se facit similitudinem omniū cognoscibilium: a se mouetur. vt dum in sensu se facit similitudinē sensibilium/in visu visibilium/in auditu audibilium/& ita de omnibus. Ideo anima ex eodem & diuerso dicitur constare: propter compræhendi motum vniuersalem omniū/& particularem diuersorū. Sic ex indiuiduo & diuiduo: quia se cōformat diuisibili & mutabili. Vnde anima vis ē illa quæ se omnibus rebus potest cōformare: & facit se causam motus corporis/ scilicet manus & pedis. sed nō semper ex discretione: quoniam & a natura est motus/vt in motu neruorum & pulmonis. In pueris vero propter debilitatem non facit se similitudinem rerum. sed post annos discretionis corpore firmato adiūcta discretione: & maxime si doctrina exercetur. Est enim ī pueris adhuc informis quo ad vsum rationis/naturæ subiecta: vt fiat fortis & perfectus homo. & eius īformitas: ad perfectionem mouetur doctrina & exercitio. Potest autem dici: animā se mouere dupliciter. Aut cum se facit causam motuum corporis/quod etiam facit dormiēdo. Aut cum se facit similitudinem rerum/ quod extra corpus humanum viuere etiam videtur esse se mouere. Vnde anima verius viuit quia ex se mouetur: q̄ homo qui mouetur ab anima. IOANNES. Hinc puto: q̄ deus verius viuat q̄ anima. CARDINALIS. Recte putas: non q̄ deus se moueat aut faciat similitudinē rerum quod facit anima/licet in eo sint omnia in quadam simplicitate. sed quia ipse verum esse rerum est: & vita vitarum. Sic enim ait. Ego sum resurrectio & vita. IOANNES. Multum placent quæ de inuentione noui: supra memorasti. In eo enim actu anima clare videtur seipsam mouere. vellem vt ad ludum applicares. CARDINALIS. Cogitaui inuenire ludum sapientiæ. consideraui quomodo illum fieri oporteret. deinde terminaui ipsum sic faciendum vt vides. Cogitatio/consideratio/& terminatio: virtutes sunt animæ nostræ. Nulla bestia talem habet cogitationem inueniemdi ludum nouum. quare non considerat aut determinat circa ipsum quicq̄. hæ virtutes sunt viuæ ratiōis quæ anima dicitur: & sunt viuæ. quia sine motu viuæ rationis nō possunt esse. In illa enim cogitatione: motum spiritus rationalis quisq̄ appræhēdit qui aduertit cogitare esse quoddam discurrere/ sic & considerare atq̄ determinare. in quo opere corp⁹ nihil præstat adiutorii. Ideo quātum potest se retrahit anima a corpore: vt melius cogitet/consideret/& determinet. Nam penit⁹ vult esse in sua libertate: vt libere operetur. Hæc autem vis libera quā animā rationalem dicimus:

But when it is outside the body it does not exist in diverse places, just as an angel, who does not give life, [does not exist in diverse places]. Therefore in the body the whole soul is in every part of the body just as its creator is in every part of the world.
JOHN: Does the soul withdraw itself from the body when a finger is cut off?
THE CARDINAL: Never, but it does cease to vivify the finger. The soul does not withdraw itself because it does not pass from one particular part of the body to another, since it is simultaneously in each and every part.
JOHN: Still, I ask that you explain the motion of the soul once again. When you say that the soul is self-moving, tell me, by what kind of motion does it perpetually move itself?
THE CARDINAL: The soul moves itself by none of the six species of motion, but equivocally.[8] The soul moves itself—that is, it discerns, it abstracts, it divides, and it assembles. The power of the soul is to reason and therefore the power to reason is the soul. In some manner the reason is perpetual and immutable as it knows that four does not equal two, because four has three in it, which two does not have. Therefore four is not equal to two. This reason is immutable. Therefore the soul is immutable. Moreover, when reason discourses in this way by calculating, its discourse is by all means rational. Therefore the rational soul is moved to reasoning from itself. For this reason the soul is the inventive power of the arts and of new sciences. Therefore it cannot be moved in its inventive motion of the new except by itself. When it makes itself the likeness of all knowable things it is moved by itself, so that when it is in the senses it makes itself the likeness of sensible things, in vision the likeness of visible things, in hearing the likeness of audible things, and so on for all the senses.

The soul is said to be composed from the same and the diverse on account of [its] seizing the universal motion of all things and the particular motion of diverse things. So it is composed from the indivisible and the divisible because it shapes itself to the divisible and the mutable. Hence the soul is that power which can shape itself to all things and it makes itself the cause of corporeal motion, as for example of the hand or the foot. But motion is not always by nature the result of a decision; for example the motion of the nerves and lungs is natural.

The soul does not make itself the likeness of things in young boys, on account of their weakness, but only after the years of discretion when the body has become strong by the addition of distinguishing power and especially if the soul exercises itself by study. For the soul is still unformed in young boys, until nature has been subjected to reason so that a strong and perfect man may be made and the boy's unformed condition is moved to perfection by study and practice. It can be said that the soul moves itself in a two-fold manner: either when it makes itself the cause of the movements of the body, which it also does while sleeping, or when it makes itself the likeness of things that live outside the human body. And so it seems that its being is self-motion. Hence the soul lives more truly because it moves itself than man, who is moved by the soul.
JOHN: Hence I think that God exists in a truer way than the soul.
THE CARDINAL: You're correct, not because God moves himself or makes himself the likeness of things, as does the soul, although all things would be in him in a certain simplicity. God exists in a truer way because he is the true being itself of things and the life of lives. As it is said: I am the resurrection and the life (*John* 11:25).
JOHN: Many things which you mentioned above concerning the invention of something new please me, for in that action it clearly seems that the soul is self-moving. I would like it if you would relate these things to the game.
THE CARDINAL: I thought to invent a game of knowledge. I considered how it should be done. Next I decided to make it as you see. Cogitation, consideration, and determination are powers of our souls.[9] No beast has such a thought of inventing a new game which is why the beast does not consider or determine anything about it. These are the powers of the living reason which is called the soul and they are alive because they cannot exist without the motion of the living soul.

Everyone who observes that to think and also to consider and to determine is a certain kind of running about understands the movement of the rational spirit through that observation. The body offers no support in this operation. For this reason the soul withdraws as much as it can from the body, so that it might better think, consider, and determine. For it wants to exist entirely in its own freedom, so that it might operate freely. Moreover, the freer this free strength that we call the rational soul is from the corporeal contractions of things, the stronger it is.[10]

tanto est fortior quanto a corporalibus contractionibus absolutior. Nõ igitur plus viuit anima in corpore q̃ extra. nec dissoluitur dissolutione harmonię seu temperamenti corporis: cum ipsa non dependeat a temperamento / sicut sanitas corporis. sed econuerso: ipsa temperatio dependet ab anima. qua non existente: non est temperatio. Anima est vita: quia ratio quæ viuus motus est. Dum igitur cogito / considero / & determino: quid aliud fit q̃ ꝙ rationalis spiritus qui est vis cogitatiua / consideratiua / & determinatiua seipsum mouet? Et dum quæro determinationem animæ quid sit anima: non cogito & considero. & in hoc reperio animam mouere seipsam motu circulari: quia supra seipsum ille motus reuertitur. Quando enim cogito de cogitatione: motus est circularis & seipsum mouẽs. Et hinc motus animæ qui vita est: perpetuus est. quia circularis supra seipsum reflexus. IOANNES. Capio sane quæ dicis. & gratissimũ est audisse tres illas virtutes animæ ĩtellectiuę: quarum vna nõ est alia. quia prima cogitatio. deinde consideratio. vltima determinatio. Cogitatio generat considerationem. & determinatio procedit ab illis. & non sunt nisi vnus viuus motus: seipsum perfecte mouens. Et in hoc vides intellectiuam vnitrinam virtutem de necessitate: si debet perfectæ viuere seu moueri. CARDINALIS. Adde adhuc ipsam esse perfectiorem: quia magis in ipsa vis illa infinita & perfectissima quæ deus est / relucet. Ideo sicut deus æternus: ita ipsa perpetua. In perpetuo enĩ æternitas melius relucet q̃ in temporali. IOANNES. Volo hæc quæ præcipis libẽtissime addere: nec adhuc vnũ dimittere mihi gratissimũ. CARDINALIS. Quid hoc? IOANNES. Si ad perfectionem spirit⁹ nostri necessario requiritur ꝙ sit vnitrinus vt optime declarasti: profecto ignorantes reputandi sunt / qui spiritum perfectissimũ / qui deus est / negant vnitrinum. CARDINALIS. Vtiq; signum est ignorantiæ: de deo non affirmare id quod simplicitatis & perfectionis est. Vnitas autem quanto magis vniens: tanto simplicior & perfectior. Hinc vnitrina perfectior: quæ sic est vna ꝙ etiã in tribus personis quarum quælibet est vna / ipsa est vna. & non esset aliter perfectissima vnitas. Careret enim natura & iis quæ ad eius perfectissimã essentiam sunt necessaria. Sed hæc altiora sunt iis quæ nunc inquirimus. IOANNES. Caute videris dixisse: hanc cogitationem ludi & considerationem atq; determinationem non esse in brutis. non negans etiam bruta in nidificatione / venationibus / & aliis quæ experimur: cogitare / considerare / & determinare. Quomodo igitur ostendes illa non esse rationalia? CARDINALIS. Quia carent libera virtute: quæ in nobis est. Nam cum ego hunc ludum inuenirem: cogitaui / consideraui / & determinaui quæ alius nec cogitauit / nec considerauit / nec determiuauit. quia quisq; hominum liber est cogitare quæcunq; voluerit: similiter considerare atq; determinare. Quare non omnes idem cogitant: quando quisq; habet liberum proprium spiritum. Bestiæ vero non sic. Ideo impelluntur ad ea quæ agunt per naturam: & eiusdem speciei similes faciunt venationes & nidos. IOANNES. Non sine ratione hæc fiunt. CARDINALIS. Natura mouetur intelligentia. Sed sicut conditor legis motus ratione / legem sic ordinauit quæ mouet subditos / non ratio legis quæ eis est incognita / sed imperium superiorum quod necessitat: ita brutum mouetur imperio naturæ necessitante ipsum / non inductione rationis quam ignorat. Ideo in vno motu specifico: videmus omnia eiusdem speciei tanq̃ ex indita lege naturæ compelli & moueri. Hac coactione non stringitur spiritus noster regius & imperialis. alioqui nihil inueniret: sed solũ impulsum naturæ exequeretur. IOANNES. Cum videam araneas vnam legem in telis & venatione seruare / &

V iiii

Therefore the soul does not exist more truly in the body than outside it, nor is it dissolved with the dissolution of the harmony or mixture of the body because it does not depend upon this bodily mixture. But, conversely, the mixture of the body does depend upon the soul. If the soul does not exist, the temperance of the body does not exist. The soul is life because it is reason which is living motion. Therefore when I think, consider, and determine, what is happening except that the rational spirit, which is the thinking, considering, and determining power, is moving itself?

And when I seek the definition of the soul – what the soul is – do I not think and consider? And in this I find that the soul is self-moving in a circular motion because its motion turns back upon itself. For when I think about thinking, the motion is circular and self-moving. And hence the motion of the soul, which is life, is perpetual, because it is circular, turned back upon itself.

JOHN: I grasp well what you are saying and it is most gratifying to have heard about these three powers of the intellective soul, of which one is not the other because thinking is the first, and the next consideration, and the last, determination. Thinking generates consideration, and determination proceeds from them. They are but one living motion moving itself perfectly. And in this I see that the intellective soul necessarily must have a ternary power in order to exist or move perfectly.[11]

THE CARDINAL: Add besides that it is more perfect because something greater, God, who is infinite and most perfect, shines forth in its power. Therefore as God is eternal so it [the soul] is perpetual, for eternity shines forth better in perpetual than in temporal things.

JOHN: I would like you most freely to add to these things that you teach. Besides, don't omit something that I regard most highly.

THE CARDINAL: What's that?

JOHN: If it is necessarily required for the perfection of our spirit that it be ternary as you have most aptly declared, then truly those thinkers who deny that the most perfect spirit who is God is ternary are to be considered ignorant.

THE CARDINAL: Certainly it is a sign of ignorance not to attribute that which belongs to simplicity and perfection to God. Moreover unity is more perfect and simple to the degree that it is more uniting. Hence the Trinity, which is one in such a way that it is also in three persons each of which is one, is more perfect. And unity would not be most perfect in any other way, for it would be lacking in nature and in those things which are necessary for its perfect essence. But this is beyond those things that we are now investigating.

JOHN: You seem to have said with certainty that the cogitation, consideration, and determination of this game is not in animals. At the same time you don't deny that animals, in making nests, in hunts, and other things we know, think, consider, and determine. How therefore would you prove that these animals are not rational?

THE CARDINAL: Because they lack the free power that is in us. When I invented this game, I thought, I considered, and I determined that which no one else thought, considered or determined, because each man is free to think whatever he wishes. In the same way he is free to consider and determine whatever he wishes. This is why everybody does not think the same thing, because each person has his own free spirit. But beasts do not have this freedom. Therefore they are impelled to [do] those things that they do by their nature so that all the members of each species hunt and make nests in the same way.

JOHN: Hunting and making nests are not irrational activities.

THE CARDINAL: Nature is moved by intelligence. But just as the author of a law, who is moved by reason, arranges the law in such a way that it is not the reason of the law, which is unknown to its subjects, that moves them, but rather the command of a superior, that obliges them, so the beast himself is moved not by the induction of reason, which he does not know, but by the necessitating command of nature. For this reason we see every member of each species to be compelled and moved in one specific motion, given, as it were, by the law of nature. Our regal and imperial spirit is not bound by this structure. Otherwise it would not invent anything, but would follow only the impetus of nature.

JOHN: Since I see that spiders observe one law in making their webs and in hunting and swallows one law in nestmaking and innumerable such things, I well understand

irundines in nidificatione/& innumera talia: bene compræhēdo vno motu singula eiusdē speciei moueri.& hunc esse ipulsium.contētus sum igitur. CARDINALIS. quando aduertis in nobis aliquā naturaliter cogitari/considerari/& determinari/ quæ nostra animalitas deposcit/& alia quæ sine corpore/spiritui tamen conueniūt/ vt illa prædicta:experimentaliter cognoscis in primis/nos libere moueri/sed ex necessitate naturæ sensibilis & corporeæ. Sed ī aliis libere:cū liberū seipsum moueat. Natura vero spiritui nostro nullam vnq̄ necessitatē imponere potest: sed bene spiritus/naturæ.vt patet in bono/in abstinentiis/& castitate:& in malo quando cōtra naturā peccamus.& desperati:in seipsos manus iniiciunt/& se interimunt.IOANNES.Vnū restat quod clarius cuperem intelligere:quomodo scilicet se habeat differēter vis sensitiua & vegetatiua in homine & brutis. Vnam enim dixisti esse substantiam quā animā appellamus/& ipsam esse virtutem multarū virtutum/scilicet vegetatiuæ & quæ in vegetatiua cōplicantur/& sensitiuæ & quæ in sensitiua cōtinentur/atq; etiam intellectiuæ/& quæ ipsius sunt. Certum est autē hāc substantiā: secūdum virtutem intellectiuā non requirere corpus.Ideo tota substātia animæ cū non depēdeat a corpore/est per se stans/sine corpore: licet alias virtutes scilicet sensitiuam & vegetatiuā non exerceat nisi in corpore.Non est igitur minoris virtutis extra corpus q̄ in corpore:licet cesset exercitatio virtutū corpus requirētium.Sed cum anima bruti sit substātia & virtus corpus requirēs/quia sine corpore nihil habet exercitii : videtur q̄ deficiente corpore deficiat. Atq; cum sit substantia quæ in homine est intellectualis/& virtus indeficiens:videtur nunq̄ deficere.Substātia enī essentia est quæ non est corruptibilis secundum Dionysium/& potest esse perpetua. quoniā in anima hominis perpetua est.CARDINALIS.Subtiliter moues: differentiam exquirēs sensitiuæ & vegetatiuæ in homine & brutis. Et primū aduertēdum puto: q̄ virtutes illę scilicet vegetatiua/sensitiua/ & imaginatiua sunt ī virtute intellectiua hominis sicut trigonus ī tetragono/vt bn̄ dicebat Aristoteles.Sed trigonus in tetragono nō habet suam trigoni formā/sed tetragoni.In brutis vero habet trigonus trigoni formā.Alterius igitur naturæ est trigonus: alterius tetragonus. Sic & virtutes vegetatiuæ/sensitiuæ/& imaginatiuæ/quæ trigonū illum quæ anima bruti dicitur constituūt:sunt imperfectioris naturæ q̄ in homine.vbi cū virtute intellectuali nobilissima & perfectissima tetragonū illum qui anima hominis dicitur constituunt. Inferiora enim in superioribus sunt secūdum naturā superioris. vt viuere nobilius in sensitiua q̄ vegetatiua:& adhuc nobilius ī intellectiua. sed nobilissime in diuina natura:quæ est vita viuētium. Nō mirum igitur si vires illæ in trigono non sunt naturæ virium illarum in tetragono : vbi in substantialem identitatem cum incorruptibili virtute intellectiua perueniunt. Sicut enim vegetatiua/sensitiua/imaginatiua/& intellectiua in diuina natura quæ est ipa æterna æternitas/sunt æterna : ita vegetatiua/sensitiua/& imaginatiua in intellectuali natura quæ est perpetua/sunt perpetua.& licet illa in bruto non sint perpetua perpetuitate naturæ intellectualis : non tamen puto aliquid de illis in substantia ex corporis varietate variari. Sicut enim in homine dum manus eius arescit substantia animæ vegetatiuæ & sensitiuæ non arescit/ sed manet semper/quia virt⁹ animæ hominis incorruptibilis licet desinat vegetatio & sensatio manus:sic forte per mortem bruti & arefactionē arboris nō perit substātia illa quę dicit̄ aīa sensitiua/aut vegetatiua/ licet nō exerceat operationē vt ante. IOAN.Quomodo igit̄ manet? CARDI.Non possumus negare hominē dici microcosmū/hoc est paruū mūdū.q habet animā.Sic

that the members of each species are moved by a single motion, and that this motion is instinctive. Therefore I am content.
THE CARDINAL: When you observe that some things which our animal nature demands are thought, considered, and determined naturally and that other things pertain to the spirit without the body, you know experimentally that we are not freely moved in those first things, but are moved from the necessity of the sensible nature and of corporeal things.[12] But in the other things we are moved freely as the soul moves itself freely. Nature can never impose necessity upon our spirit, but the spirit can impose necessity upon nature, as is very evident in the good, in self-restraint, and in chastity, and in evil, when we sin against nature, and the desperate throw their hands upon themselves and destroy themselves.
JOHN: One thing remains which I would like to understand more clearly: in what manner do the sensitive and vegetative powers exist differently in man and in beasts? You have said that there is one substance that we call the soul and it is the power of many powers, as for example of the vegetative power and of those things that are enfolded in vegetative power, and of the sensitive power and of those things that are contained in the sensitive power, and also of the intellective power and of those things that are contained in it.

However it is certain that this substance, in that it is the intellective power, does not require a body. Since the entire substance of the soul does not depend upon the body, it subsists through itself without the body, although its other powers such as the sensitive and the vegetative function only in the body. Therefore the power of the soul is not lesser outside the body than it is within it, even if the function of the powers requiring the body ceases. But since the soul of a beast is a substance and a power that requires a body because it does not function without the body, it appears that it [the soul of the beast] declines when its body declines. Since the substance of the soul in man is an intellectual and unfailing power, it appears that it never declines. For, according to Dionysius, substance is essence, which is not corruptible and can exist perpetually, since it is perpetual in the soul of man. (*De div. nom.* 4.2)
THE CARDINAL: You are moving subtly, searching out the differences between the sensitive and vegetative in man and beasts. I think that the first thing worth noting is that the vegetative, sensitive, and imaginative powers are in the intellective power of man as a triangle is in a quadrangle, as Aristotle has rightly said (*De anima* 2.3.414b). But the triangle in the quadrangle does not have the form of a triangle but that of a quadrangle. But in beasts the triangle has the form of a triangle, therefore the triangle is one of nature, the tetragon of another. So also the vegetative, sensitive, and imaginative powers which constitute that triangle which is called the soul of a beast, are of a more imperfect nature than they are in man where with the most noble and most perfect intellectual power they constitute that quadrangle that is called the human soul.

Inferior things are in superior things according to the nature of the superior thing, so that it is more noble to live in the sensitive than in the vegetative power and still more noble to live in the intellective power and most noble to live in the divine nature which is the life of living things. Therefore it is not extraordinary if those powers in the triangle are not of the nature of those powers in the quadrangle where they reach substantial identity with the incorruptible intellective power.

Just as the vegetative, sensitive, imaginative, and intellective are eternal in the divine nature which is eternal eternity itself, so the vegetative, sensitive, and imaginative are perpetual in the intellectual nature which is perpetual. And although they are not perpetual through the perpetuity of the intellectual nature in beasts, nevertheless I think that they cannot be substantially varied in accordance with the variations among different bodies. When a man's hand withers the substance of the vegetative and sensitive soul does not wither but always remains because the power of the soul of man is incorruptible although the enlivening and feeling of the hand ceases. So also perhaps that substance which is called the sensitive or vegetative soul does not perish through the death of an animal or the withering of a tree although it does not operate as before.
JOHN: In what way then does it remain?
THE CARDINAL: We cannot deny that man is called a microcosm: that is, a little world which has a soul.

& magnũ mundũ animã habere ferunt:quã naturã quidã dicunt.alii spiritũ vniuersorum:q oĩa intus alit/vnit/connectit/fouet/& mouet. Vis enĩ illa mundi quæ seipsam & oĩa mouet/de qua diximus: est perpetua.quia motus rotundus & circularis: omnem ĩ se habẽs motũ.sicut circularis figura/omnẽ figurã ĩ se complicat. Dicitur etiã hæc aĩa:necessitas cõplexionis a plærisq;. Ab aliis autẽ:fatũ appellatur ĩ substãtia/oĩa ordinate explicãs.Ad quã se habet totus corporalis mundus:sicut corpus hominis se habet ad animã.Illa est sensitiua anima ĩ sensitiuis/vegetatiua ĩ vegetatiuis & elemẽtatiua ĩ elemẽtis.quæ si desinit vegetare arborẽ aliquã / aut viuificare brutum:non tamẽ propterea desinit esse.vt de anima hominis dictum est. IOANNES. Non ergo est alia aĩa vnius bruti aut arboris/& alia alterius? CARDINALIS. Hoc secundũ substantiã hac via concedi oportet. Quoniã non est nisi vna omniũ aĩa.sed per accidẽs omnes differunt.Sicut enĩ vis visiua ĩ homine secundũ substantiã nõ differt a virtute auditiua:quia vna est aĩa quæ est vis visiua & auditiua.per accidẽs autẽ differũt:quia accidit virtuti visiuæ esse ĩ oculo & non ĩ aure/& ĩ vno oculo magis apto q̃ ĩ alio ad operationẽ suã exequẽdam. IOANNES. Secundum hanc opinionẽ: concedi potest ꝙ triplex est mundus.Paruus:q homo.Maximus:q est deus.Magnus: qui vniuersum dicitur. Paruus:est similitudo magni.magnus : similitudo maximi. Sed dubito.cũ homo sit mundus paruus:si etiã sit pars mundi magni.CARDINALIS.Vtiq; homo sic est mũdus paruus:ꝙ & pars magni.In omnibus enĩ partibus relucet totũ:cũ pars sit pars totius.Sicut totus homo relucet ĩ manu ad totũ proportionata.Sed tamen ĩ capite:pfectiori modo tota pfectio hominis relucet.Sic vniuersum ĩ qualibet eius parte relucet . Omnia enĩ ad vniuersum suã tenẽt habitudinẽ & proportionẽ.plus tamẽ relucet ĩ ea parte quæ homo dicitur/q̃ ĩ alia quacunq;.Perfectio igitur totalitatis vniuersi quia plus relucet ĩ homine:ideo & homo est perfectus mundus.licet paruus:& pars mundi magni. Vnde quæ vniuersum habet vniuersaliter:habet & homo particulariter/proprie/& discrete.Et qa nõ potest esse nisi vnũ vniuersum/& plura particularia & discreta esse possunt:ideo vnius perfecti vniuersi/plures particulares & discreti hoĩes/speciem gestant & imaginẽ.vt stabilis vnitas magni vniuersi:ĩ tã varia pluralitate multorũ paruorũ fluidorũ mũdorũ sibi iuicẽ succedentium pfectius explicet. IOANNES. Si recte capio/tũc sicut vniuersum est vnũ regnũ magnũ:sic & homo est regnũ/sed paruum ĩ regno magno.sicut regnum Bohemiæ ĩ regno Romanorũ/seu vniuersali ĩperio. CARDINALIS. Optime.Homo enĩ est regnũ simile regno vniuersi:fundatum ĩ parte vniuersi . Dum enĩ est embrio ĩ vtero matris:nondũ est regnũ propriũ.sed creata aĩa ĩtellectuali quæ creando imponitur/regnũ fit/regẽ habẽs propriũ:& homo dicitur.Recedẽte vero aĩa:desinit esse homo & regnũ.Corpus autẽ sicut ante aduẽtum aĩæ ĩtellectiuæ fuit de vniuersali regno magni mundi:ita & reuertitur ad illud.sicut Bohemia erat de ĩperio/ anteq̃ haberet propriũ regẽ:sic & manebit proprio rege sublato.Homo igitur ĩmediate suo proprio regi qui ĩ ipso regnat subest:sed mediate subest tunc regno mundi.Quãdo autẽ nondũ habet regẽ aut esse desiit:ĩmediate subest regno mũdi.Quare vegetatiuã virtutẽ/in embrione natura/seu mundi aĩa exercet:sicut ĩ aliis vegetatiuã vitã habẽtibus.& etiã continuat hoc exercitium ĩ nonnullis mortuis:quibus capilli & vngues crescunt.& ea facit ĩ illis/sicut ĩ aliis corporibus proprio rege carẽtibus.Quomodo vero homo sit regnũ proprium/liberũ & nobile:alibi latius tractaui.& pulchra est speculatio:per quã homo seipsum cognoscẽs/ĩ suo regno licet paruo/omnia abunde sine defectu reperiens/fœlicẽ se vidẽs si velit/optime contẽtus est.

E X A L I E N I S P A R T I M

V V.

And likewise they say that the great world has a soul, which some men call nature and others the spirit of the universe. This world soul nourishes, unites, connects, warms, and moves all things from within. Truly that power of the world of which we have spoken and which moves itself and all things, is perpetual. Because its motion is round and circular it has in itself all motion just as the circular figure enfolds all other figures in itself. This soul of the world is also called the necessity of connection by many men. Moreover, by others it is called fate in substance, unfolding all things from itself in an orderly manner.

The entire corporeal world is related to the world soul just as the body of man is related to is soul. The world soul is the sensitive soul in sensitive things, the vegetative soul in vegetative things, and the elemental soul in elemental things. Nevertheless if it ceases to animate any specific tree or any individual beast, the world soul does not cease to exist on account of this. The same was said concerning the soul of man.[13]

JOHN: Therefore doesn't each beast or tree have its own soul?

THE CARDINAL: It must be conceded that in terms of substance there is only one soul for all things. But all things differ through accidents. For instance, the visual power in man does not differ in substance from the auditory power because there is only one soul which is both the visual and the auditory power. However these powers differ accidentally, because it happens that the visual power exists in the eye and not in the ear and more in one eye that is more apt than another in the exercise of its operation.

JOHN: According to this opinion, it can be conceded that the world is trinary; the small world which is man, the greatest which is God, and the large which is called the universe. The small is the likeness of the large, the large the likeness of the greatest. But since man is the small world, I doubt whether he would actually be part of the large world.

THE CARDINAL: By all means man is the small world in such a way that he also is part of the large world. For the whole shines forth in all its parts since each part is part of the whole, and so the whole man shines forth in the hand proportionately to the whole. But still the whole perfection of man shines forth in a more perfect manner in the head. The universe shines forth in each of its parts in the same way, for all things maintain their status and proportion in relation to the universe. Yet it shines forth more in that part which is called man than in any other.

Therefore, because the perfection of the entire universe shines forth more in man, man is the perfect world, although small and a part of the large world. Hence those things which the universe has universally, man also has particularly, individually, and separately. And because there can be only one universe and there can be many particular and individual beings, particular and individual men bear the appearance and image of the one perfect universe. In this way the stable unity of the great universe is more perfectly unfolded in such a varying plurality of many small fluid worlds succeeding each other in turn.

JOHN: If I grasp you correctly, then it follows that the universe is one great kingdom and so also man is a kingdom, but a small one within a great kingdom as the kingdom of Bohemia is a small kingdom within the great kingdom of the Romans, or the universal empire.

THE CARDINAL: Excellent! A man is a kingdom similar to the kingdom of the universe, established in part of that universe. As long as the embryo is in the mother's womb it is not yet its own kingdom, but when the intellectual soul, which is put in the embryo in the process of creation, is created, the embryo becomes a kingdom, having its own king, and is called a man. But when the soul departs, the man and the kingdom cease to be. However, as the body was part of the universal kingdom of the large world before the advent of the soul, so also, it returns to it. Just as Bohemia was part of the Empire before it had its own king, so also it will remain if its own king is taken away.

Therefore man is directly subject to his own king who rules in him, then he is subject to the kingdom of the world in an indirect way. But, when he has not yet a king or when he ceases to be, he is directly subject to the kingdom of the world. This is why nature or the world soul exercises vegetative power in the embryo as in other things having vegetative life. And this exercise of the vegetative power actually continues in certain dead men in whom the hair and nails continue to grow. The world soul exercises this vegetative power in other bodies lacking their own ruler as well as in dead bodies. I have dealt extensively elsewhere with the way man is his own kingdom, free and noble. And speculation, through which man, knowing himself, finding all things abundantly and without defect in his own kingdom though it be small, seeing himself happy if he wishes, is contented in the best way, is beautiful.[14]

Hæc nunc vt tepus dedit/tacta sint. IOHANNES. Non pigriteris istis pulcherrime dictis adiicere: quomodo maximus mūdus q deus est/ī vniuersali relucet. CARDINALIS. Alta petis: nescio si sufficiā. Iuuabo me tamen ex globo: quātum potero. Nā globus visibilis est inuisibilis globi q ī mēte artificis fuit: imago. Attēte igitur ad uertito: mētem ī se fingēdi virtutē habere. In seipsa enī mēs concipiendi liberā habēs facultatē: artē repperit pādēdi conceptum/quæ nūc fingēdi vocetur magisterium. quā artē: habent figuli/statuarii/pictores/tornatores/fabri/textores/& tales similes artifices. Esto igit̃ ꝙ ipse figulus velit ollas/patellas/vrceos/& quæq; talia quæ mente concipit: exprimere/& visibiliter ostēdere ad finē vt cognoscat̃ magister. primum studet possibilitatē inducere / seu materiā aptā facere ad capiendā formā artis/qua habita videt sine motu non posse hāc possibilitatē in actum deducere/vt habeat formā quā mēte concepit. & rotā facit: cuius motu educat de possibilitate materiæ formam ꝑconceptā. Et quia vna materia est aptior alia: nulla possibilitas perfectissima esse potest. Ideo in nulla materia: immaterialis & mentalis forma potest veraciter fingi/vti est. sed similitudo & imago manebit omnis visibilis forma: veræ & inuisibilis formæ/quæ ī mēte mens ipsa existit. Sic igitur ī mēte tornatoris/globus iste mēs ipsa existēs/dū mēs ī se ī ea forma quā cōcepit/& cui cōceptui se assimilauit visibilē facere vellet: adaptauit materiā scilicet lignū/vt illius formæ capax esset. Deinde tornatili motu: formā in ligno ītroduxit. Fuit igitur globus ī mēte: & ibi globus archetypus mēs est. Fuit ī rudi ligno possibiliter: & ibi fuit materia. Fuit ī motu dū de potētia ad actum duceretur: & ibi fuit motus. Et producta est possibilitas eius ad actū: vt sit actu per determinationē & diffinitionē possibilitatis. quæ actu est sic determinata: vt sit visibilis globus. Habes igitur ex hac similitudīe humanæ artis: per quod/ artē diuinā creatiuā aliqualiter coiicere poteris. licet īter creare dei & facere hominis tātum īter sit: sicut īter creatorē & creaturā. Mens igitur diuina mūdum ī se cōcipiēs/qui conceptus est mens ipsa æqualis conceptui: mundus dicitur archetypus. Voluit autē deus pulchritudinē conceptus sui manifestare. Creauit eñ possibilitatē seu posse fieri mundū pulchrum/& motum per quē de possibilitate duceretur: vt fieret hic mundus visibilis. ī quo possibilitas essendi mundū: est sic vt deus voluit & fieri potuit/actu determinata. IOHANNES. Intelligis ne per posse fieri/possibilitatē/seu materiā: aliquid de quo factus est mūdus/vt de ligno globus? CARDINALIS. Nequaq̃. Sed ꝙ mundus de modo quæ possibilitas seu posse fieri aut materia dicitur: ad modū qui actu esse dicitur/transiuit. Nihil enī fit actu: qđ fieri non potuit. Impossibile enī fieri: quomodo fieret? Materia vero si aliqđ actu esset: vtiq; ipā æternitas esset/aut æternitatis factura. Non potest dici ꝙ sit æternitas. qa æternitas deꝰ est: q est omne id qđ esse potest/sic non est materia quæ est possibilitas/seu fieri posse/siue variabilitas. Nec æternitatis factura. nam si facta esset: fieri potuisset. tūc fieri posse scilicet materia/de materia facta esset. & sic de ipā: quod est impossibile. Non est igitur aliquid actu materia. Sed res quæ fit: dicitur ex materia fieri: quia fieri potuit. Non enim esset mens diuina omnipotēs: si non nisi de aliquo aliquid facere posset/quod mens creata/nequaq̃ omnipotens/quotidie facit. IOANNES. Non negas posse fieri: licet non sit aliquod esse/posse fieri aliquid. Non est igitur penitus nihil: cum de nihilo nihil fiat. & cum non sit deus/nec aliquid actu/nec de aliquo/nec nihil: ideo quicquid est/de nihilo est. non enī ex seipso: cum se de nihilo creare nequeat. Dei igitur creatura videtur. CARDINALIS. Optime concludis. Hoc enī sic concedi debere/viua ratio necessitat. licet quomodo hoc concipi possit: non reperiat. Sicut

Time allows us only to touch upon these things now.
JOHN: Don't shrink from adding to these things of which you have spoken most beautifully how the greatest world, which is God, shines forth in the universe.
THE CARDINAL: You demand deep things and I don't know if I can satisfy you. Nevertheless I will be pleased to derive what I can from the ball, for the visible ball is the image of the invisible ball which was in the mind of the inventor. Therefore, take note that the mind has within itself the power of inventing. For the mind, having the ability of freely conceiving, finds within itself the art of unfolding its conceptions, which now may be called the mastery of inventing. The potters, sculptors, painters, turners, metalworkers, weavers and similar artisans all possess this art. Thus it is that the potter wishes to express and make visibly manifest the pots, dishes, pitchers and other things that he conceives in his mind so that he will be known as a master. First he tries to determine the possibility or to prepare the matter suitable for receiving the form of the art. Having done this, he sees that without motion he cannot draw this possibility into actuality so that it will have the form that he has conceived in his mind. And he makes a wheel, by whose motion he brings the preconceived form out of the possibility of matter.

And because one material is more suitable than another no possibility can be the most perfect. Therefore the immaterial and mental form cannot be shaped as it truly is in any material. Every visible form remains the image and likeness of the true and invisible form which exists in the mind as the mind itself. So therefore, the ball exists in the mind of the turner as the mind itself. When the mind wishes to make itself visible in that form which it conceives and in the conception to which it assimilates itself, it adapts the material, namely the wood, so that it becomes capable of assuming that form. Hence the turner introduces the form into the wood by a rotary movement.

Therefore the ball was in the mind and there the archetypal ball is the mind. It was in the raw wood in possibility and there it was matter. It was in motion while being led forth from potentiality to act and there it was motion. And its possibility was induced into act so that it would become an act through the determination and definition of the possibility. It is thus determined by this act so that it is a visible ball. You have therefore from this likeness of human art a way of conjecturing somehow concerning the nature of the divine creative art, although there is as much difference between the creativity of God and man's fabrications, as there is between creator and creature.

Therefore the divine mind conceived the world within itself and this conception is an equality of the divine mind itself and its conception and it is called the archetypal world. God wished to manifest the beauty of his conception. He created the possibility that the world could be made beautiful and the motion by which the world would be led forth from possibility so that this visible world would come to be. In the world, the possibility of the world's being the world was actually determined just as God intended it and as it was able to become.
JOHN: Do you mean by "the capacity to be made," possibility or matter, something from which the world is made, as the ball is made from wood?
THE CARDINAL: Not at all. I mean that the world crosses over from that mode [of being] that is called possibility or capacity to be made or matter to that mode of being that is called being in act. For nothing actually is made that could not be made. For how would anything that it is impossible to make, be made? But matter, if it were to exist in act at all, would by all means be eternity itself or the work of eternity. It cannot be said that it [matter] is eternity, because God is eternity. He is all that can be. So he is not matter, that is, possibility or the capacity to be made or variability, nor is matter the work of eternity, for if it were made it could have been made. Then the capacity to be made that is matter would be made from matter and thus from itself which is impossible. Therefore matter does not exist in act at all. But the thing which is made because it could be made is said to be made from matter. The divine mind would not be omnipotent if it could make something only out of something, which the not-at-all omnipotent created mind of man does daily.
JOHN: You do not deny the capacity to be made although the capacity to be made would not be anything that exists at all. Therefore it is not entirely nothing since nothing is made of nothing. And since it would not be God, nor anything in act, nor from anything, nor from nothing, therefore whatever it is, it is out of nothing. It is not from itself because it is unable to create itself from nothing. Therefore it seems that the creature is made by God.
THE CARDINAL: You have concluded very well. The living reason necessitates that it should be thus conceded, although it does not discover how this can be conceived.

enĩ conceptus de deo/omnẽ excellit conceptum:ſic de materia/omnẽ fugit cõceptũ.
IOANNES.Latẽt ne formæ in materia:vt globus latuit ĩ ligno?CARDI.Nequaq̃.
Nã dum tornator globũ facit abſcindẽdo partes ligni vſqꝫquo pueniat ad formã glo
bi:poſſibilitas quã vidit tornator ĩ ligno/quãdo ſe cõformat cũ globo mẽtis/trãſiuit
de poſſibili modo eſſendi ad actu eſſe.Cuius cauſa materialis:eſt lignũ.& efficiẽs:ar-
tifex.& formalis:exemplar in mẽte artificis.& finalis:ipſe artifex/q propter ſeipſum
operatus eſt.Tres igit̃ cauſæ concurrunt ĩ artifice:& quarta eſt materialis. Ita deus
eſt tricauſalis:efficiẽs/formalis/ & finalis om̃is creaturæ & ipſius materiæ.quæ cau
ſat aliquid:cũ non ſit aliquid.Sed ſine ipa/id qđ fit:fieri non poſſet.Nã cum id quod
eſt ĩ mẽte dei ſit deus q eſt æternitas:vtiqꝫ id fieri nõ poteſt.neqꝫ fit aliquid quod nõ
eſt ĩ mẽte & conceptu dei.Oportet igitur ꝙ veritas omnis rei quæ fit:nõ ſit niſi exemplar eius quæ mẽs dei eſt.Ideo qđ fit:erit imago exemplaris formæ. nã imaginis
veritas non eſt imago:ſed exemplar.Si igitur non eſt veritas/ſed eius imago:tũc neceſſe eſt id qđ fit cum deſcẽdat a ſtabili æternitate/ĩ variabili ſubiecto recipi. vbi nõ
recipitur vti eſt ĩ æternitate:ſed vti fieri poteſt. IOANNES. Si bene cuncta capio:
omnia ſunt ĩ deo.& ibi ſunt veritas:quæ nec eſt plus/nec minus. Sunt ibi complicite
& ineuolute:ſicut circulus ĩ puncto.Omnia ſunt ĩ motu:ſed ibi ſunt vt euoluuntur/
ſicut cũ punctus vnius pedis circini ſup̃ alio euoluitur. Tunc enĩ punctus ille explicat circulum prius cõplicatum.Omnia ĩ poſſe fieri:ſicut circulus in materia quæ in
circulum duci poteſt.Et oĩa ſunt ĩ poſſibilitate determinata : ſicut circulus actu de-
ſcriptus.CARDINALIS.Satis ſummarie hæc reſumpſiſti:quæ neſcio quomodo &
extra propoſitum ĩ ſermonẽ peruenerunt.Igitur reuertamur nunc ad ludũ noſtrũ:
& ĩtentum breuiſſime pãdam.IOANNES.Niſi te viderẽ abunde & amplius q̃ ſpe-
rauimus ſatiſfeciſſe/& doctrinã pandiſſe magnæ ſpeculationi congruã : pro magno
noſtro audiendi deſiderio/te q̃uis fatigatum ſollicitarẽ/vt hæc quæ cœpiſti ĩ longos
tractatus extẽderes.Sed nunc vt proponis facito:q̃remus libros tuos/quos his api-
cibus refertos ſperamus. CARDINALIS. Credo me ſæpius iſta & alia & dixiſſe &
ſcripſiſſe:melius forte q̃ modo/cũ amplius vires deficiant/& memoria tarde reſpon
deat.Fuit autẽ propoſitum meum hunc ludũ recẽter ĩuentum/quẽ paſſim omnes fa
cile capiunt & libẽter ludunt:& nunq̃ certo curſu contigit ĩ ordinẽ propoſito vtilẽ
redigere.& feci ſignũ vbi ſtamus globum iacientes:& circulum ĩ medio plani.ĩ cuius medio eſt ſedes regis:cuius regnum eſt regnũ vitæ ĩtra circulum ĩcluſum/ & in
circulo nouẽ alios.Lex autẽ ludi eſt:vt globus ĩtra circulum quieſcat a motu. & pro
p̃iquior cẽtro plus acquirat:iuxta numerũ circuli vbi quieſcit.Et q citius xxxiiii ac-
quiſierit q ſunt anni CHRISTI:victor ſit.Iſte ĩnquã ludus ſignificat motum aĩæ no
ſtræ:de ſuo regno ad regnũ vitæ ĩ quo eſt quies/& fœlicitas æterna.In cuius centro:
rex noſter & dator vitæ IHESVS CHRISTVS p̃ſidet.Qui cũ ſimilis nobis eſſet:
perſonæ ſuæ globũ ſic mouit/vt ĩ medio vitæ quieſceret. nobis exemplũ relinquẽs:
vt quẽadmodũ fecit faciamus.& globus noſter:ſuum ſequatur/licet ĩpoſſibile ſit/ꝙ
alius globus ĩ eodẽ cẽtro vitæ ĩ quo globus CHRISTI quieſcit/quietẽ attingat. Intra circulum enĩ:ſunt ĩfinita loca & mãſiones.Quieſcit enĩ locus cuiuſqꝫ ĩ puncto &
atomo ſua propria:quã nullus vnq̃ attingere poterit. Neqꝫ duo globi poſſunt æque
diſtare a cẽtro:ſed ſemp̃ vnus plus/alius minus.Oportet igitur quẽlibet Chriſtianũ
cogitare/quomodo quidã non habent ſpem alterius vitæ:& ii globum ſuum mouẽt
in his terrenis.Alii ſpem habent fœlicitatis/ſed ſuis propriis viribus & legibus ſine
CHRISTO cõtẽdũt peruenire ad vitã illã:& ii globũ ſuũ ſequẽdo ĩgenii vires & ſuo-

For just as the concept of God surpasses all conceiving, so does every concept concerning matter escape all conceiving.
JOHN: Are not forms hidden in matter as the ball was hidden in the wood?
THE CARDINAL: Not at all. For when the turner makes the ball by cutting off parts of the wood until he arrives at the form of a ball, the possibility which the turner saw in the wood when it conforms to the ball in his mind crosses over from the state of possible being to actual being. Its material cause is the wood and the efficient cause the artisan and the formal cause the exemplar in the mind of the artist and the final cause the artisan himself who brings it about for himself. Therefore three causes come together in the artisan and the fourth is the material.

God is tricausal – the efficient, formal, and final cause – of all creatures and of matter itself, which causes something although matter is not anything. But without it that which is made could not be made. That which is in the mind of God is God, who is eternity; certainly neither it nor anything else which is not in the mind and conception of God could be made.

Therefore it is necessary that the truth of everything that is made is nothing but its exemplar which is the mind of God. For this reason, what is made, is the image of the exemplary form, for the truth of an image is not the image, but the exemplar. If therefore what is made is not truth but its image, since it descends from stable eternity, then it is necessary that it be received in a variable subject, where it is not received as it is in eternity, but as it can be made.
JOHN: If I rightly understand this whole argument, everything is in God. And there these things are the truth, which is neither more nor less. They exist there in an enfolded and unevolved way, as a circle exists in a point. All things exist in motion but here they exist in the way that they are unrolled, just as when the point of one foot of a pair of compasses is rolled out above the other. For then that point unfolds the circle which was enfolded before. All things exist in the capacity to be made as the circle exists in the matter which can shape the circle. All things exist in a determinate state in possibility in the same way that the circle, once having been described, actually exists.
THE CARDINAL: I don't know how these things entered our talk and they are outside our purpose; you have resumed them satisfactorily enough. Therefore let us return now to our game and I will most briefly expand upon its meaning.
JOHN: Except that I see you have abundantly and more fully satisfied us than we had hoped and have revealed this doctrine suited to a great speculation, I would solicit you, although you are tired, to expand upon what you have begun in a long treatise because of our great desire to hear. But now do as you propose. We ask about your books which we hope refer to these deepest highest things.
THE CARDINAL: I believe that perhaps I have spoken and written better and more frequently concerning these and other things than I did just now since my faculties are declining further and my memory responds slowly. However, it was my purpose to apply this game, which everyone easily understands and gladly plays because of the frequent laughter which occurs from the varied and never certain course of the ball, in a manner suited to our purpose.[15] I marked the spot where we stand when throwing the ball and I drew a circle in the middle of the flat surface [upon which the game is played]. In the middle of that circle, enclosed inside it, is the seat of the ruler whose kingdom is the kingdom of life. And inside that circle there are nine others. The rule of the game is to make the ball stop moving within the circle and the closer to the center it comes to rest the more nearly it acquires the number of the circle where it comes to rest. And he who gets the number 34, which are the years of Christ's life, the quickest would be the winner.

This game, I say, represents the movement of our soul from its kingdom to the kingdom of life in which is peace and eternal happiness. Jesus Christ, our king and the giver of life, presides in its center. Since he was similar to us, Christ moved the sphere of his person so that it came to rest in the middle of life, leaving us the example so that we would do just as he had done. And our sphere would follow him although it would be impossible that another sphere attain peace in the same center of life where the sphere of Christ rests. There is an infinity of places and mansions within the circle, for each person's sphere rests on its own point and atom which no other could ever attain (cf. *John* 14:2).[16] Nor can two spheres be equally distant from the center, but one is always more distant, the other less so.

Therefore it is necessary that all Christians contemplate in fact how some men do not have the hope of another life and that they move their sphere in these terrestrial lands. Others have the hope of happiness but they strain to reach that life by their own powers and laws without Christ. These make their sphere run to higher things by following the powers of their own genius and the precepts of their own prophets and masters and their sphere does not reach the kingdom of life.

rũ prophetarum & magiſtrorum pcepta ad alta currere faciunt.& horum globi ad regnũ vitæ non perueniunt.Sunt tertii:qui viam quã CHRISTVS dei vnigenitus filius prædicauit & ambulauit amplectuntur.ii ſe ad medium vbi eſt ſedes regis vir tutũ mediatoriſq; dei & hoĩm conuertunt/& globũ ſuum/ĩſequẽdo veſtigia CHRI STI/mediocri curſu ĩpellunt:q ſolum ĩ regno vitæ mãſionẽ adquirunt.Solus enĩ dei filius de cœlo deſcẽdens ſciuit viam vitæ:quã verbo & opere credentibus patefecit. IOANNES. Dicis credentibus:qui ſunt ii? CARDINALIS. Qui credunt ipſum dei filium/& euãgelium eſſe per ipſum prædicatũ:illi de veritate euãgelii certi ſunt quia filius dei non mẽtitur.Ideo præferunt promiſſa euãgelii huic vitæ.Gaudẽt hic mori:vt ĩtrent cũ CHRISTO ĩ vitã æternã.Moriendũ omnino eſt.Mori igitur pro pter fidẽ filii dei:habet retributionẽ vitæ æternæ.Quomodo enĩ deus q eſt iuſtus & pius:fidelitatẽ pro ipſius dei gloria moriẽtis non remuneraret?aut quã daret remu nerationẽ niſi vitæ/ei q pro eo vitã dedit?eſt ne deus ignobilior homine nobili/fideli tatẽ ſerui abunde remunerãte vſq; ad conſortium regni? Etſi fidelis pro gloria filii eligit pati etiã æternã mortẽ:quomodo dabitur ei retributio niſi vitę/vbi ſemper & æternaliter ſe ſciat veraciter viuere & lætari?IOANNES.Nõ ergo ſunt veri chri ſtiani:q non moriuntur vt CHRISTVS/pro gloria dei. CARDINALIS.Ille chri ſtianus eſt q præfert gloriã CHRISTI propriæ vitæ & gloriæ: & taliter præfert/ꝙ ſi probaretur ĩ pſecutione/talis inueniretur.In illo viuit CHRISTVS:& ipſe nõ vi uit.contẽptor igitur huius mũdi & vitæ eſt:in quo per fidẽ eſt ſpũs filii dei IHESV CHRISTI.q mortuus mũdo:viuit ĩ CHRISTO.IOANNES. vt video difficile eſt dirigere globũ curuum/vt ſequaẽ viã CHRISTI:ĩ quo fuit ſpiritus dei q ipſum de duxit ĩ centrum & fontẽ vitæ.CARDINALIS. Facile valde eſt habẽti verã fidẽ/vt prædixi.Igitur ſi globus perſonæ tuæ ſpiritu fidei ĩpellitur:firma ſpe ducitur:& cha ritate CHRISTO aſtrĩgitur/q te ducet ſecũ ad vitã.ſed ĩpoſſibile eſt ĩfideli. IOAN NES.Certiſſimũ hoc eſſe video:q non credit CHRISTO vti dei filio mundo adhæ ret/& meliorẽ vitã non expectat.Sed fidelis ĩ aduerſitate gaudet:qa ſcit mortẽ glo rioſam præſtare ĩmortalẽ vitã.Videtur tamẽ vix poſſibile ꝙ globus ſecũdũ natu rã ſuam ĩclinatus deorſum:non ſic moueaẽ & ĩcuruetur/& vnus plus q̃ alius.CAR DINALIS.Hæc eſt ſumma myſteriorũ huius ludi : vt diſcamus has ĩclinationes & naturales ĩcuruationes taliter rectificare ſtudioſo exercitio/vt tandem poſt multas variationes & ĩſtabiles circulationes & ĩcuruationes quieſcamus ĩ regno vitæ. Vi des enĩ ꝙ vnus ĩpellit globum vno modo/alius alio:manẽte eadẽ curuitate in globo. Secundũ varium ĩpulſum varie mouetur & quieſcit : & nunq̃ certũ eſt ante quietẽ/ vbi demũ quieſcat.Vidẽs igitur globum ĩpulſum per aliquẽ attigiſſe prope cẽtrum cogitat ſequi velle illius modum & pluries attẽtat & proficit. IOANNES. Quiſq; globus eſt proprius/& aliter q̃ alius ĩcuruus.Igitur nõ poteſt vnus aliũ ſequi.CAR DINALIS. Verũ eſt. Nullus:alterius ſemitã præciſe ſequi poteſt. ſed neceſſe eſt vt quiſq; dominetur ĩclinationibus globi ſui & paſſionibus:ſeipſum exercitãdo.demũ taliter moderatus/ſtudeat viam ĩuenire:ĩ qua curuitas globi non ĩpediatur/quo mi nus ad circulũ vitæ perueniat.Hæc eſt vis myſtica ludi ſtudioſo exercitio poſſe etiã curuum globũ regulari:vt poſt ĩſtabiles flexiones motus/ĩ regno vitæ quieſcat.IO ANNES.Negare nequeo:vna globi gibboſitate ſtãte ſecundũ diuerſum ĩpetum cu iuſq; ipſum proiicientis/differẽter ſemper moueri.poſſeq; eundẽ globum per quenq̃ iuxta libitũ varie ĩpelli:ita ꝙ licet curua reuolutio ſemp maneat:tamen motus eius varietur. Dicimus tamẽ/cum non ſemper ĩ cẽtro circuli quieſcat vbi quiſq; ludens

There is a third group who embrace the life that Christ the only begotten son of God preached and walked. They turn themselves towards the middle where the seat of the king of virtue and of the mediator of God and men is, and, following the vestige of Christ, they move their sphere by a moderate course. These men alone acquire a mansion in the kingdom of life. For only the son of God, descending from heaven, knew the way of life, which he revealed to the believers by word and deed.

JOHN: You say the "believers;" who are they?

THE CARDINAL: Those who believe that Christ is the son of God and that the gospel was preached by him. These believers are certain of the truth of the gospel because the son of God does not lie. For this reason they prefer the promises of the gospel to this life. They enjoy dying here so that they may enter the eternal life with Christ. Dying is universal. Therefore to die on account of their faith in the son of God has the reward of eternal life.

For how would God, who is just and pious, not reward the fidelity of those dying for the glory of God himself? And what reward would God give except life to him who gave his life for Him? Is God less noble than the noble man who abundantly rewards the fidelity of his servant by making him a consort of his kingdom? And if the faithful one chooses to suffer even eternal death for the glory of the son of God how can he be given a reward other than the life where he knows always and eternally that he will truly live and rejoice?

JOHN: Therefore those who do not die for the glory of God as Christ did are not true Christians.

THE CARDINAL: He is a Christian who prefers the glory of God to his own life and glory and prefers it in such a way that if he were tested in persecution he would be found to be such a man. Christ lives in him and he himself does not live (cf. *Gal* 2:20). Therefore he in whom the spirit of Jesus Christ the son of God exists through faith is contemptuous of this world and of life. He who is dead to the world is alive in Christ.

JOHN: You see how difficult it is to direct the curved sphere so that it follows the way of Christ in whom was the spirit of God, who himself led to the center and font of life.

THE CARDINAL: It is very easy for those having true faith as I have already said. Therefore if the sphere of your person is set in motion by the spirit of faith, it is led by firm hope and bound by the charity of Christ who will lead you with him to life. But this is impossible for the infidel.

JOHN: I see that this is most certain. He who does not believe in Christ as the son of God clings to the world and does not expect a better life. But the faithful man delights in adversity because he knows that a glorious death gives immortal life. Nevertheless it is hardly possible that the sphere, which is naturally inclined downwards, should not therefore be moved and curved downwards, and that this be so in one sphere more than another.

THE CARDINAL: This is the sum of the mysteries of this game: that we learn to rectify these inclinations and natural curvings by studious practice so that at last after many variations and unstable circlings and curvings we come to rest in the kingdom of life.[17] For you see that one person throws the ball in one way, another in another, with the same curvature remaining in the ball. It is moved and comes to rest in various ways according to the variety of impetus, and it is never certain before it comes to rest just where it comes to rest. Therefore someone seeing that the ball thrown by another comes near the center, thinks that he wants to follow that person's method and he frequently practices it and improves it.

JOHN: Each ball is peculiar and is differently curved than any other. Therefore one cannot follow another.

THE CARDINAL: It is true, no one person can precisely follow another's path. But it is necessary that each person master the inclinations of his sphere and its tendencies through practice. The moderate person applies himself in precisely this way so that he at last finds the path which the curvature of the ball does not impede, a path from which he may arrive at the circle of life. This is the mystical power of the game: that through studious practice, the curvature of the sphere can actually be regulated, so that after unstable fluctuations, its motion comes to rest in the kingdom of life.[18]

JOHN: I cannot deny that one ball is always differently moved according to the diverse impetus of the throws with the crookedness of the ball remaining. And I cannot deny that the same ball can be impelled in various ways according to the pleasure of the players, so that although its revolution always remains curved, nevertheless its motion is varied. We say nevertheless that it seems that the ball is not

ipsum ponere itendit/& iter ludentes vnus nunc ipsum i propinquo/centro locat/& postea eandē vt prius habens itentionē globus remote a cētro declinat: videri ꝙ nō secundū pellentis itentionē/sed etiā fortunā moueatur. CARD. Fortuna potest dici id: qđ præter itentionē euenit. & cum quisq̄ ludēs petat cētrum circuli: nō est fortuna si tetigerit. Neq̄ est i potestate nostra: ꝙ volūtas nostra ꝑficiat. Dū enī globus currit: attēti sumus vt videamus si ad cētrum accedit. & vellemus iuuare ipm si possemus: vt tādem ibi quiesceret. Sed quia non possumus eum i via/nec ipetum adhibuimus ad hoc necessarium: ideo cum itentione superueniente cursum quem ipressimus/moderari nequimus. Sicut q de monte currere icepit: dum est i veloci motu/ etiā si vellet nō potest se cōtinere. Oportet igitur: circa pricipiū motus attentū esse. Quare mala consuetudo quæ motus est/nō sinit aliquē benefacere: nisi ipsa deposita/ virtutis motum i bona consuetudine ponat. Non habēt igitur male currētes/etiā si in cursu pœniteant: alicui dispositioni quæ aut fatū aut mala fortuna nominari consueuit iputare si male cursum termināt/sed sibiipsis qui iconsulte se ꝓcipitarūt. Bene vides: ꝙ globum quādo vis/& quo modo vis i motu ponis. etiā si constellatio cœli haberet globū fixum debere persistere: non tenebit cœli ifluxus manus tuas / quin si velis globū moueas. Regnum enī cuiusq̄ liberū est: sicut & regnū vniuersi/i quo & cœli & astra continētur/quæ i minori mūdo etiā sed humaniter cōtinētur. IOANNES. Secūdū hoc igitur: nemo nisi sibiipsi aduersos etiā casus iputare debet. CARDINALIS. Ita est i moralibus atq̄ iis operib⁹ quæ sunt hominis vt hominis. Nemo enī viciosus: nisi sua culpa. IOAN. Quomodo tunc dicunt fortunā omnipotentem? CARD. Hoc poeta dicebat: sciens sic philosophos platonicos affirmare. hi enī fortunā aiunt ordinē & dispositionē rerum omnium i suo proprio esse. & illā vocāt necessitatē complexionis: quia nihil illi dispositioni resistere potest. Nec aduersa nec prospera dicitur dispositio seu fortuna illa: nisi quantū ad nos/& secundū explicationes rerū actu & opere. puta dispositio & ordo essendi hoiem/si se habet vt sic fiant omnia vt fieri solēt: alioqui nō fieret homo. Est ergo ineuitabilis necessitas: cui nihil resistere potest. ideo omnipotēs. Cum autē Socrates & Plato actu homines / sint dispares: hoc non euenit quia fortuna seu ordo & dispositio sint prospera & aduersa/nisi quātū ad illos homines quorū vnus assequitur prospera respectu alterius. Sed neq̄ hæc fortuna quæ aīa mundi/supra nominatur: i nostro regno disponit illa quæ hominis sunt. Quisq̄ enī homo: liberū habet arbitrium/velle scilicet/& nolle. cognoscēs virtutē & vicium: quid honestū/quid inhonestū/quid iustum/& quid iniustū/quid laudabile/quid vituperabile/quid gloriosum/quid scandalosum. & ꝙ bonū eligi debeat & malū sperni: habēs itra se regē & iudicē horum. quæ omnia/cum bruta ignorent: ideo sunt hoīs vt hoīs. & i supradictis est nobile regnū / nequaq̄ vniuerso aut alteri creaturæ subiectum: non iis extrinsecis bonis quæ fortuita dicuntur. de qbus nō potest homo quantū vellet/quoniā libere voluntati non subsunt sicut bona præfata imortalia quæ voluntati subiiciuntur. Nam si vult/reperit & eligit libere virtutes imortales imortalis anima/propriȩ vitæ suæ cibum imortalem: sicut vegetatiua corporis pastum sibi aptum corporalē. Et licet sit ipossibile/dum globus mouetur præscire i quo puncto quiescat/neq̄ propterea semper i circulo quiescit quia circulū aliquoties subintrat: non minus tamē ex cōsuetudine & cōtinuata practica præuideri poterit coniectura verisimili/i circulo globum quietē accepturū. Difficilius tamen in quo ordine per circulos distincto: & penitus ipossibile/i quo puncto. Terreno igitur hominu & eius peregrinationi: globus habens ponderosum corpus/& latus ter-

moved according to the intention of the thrower but rather by fortune since it does not always come to rest in the center of the circle where each person playing the game intends to put it. Among those playing the game one player now places the ball near the center and then later, with this player having the same intention, the ball stops moving far from the center.
THE CARDINAL: Fortune can be called that which happens outside of intention. And since each player aims for the center of the circle, if he hits it, it is not by fortune. Nor is it in our power that our will is carried out. When the ball is rolling we are attentive so that we may see if it will reach the center and we would help it if we could so that it would finally come to rest there. But since we did not initially put it on the right path and did not apply the impetus necessary for it to reach the center, we cannot modify its course by a later effort. It is just as if someone begins to run down a mountain; once he is in rapid motion, he cannot stop, even if he wishes to.

Therefore it is necessary that attention be paid to the origin of motion. Hence bad habit, which is a motion, does not allow anyone to do good things unless, having put aside the bad habit he places the motion of virtue in good habit. Therefore those running badly, even if they repent during the course, may not blame some disposition that it is customary to name fate or bad fortune if they finish the course badly, but only themselves, who raced forth precipitously without thinking. You can well see that you put the ball in motion when and how you wish. Even if a heavenly constellation were able to make the ball remain in a fixed point, the influence of the heavens will not keep your hand from moving the ball if you wish, for the kingdom of each [man] is free and so is the kingdom of the universe in which the heavens and the stars are contained. These are also contained in the lesser world but indeed, humanly.
JOHN: Therefore according to this no one ought in fact to attribute adverse events to anything except to himself.
THE CARDINAL: This is so in moral things and in the works that are of man as man. For no one is corrupt except by his own fault.
JOHN: In what way then do they say that fortune is omnipotent?
THE CARDINAL: This the poet said, knowing that the Platonic philosophers agree.[19] For these [Platonic philosophers] called fortune the order and disposition of everything in its own being, and they called it the necessity of the combination of things because nothing can resist that disposition. Nor is that fortune or disposition called either prosperous or adverse except in as much as it relates to us and to the unfolding of things in act and work. For example the disposition and order of human existence is such that all things are made in the way that they are made, otherwise man would not be made. The disposition and order of human existence is therefore inevitable necessity which nothing can resist. For that reason it is omnipotent. But, although one of them may become more prosperous than the other, it does not happen that Socrates and Plato are actually different men because of the prosperity or adversity of fortune or order and disposition.

This fortune, which is called *anima mundi* above, does not determine those things in our kingdom which are man's. For each man has free will, willing or not willing, knowing virtue and vice, what is upright, what shameful, what is just and unjust, what is laudable and what is blameworthy, what is glorious and what is scandalous. And he ought to choose that which is good and spurn the bad, having within himself the rule and judgment over these things, which, since the beasts are ignorant of them, are in man as man's. And in these matters the noble kingdom is never subject to the universe or to another creature. The noble kingdom is not in these extrinsic goods that are called fortuitous which man cannot influence no matter how much he would like to since they are not subject to the will as are the aforementioned good immortal things. For if the immortal soul wishes, it freely discovers and chooses the immortal powers, the immortal nourishment of its own life, just as the vegetative power of the body chooses the corporeal food suitable for it.

Although it would be impossible to have foreknowledge of the point at which the ball will come to rest when it is moved, nor does it always come to rest in the circle because it steals into it several times, nonetheless, through habit and continuous practice, the place in the circle where the ball would stop might be foreseen by a verisimilar conjecture. Nevertheless it would be difficult to foresee in which distinct order the ball would pass through the circles and entirely impossible to foresee at what exact point it would come to rest. Therefore the ball, having a heavy body and a

renum inclinatum/& eius motus quia per hominis fit impulsum/aliqualiter simila tur.Non enī potest ī rectitudine persistere motus humanus. Cito declinat/propter terrestreitatem/inconstanter & varie semper fluctuans:qui nihilominus potest exer citio virtutis reuolutionem in circulo terminare.& bonam & perseuerantem inten= tionem adiuuat deus qui in motu quæritur:& perficit bonam voluntatem. Ipse enī est qui fidelem dirigit & ad perfectum perducit/& qui īpotentiam in ipsum speran= tis sua omnipotenti supplet clæmentia.Christianus igitur qui facit omnia quæ ī ip= so sunt/licet sentiat globum suum inconstanter currere:ī deo tamen confidens non confundetur/qui non derelinquit sperantes in se.Et hoc est huius ludi mysterium sa tis nunc pro tam breui hora declaratum:vt de his paucis/multa elicias & proficias in motu/vt tandē quietē simul ī regno vitæ cū CHRISTO rege nostro fœliciter as= sequamur.Eo præstante:q̄ solus potēs est/& ī sæcula sæculorum benedictus. Amen.

Versus de laude libri.

QVi cupis ingenium præsentis nosse libelli:
Redde prius mensis/terq3/quaterq3 sacrū. id est eucharistiam deo liba
Et semel atq3 iterū/sensus vbi legeris altos:
Ad caput & titulos/mente vacante redi.
Ne pigeat/quocunq3 situ salebrosa videbis
Esse loca/& trepido non adeunda pede:
Poscere opem/& sancti per florida prata magistri
Ire licet.multa doctior arte senex.
Vtribus hæc crassis non sunt condenda vehendis.
Pinguis aqualiculi/non capit alta locus.
Attritas subeunt vix post conamina mentes.
Purgatum hæc tantum dogmata pectus habet.
Luditur hic ludus:sed non pueriliter.at sic
Lusit vt orbe nouo:sancta sophia deo.
Sic ludit quisquis per cœli aprica/domosq3
Aethereas:quid agant cernere sancta venit.
Sol oriens ludis sic Augustine canendo
Musica cum nobis/te modulante data est.
Sic omnes lusere pii:Dionysius/& qui
Increpuit magno mystica verba sono.
Et nos magne pater ludum celebremus amicum:
Noster vt æterna sit globus æde sedens.
Istic perpetuo post longa volumina centro
Hæreat:& nullo fine perennis agat.
I prior.at tecum nos sedibus optime castis
Siste pater:stat vbi lusus & ara dei
Tu quoq3 cara ducum soboles dux inclyte lude:
Principibus famam quo tua mens pariat
Nam bene Cæsareos q̄q̄ ornent stemmata cippos
Inq3 palatinis gloria maior eat.
Et tibi consurgat comitum fœcunda propago:
Occiduas Rhenus qua pater auget aquas.

side inclined towards the earth, is somewhat similar to the earthly condition of man, and its movement, because it is thrown by man, is somewhat similar to man's earthly pilgrimage.

Human motion cannot persist in a straight line. It quickly declines, always fluctuating inconstantly and variously on account of its terrestrial nature. Man can nevertheless terminate the revolution in a circle through the exercise of his virtue. And God, who is sought in this motion and who perfects that good will, aids the good and perseverant intention. God is the same one who directs the faithful man and leads him forth towards perfection and who by his omnipotent clemency overcomes the impotence of him who hopes in Him.

Therefore that Christian who, confident in God, does all the things which are in him, will not be disturbed although he perceives that his sphere rolls capriciously and inconstantly. God will not abandon those who place their hope in Him. And I have now spoken enough concerning the mystery of this game in this so very brief hour so that you may elicit much from these few words and become proficient in motion, and so that finally we may also felicitously attain, by His provision, peace in the kingdom of life with Christ our king who alone is powerful and is forever blessed. Amen.

Anglica sint q̄uis consanguinitate propinqua
  Sceptra tibi: & quicquid gallia pinguis arat.
Et genitrix tibi sit ditis germana tyranni.
  Præluſtres ſpectent & tua iura duces.
Nec minus in CHRISTI ſortem/templiſq; ſacratis:
  Hinc atq; inde vocet te pius ordo patrum.
Vt nihil in pulchra ſine te germania gente
  Euehat: & claris clarior vt niteas.
Teq; decus patriæ magnus generauerit Otto
  Siluarum terror/cui lupus ingemuit.
Vt Baioahariæ tua cingant tempora frondes:
  Maſcula belligero quas tulit enſe cohors
Et quicquid tantis titulis memorande reliqui:
  Claudicet vt nulla parte ſuperba domus.
Hæc ne iure ſuo volucris fortuna repoſcat:
  Q; ſeries patrum nil niſi nomen habet.
Surge tuo marte/hic princeps digniſſime ſurge:
  Ingenii dotes laudibus adde ducum.
Aurea ſit liceat: lituum tamen aurea flatum
  Corrogat: effundat quo tuba rauca ſonum.
Quid tibi conueniat: melius te nemo videbit.
  Tu modo non aliis q̄ tibi crede magis.
Candidus æoo ſurget dum lucifer axe/
  Et bibet occiduas veſpere phœbus aquas/
Dum niuibus longas hyemes germania ducet/
  Et veſpertinam gallus amabit humum/
Dūq; homines tellus/piſces mare/ſydera cœlum
  Reddet: doctorum hic ludus honeſtus erit.
Tu quoq; magnanime princeps mihi crede Ioannes:
  Semper eris/ſemper viuus in ore virum.
Effice quod ſolum tibi te monitore gerendum eſt:
  Ne tantum in chartis ſit tibi grande σοφῶσ.
Et mecum refer O grates memorande magiſtro:
  Eſt cui (ſi cuiq̄ eſt) mens patefacta dei.

PRIMI LIBRI DE LVDO GLOBI
DOCTISSIMI PATRIS NI-
COLAI DE CVSA CAR.
FINIS.

Nicholas of Cusa – THE GAME OF SPHERES II

Dialogi de ludo globi Liber Secundus. Interlocutores ALBERTVS adolescens. dux Bauariæ. & NICOLAVS cardinalis. ALBER.

V nosti pater me aduenisse summa fiducia: vt papæ nostro Pio: atq; tibi & aliis cardinalib⁹ notior fierẽ & proficerẽ. Cũ nunc illustrẽ ducem Ioannem consanguineum meũ charissimũ in hac vrbe reperissem / & inter nos post cõmunia amicorũ colloquia ipsum vacare viderẽ lectioni libelli de ludo globi: admiratus tã de ludo q̃ de libello / nisus sum cõpræhendere non nihil iuxta meã iuuenilem capacitatẽ. Sed non est mihi visum: te circulorũ regionis vitæ mysticã sententiã explanasse. Rogo igitur tuã pietatẽ: ne in me despicias tanti mysterii incapacitatẽ. Dabitur vt doctior rememorẽ quæ audiuero: & dei dono proficiam. CARDINA. Multo gaudio te cũ fratre Volfgango hoc loco vidi. Pater enĩ tuus Albertus Illustris comes Palatinus & Bauariæ dux / multis annis me singulariter amauit. & hoc ostendit. Videre tantũ amicũ viuere in illustribus & optime nobiliterq; cõpositis & eruditis filiis: mihi periocundũ est. Et hinc quæq; possibilia: libẽs impertiar. De ludo globi inquiris ea: quæ dum audieris / non poteris (ætate obstante) fortasse discutere. Admiraberis tamẽ / & violentia quadã incorporabis altissima / quæ te habilem reddẽt / vt ad cuncta scibilia melius volare queas. Oportet autem vt mẽtis oculũ aperias / & visum illum totaliter eleues: vt quæ dicturus sum potius videas q̃ audias. ALBERTVS. Faciam omnia: quantũ natura & ĩgeniũ concesserint. CARDINA. Circulorũ mysterium: qđ vt capias insige tuæ memoriæ propositionẽ quæ sequitur. Eo qđ in omnibus & in quo omnia: nihil maius aut minus esse potest. quare: omniũ exemplar. ALBERTVS. Habeo iã hanc in memoria fixam propositionẽ. Sed vt mens eius videat veritatẽ: declaratione opus habet. CARDINALIS. Parua sufficiet. Nam quomodo esset aliquid minus eo qđ in omnibus: aut quomodo maius eo in quo omnia? Si igitur nihil omniũ est aut minus aut maius eo: necesse est omnia illius vnius exemplaris esse exemplata. ALBERTVS. Breuissime declarasti. Nam certissime video / cũ exemplatum nihil habeat nisi ab exemplari / sitq; vnum omniũ exemplar / qđ in omnibus & ĩ quo omnia: clara est ostẽsio / q̃ postq̃ videro vnitatẽ exemplaris omniũ variorũ exemplatorũ / me ad altã contẽplationẽ deduxeris. CARDINALIS. tu probe mente conspicis: exemplatũ non posse esse nisi in ipso sit exemplar. ALBERTVS. Certissime. CARDINALIS. Sed quomodo est exemplatũ: nisi sit in eodẽ suo exemplari? Nam exemplatũ si est extra suũ exemplar: quomodo manet exemplatũ? ALBERTVS. Nihil obest: quo minus hoc videam. Nam necesse est vtiq; exẽplatũ in exemplari suo contineri: alioqui non esset verũ exemplatũ. Ideo perfecte intueor / exemplar necessario esse ĩ exemplato: & exemplatũ contineri seu esse in exemplari. CARDINA. Exemplar igitur est in omnibus exemplatis: & in quo omnia exemplata. Nullum igitur exemplatũ est minus aut maius eo. Quare exemplata omnia: sunt vnius exemplaris exemplata. ALBERTVS. Verissime: sic esse video. CARDINALIS. Nec est necesse propter pluralitatẽ exemplatorum esse plura exemplaria: cũ vnũ infinitis sufficiat. Præcedit enĩ naturaliter exẽplar exemplatũ: omnẽ pluralitatẽ vnitas / quæ est omnis exemplatę multitudinis exemplar. Ideo si essent plura exemplaria: necesse esset vnitatẽ exemplarem / illã pluralitatẽ præcedere.

The second book of the dialogue on the game of spheres. The interlocutors are the young man Albert, Duke of Bavaria and the Cardinal Nicholas.

ALBERT: You know, father, that I have come with the highest confidence that I will become better known to our Pope Pius and to you and the other cardinals, and will make progress. Now when I found the illustrious Duke John, my most dear relative in this city, after we had a general conversation, I saw that he was devoting his time to the reading of the book on the game of spheres, admiring both the book and the game. I have striven to comprehend something of it according to my youthful capacity, but it didn't seem to me that you explained the mystical meaning of the circles of the region of life. Therefore I appeal to your piety not to despise my incapacity for such a great mystery. May it come to pass that I, becoming more learned, remember what I have heard and profit by the gift of God.
THE CARDINAL: It is with great delight that I have seen you here with your brother Wolfgang. As is obvious, your father Albert, the illustrious Count Palatine and Duke of Bavaria, has been very close to me for many years. It is most pleasing to me to see so great a friend alive in illustrious and most nobly composed and learned sons. And hence I will willingly share whatever I can. You inquire about these things concerning the game of spheres, but when you hear about them, you will perhaps not be able to discuss them since your age stands in the way. Nevertheless with a certain effort you will admire and incorporate some deep things which will make you fit so that you are better able to fly toward everything that is knowable. However it is necessary that you fully open the eye of the mind and its vision so that you will see rather than hear the things that I shall say.
ALBERT: I will do all [these] things, to the extent that [my] nature and character permit.
THE CARDINAL: In order to understand the mystification of circles, impress upon your memory the proposition that follows: nothing can be greater or lesser than that which is in all things and in which all things are, therefore it is the exemplar of all things.[20]
ALBERT: I have already fixed this proposition in my memory but in order that the mind see its truth it needs an explanation.
THE CARDINAL: A small explanation will suffice; how would anything be smaller than that which is in all things or how would anything be larger than that in which are all things? If therefore nothing is either greater or lesser than it, it is necessary that all things are exemplifications of this one exemplar.
ALBERT: You have expressed yourself most succinctly. Most certainly I see that since the exemplified thing has nothing except from the exemplar and since there is only one exemplar of all things, which is in all things and in which all things are, the proof is clear. Since I have seen the unity of the exemplar of all the various exemplified things, you have led me into high speculation.
THE CARDINAL: You correctly observe in the mind that the exemplified thing cannot be unless the exemplar would be in it.
ALBERT: Most certainly.
THE CARDINAL: But how does the exemplified [thing] exist save in its own exemplar? For if the likeness is outside its exemplar, how does it remain a likeness?
ALBERT: Nothing prevents me from seeing this. By all means it is necessary that a likeness be contained in its exemplar, otherwise it would not be a true likeness. For this reason I observe perfectly well that it is necessary that the exemplar be in the exemplified and that the exemplified exist or be contained in the exemplar.
THE CARDINAL: Therefore the exemplar is in all exemplifications and all exemplifications are in it. Therefore no exemplification is lesser or greater than its exemplar, which is why all exemplifications are exemplifications of one exemplar.
ALBERT: I see this to be most truly so.
THE CARDINAL: It is not necessary that there be many exemplars on account of the fact that there are many exemplifications since one [exemplar] suffices for infinite likenesses. The exemplar naturally precedes the exemplification and unity, which is the exemplar of every exemplification of multitude, exists before all plurality. For this reason if there were many exemplars it would be necessary that one exemplar—of unity—precede that plurality [of exemplars].

Non essent igitur illa plura exemplaria / æque prima exemplaria: sed vnius primi exemplaris exemplata. Non potest igitur esse nisi vnũ primum exemplar: qđ est ĩ omnibus exemplatis / & ĩ quo omnia exemplata. ALBERTVS. Ostendisti nunc mihi quæ videre concupiui. Nã nihil mihi obsistit: quin videam omnis multitudinis vnitatem principium . ex quo intueor vnitatem exemplar omnium exemplatorum. CARDINALIS. Dixi vnitatẽ esse exemplar omnium numerorum: seu omnis pluralitatis aut multitudinis. In omni enĩ numero vides vnitatẽ : & omnem numerum in vnitate contineri. Omnis enĩ numerus est vnus: binarius / ternarius / denarius / & ita de omnibus / quisq; est vnus numerus. Nec esse posset quisq; vnus: si ĩ eo non esset vnitas / & nisi ipse in vnitate contineretur. ALBERTVS. Hactenus non aduerti ad hæc: quando mihi visum fuit denarium maiorem vnitate / & ideo in vnitate non contineri. Sed nunc video denarium: cum sit vnus denarius / nõ posse hoc esse nisi in vnitate contineatur. CARDINALIS. Attendas etiam oportet quomodo vnitas non potest esse nec minor nec maior. Q2 non minor: statim admisisti. Q2 non maior etiã vides: quãdo aduertis id quod esset maius vno non esse vnum. Ac q; sic est de denario: quẽ siue videas ipsum minoratum siue auctum / non vides denarium. Hoc autẽ habet omnis numerus ab vnitate. quia numerus est exemplatum exemplaris vnitatis. ALBERTVS. Propositio quã præmisisti: clauis esse videtur ad intrandam intelligentiam absconditorum / quando quærens ipsam / recte applicat. CARDINALIS. Nec est applicatio difficilis. Nam si te interrogo seriatim : sola interrogatione duceris ad visionem veri. Puta. Interrogo te: an cuncta quæ vides putas aliquid existere? Credo dices: cuncta existere. ALBERTVS. Cum sint aliquid: oportet existere. CARDINALIS. In existentibus: est ne ipsum esse? ALBERTVS. Vtiq;. alias si non esset in ipsis ipsum esse: quomodo existerent? CARDINALIS. Nonne quæ existunt: in ipso esse existunt? ALBERTVS. Extra esse ipsum vtiq; non existerẽt. CARDINALIS. Esse igitur omniũ in omnibus existentibus est: & omnia existentia in ipso esse existunt. ALBERTVS. Nihil certius video: q̃ q; & esse ipsum simplicissimum est omnium existentiũ exemplar. CARDINALIS. Hoc est esse absolutũ. quẽ creatorẽ omniũ quæ sunt credimus. ALBERTVS. Quis non videret hæc quæ dixisti ita se habere? CARDINALIS. Sic vides ĩ animato animã: & simul ipsum animatũ in aĩa. Et ĩ iusto iustitiã: & ipsum ĩ ea. Sicut ĩ albo albedinẽ: & ipsum in ea. Et generaliter ĩ contracto absolutũ: & ipsum cõtractũ ĩ absoluto . Humanitatẽ in hoĩe: & ipsum ĩ humanitate. ALBERTVS. Video certe ista oĩa necessaria: sed imaginatio non capit quomodo hoc fiat. Quis enĩ conciperet vnũ esse ĩ alio: & id aliud ĩ eodẽ vno? CARDINALIS. Hoc est ideo ĩimaginabile: quoniã hæc virtus imaginatiua ĩ quãto terminatur. Nã non quantũ imaginatio non attigit. Vnde q; continens sit ĩ contẽto: quãdo imaginatio ad locũ se cõuertit q quãtus est / nõ capit. Videturq; ei ac si diceret quis: q; esse aliquẽ in domo sit esse domũ ĩ ipso. Sed oculus mẽtis ad ĩtelligibilia quæ supra imaginationẽ sunt respiciens: non potest negare quĩ videat in esse ipso quod est supra imaginationẽ / omnia / etiã imaginationẽ ipsam cõtineri. & nisi ĩ contẽtis esset hoc verum: non essent. ALBERTVS. Vtiq; hæc vera video. & occurrit mihi manifestũ exemplũ. Omnia quæ sensu & imaginatione attingunt: sunt circa substantiã / quæ accidẽtia dicunt. quæ nisi continerẽtur per substantiã: nõ subsisterẽt. Necesse est igitur continẽs illa accidẽtia esse ĩtra accidẽtia: & substare / vt ĩ ipso illa subsistant. Substantia igitur ĩtelligibilis naturæ supra sensum & imaginationẽ existens: omnia accidẽtia continet & in contentis existit. Nec est aliud accidentia

x

Therefore these many exemplars would not all be first exemplars, but exemplifications of the one first exemplar. Therefore there can be only one first exemplar which is in all exemplifications and in which are all exemplifications.

ALBERT: Now you have shown me that which I have longed to see. For nothing remains for me but that I see unity as the principle of all multiplicity, from which I contemplate the unity as the exemplar of all exemplifications.

THE CARDINAL: I have said that unity is the exemplar of all numbers or of all plurality or multiplicity for you see that unity is contained in every number and every number is contained in unity. For every number is one— two, three, ten, and so on for all [numbers]. Each number is one number. It would not be possible that each number were one if unity were not in it and unless it were contained in unity.

ALBERT: So far I have not observed this since to my vision ten was greater than unity and for that reason is not contained in unity. But now I see that ten, since it is one ten, cannot be thus unless it were contained in unity.

THE CARDINAL: It is also necessary that you observe how unity cannot be greater or lesser. You immediately admitted that it cannot be smaller. You also see that it cannot be larger when you observe that what is greater than one is not one. And so it is concerning ten: whether you see it become smaller or larger you do not see ten. Every number has this from unity because number is the exemplification of the exemplar of unity.

ALBERT: When the inquirer correctly applies the proposition that you have premised it seems to be the key to the entrance into the understanding of hidden things.

THE CARDINAL: And this application is not difficult. If I question you in an orderly way you will proceed to the vision of the truth by the interrogation alone. For example if I ask you whether you think that everything you see is something that exists, I believe that you will say that everything that you see exists.

ALBERT: Since the things that you see are something, it is necessary that they exist.

THE CARDINAL: Is being itself in the things that exist?

ALBERT: Certainly, if being itself were not in them, how would they otherwise exist?

THE CARDINAL: Do not those things which exist exist in being itself?

ALBERT: Certainly they would not exist outside of being itself.

THE CARDINAL: Therefore the being of all things is in all existing things and all existing things exist in being itself.

ALBERT: I see that nothing is more certain than that the most simple being itself is the exemplar of all existing things.

THE CARDINAL: This is the absolute being that we believe is the creator of all things that exist.

ALBERT: Who would not see that it is as you have said?

THE CARDINAL: So you see the soul in the animated thing and at the same time the animated thing itself is the soul, and justice in the just and the just in justice, just as whiteness is in a white thing and the white thing in whiteness, and generally the absolute is in the contracted and the contracted in the absolute, humanity in the man and the man in humanity.

ALBERT: Certainly I see that all these things are necessary, but the imagination does not understand how this is. For who would conceive that one is in another and that that other is in the same one?

THE CARDINAL: This is unimaginable because the imaginative power is terminated in quantity. The imagination does not attain non-quantity. When the imagination turns itself to the quantifiable, it does not understand that the containing would be in the contained. To the imagination it appears as if someone said: a-man-in-a-house would be a house-in-a-man. But the eye of the mind, looking towards intelligible things which are above the imagination cannot deny that it sees that all things and also imagination itself are contained in being itself which is above imagination and unless this were true in contained things they would not be.

ALBERT: Certainly I see this to be true and an obvious example suggests itself to me. All things which are attained by sense and imagination are in the region of substance. These things are called accidents; they would not subsist unless they were contained by substance. Therefore it is necessary that that which contains those accidents be within the accidents and that it subsist in such a way that those accidents subsist in it. Therefore the substance of the itelligible nature, existing in it above sense and imagination, contains all accidents and exists in the contained things. That the

esse in subiecto qđ est substãtia: q̃ substãtiam in accidentibus. Et hoc potissimũ verũ video: quia accidẽtia non sunt in subiecto seu substãtia quasi in loco/cum locus nõ sit substãtia sed accidens. CARDINALIS. Gaudeo te sanum mẽtis visum habere. Et quãdo hanc speculationẽ extendis ad animã rationalem quæ est substãtia omniũ virium & potẽtiarum suarum: tu vides ipsam illas continere/ & in omnibus suis viribus & potentiis esse. ALBERTVS. Incipio gustare hãc scientiã sapidissimã: exercitabo me in ipsa vt habitum acquirã. Sed ne te nimium in hac necessaria mihi digressione teneã: amplius pergere poteris ad institutum. CARDINALIS. Nunc puto facile capis hãc regionẽ viuorum. Nam in omni viuẽte: necesse est esse vitã/ & viuens in ipsa. Vita igitur christiformium eorũ omnium scilicet qui in regione sunt viuentium sic se habet/ꝙ vita quæ CHRISTVS est qui aiebat/ego sum vita: est in omnibus ibi viuẽtibus/& ipsi oẽs viuẽtes ĩ vita quæ CHRISTVS est. & ideo vita CHRISTI: est forma exemplaris omniũ ibi viuẽtium q sunt huius formæ exemplata. ALBERTVS. Bene video oportere viuentẽ christianum sic se habere vt ais. nã oportet ĩ ipso esse vitã CHRISTI: & ipsum ĩ eadẽ ipsa vita. CARDINALIS. Figuratur hæc vita regionis viuẽtium ĩ figura quã rotundã vides. & vt circuli oẽs habẽt idem centrũ: circuli sunt figuræ rotunditatis. Rotunditas: circulatio est motus vitæ perpetuæ & infinibilis. In omni rotundo necesse est esse rotunditatẽ: in qua sit ipsum rotundũ. Vnde sicut nec notitia nec essentia rotundi seu perpetui sciri aut haberi potest nisi a cẽtro super quo voluitur motus perpetuus/ita ꝙ eo nõ existẽte/non potest nec perpetuitas nec motus vitæ perpetuæ qui ĩ æqualitate ad idẽtitatẽ centri refertur/aut nosse aut esse: sic se habet centrũ qui CHRISTVS est ad omnes circulationes. Circuli igitur: hic motũ vitæ figurãt. Et viuaciores motus designãtur per circulos cẽtro qđ est vita: propinquiores. quoniã vita qđ cẽtrum est/qua nec maior nec minor dari potest. In ipso em̃ continetur omnis motus vitalis: qui extra motum esse nequit. Nisi enĩ sit in omni motu vitali vita: nequaq̃ vitalis erit. Est autẽ circularis & cẽtralis motus: qui vita est viuentium. Quãto autẽ circulus cẽtro est propinquior: tãto citius circũuolui potest. Igitur qui sic est circulus ꝙ & cẽtrum: in nunc instãti circũuolui potest. erit igitur motus infinitus. Cẽtrum autem punctus fixus est: erit igitur motus maximus seu infinitus/& pariter minimus/vbi idẽ est centrum & circunferentia. & vocamus ipsum vitã viuentium: in sua fixa æternitate omnem possibilem vitæ motum complicantẽ. ALBERTVS. Intelligo te dicere velle paruitatẽ circulorũ velociorẽ seu viuaciorẽ motum vitæ figurare: quoniã ad centrũ quod est vita viuentium propius accedunt. Sed dicito: cur nouẽ circulos figurasti? CARDINALIS. Scimus aliquos in rationis motu veloces/alios tardos/sed differẽtes: vt ex varietate ingeniorum experimur. Quorum quidã tanta gaudẽt viuacitate: vt breuissime discurrant. Alii tardius: & vix vnq in aliquo proficiunt. CHRISTVS qui est vita: est & sapientia/hoc est sapida scientia. Scientia in eo quia sapida: ostenditur viua appræhẽsio. Et vita intellectualis: est appræhẽsio sapientiæ seu sapidæ scientiæ. Omnis igitur motus viuus rationalis: est vt suæ vitæ causam videat/ & tali sapientia ĩmortaliter pascatur. ꝙ si ad hoc non peruenerit: non viuit/quãdo suæ vitæ causam ignorat. Deus autẽ est dator vitæ: quẽ nisi CHRISTVS dei filius ostendat nemo videbit. Ostẽdere enĩ: ad ipsum solũ spectat. quia non potest patrẽ vt patrẽ ostendere: nisi filius. Vnus est autẽ pater CHRISTI & noster/q est ipsa æternitas: quæ est in oĩbus patribus/& ĩ quo oẽs patres sunt & continẽtur. Sed vt clarius videas ipsum ostensorẽ patris/aduerte qa ipse est veritas. Dicebat enĩ se viã & ostium/vitã & veri

accidents are in the subject which is substance in nothing other than that the subtance is in the accidents.
And I see this to be true because the accidents are not in the subject or substance as if they were in a place, since place is not substance but accident.
THE CARDINAL: I rejoice that you have sound vision of the mind. And when you extend this speculation to the rational soul which is the substance of all powers and of their potentialities, you see that it [the rational soul] contains them and that it is in all their power and potentialities.
ALBERT: I am beginning to taste this most savory knowledge. I will practice in it so that I acquire the habit. But I insist that you don't linger too much in this digression that is necessary to me in order that you will be able to progress more fully towards that which you have undertaken.
THE CARDINAL: Now I think that you easily understand this region of living things, for it is necessary that there be life in every living thing and that the living thing in it is life. Therefore the life in the region of the living of all of those who are formed in Christ is so constituted that the life which is Christ who said, "I am life," is in all things living here and all living things are in the life which is Christ (*John* 11:25; 14:6).
ALBERT: I see well that it is necessary that the living Christian is as you say. For it is necessary that the life of Christ be in him and that he be in that same life.
THE CARDINAL: This life of the region of living things is represented in the round figure which you see. And as all circles have the same center, circles are the representations of roundness. Roundness is the circulation of the motion of perpetual and unending life. In every round thing it is necessary that there is roundness in which the round itself is. Hence, neither the knowledge nor the essence of the perpetual or the round can be known or exist except from the center about which perpetual motion is turned, and this in such a way that if it does not exist neither the perpetuity nor the motion of perpetual life, which is equally related to the identity of the center, can be known or exist.

The center which is Christ also exists in such a relation to all circulations. Therefore circles represent the movement of life here. And more lively motions are designated through the circles that are closer to the center that is life since life, than which nothing greater nor lesser can be given, is the center. For every vital movement which cannot exist outside of life is contained in it. For unless there were life in every vital motion, it [the motion] would never be vital.[21]

The motion which is the life of the living is therefore circular and central. The closer the circle is to the center the more rapidly it can orbit around the center. Therefore the circle that is also the center can orbit instantaneously. Therefore it would be infinite motion. The center is a fixed point. It will therefore be the greatest or infinite motion and likewise the smallest, where the center and circumference are the same. And we call it the life of the living which enfolds all possible motion of life in its fixed eternity.
ALBERT: I understand you to mean that the smallness of the circles represents the more rapid or lively motion of life since they more closely approach the center which is the life of living things. But tell me, why have you drawn nine circles?
THE CARDINAL: We know that some people are quick in the movement of reason and we experience that others are slow and differ because of the variety of character. Of these people, certain ones enjoy such great vivacity that they discourse very concisely. Others discourse more slowly and hardly make any progress in anything at any time.

Christ, who is life, is also the wisdom that is savory knowledge. Because knowledge is savory in him it is made manifest as living apprehension, and intellectual life is the apprehension of wisdom or savory knowledge. Therefore every living rational motion exists so that it may see the cause of its life and be immortally fed by such wisdom. If it does not attain this it does not live because then it is ignorant of the cause of its life.

God is the giver of life whom no one sees unless Christ, the son of God, shows him. For it belongs only to Christ to show him because only the son can show the father as father. Our father and Christ's father, who is eternity itself which is in all fathers and in which all fathers exist and are contained, are one and the same. But in order that you may more clearly see this manifestation of the father, notice that he himself is the truth. For he said that he is the way and the door, life and truth (*John* 14:6).

tatē.Oſtēſio certa & vera:non niſi per veritatē fieri poteſt.Falſitas vero errat & de-
uiat/quę mēdaci diabolo ſeductori tribuitur.filiatio dei ī CHRISTO:ſeipſam/qa ve
ritas oſtēdit.Et q CHRISTVM vere videt:in eo patrē & ipſum ī patre videt.Cir-
culi igitur:ſunt viſionis gradus.In omni circulo videtur cētrū oībus cōmune: pro-
pinquius ī propinquiori/remotius ī remotiori.Extra quē/cū centrū videri nequeat
quod non niſi ī circulo videtur:extra viſionis æternæ gradus & ſine CHRISTO nō
videtur vita viuētiū/ſeu lux luminū intellectualiū.Ideo ī tenebris & ī vmbra mortis
ſic carēt vita:ſicut oculus īteger ī tenebris caret vita.qa videre:eſt illi viuere.In carē
tia autē lucis/nihil videre poteſt:licet ſit oculus ſanus.Ita aīa licet īcorruptibilis luce carēs oſtēſiua quæ CHRISTVS eſt:non videt/nec ītellectuali vita viuere poteſt.
Sicut enī ſenſibilis viſio vt ſit vera & viua ſenſibili luce īdiget oſtēſiua:ita & intellectualis viſio ītellectuali veritatis luce opus habet/ſi videre ſeu viuere debet. Et quia
in denario terminatur omnis numerus : per nouē circulos ī decimū qui ſic circulus
ꝙ cētrū/figuraui aſcēſum. ALBERTVS. Cuncta cōpetēter quæ dixiſti/& ſi nō cœ
pi ī guſtu ītelligētiæ:vidi tamē vera eſſe.Solū admiror:poſtꝙ īfinitas cētralis lucis li
beraliſſime ſe diffundit/quomodo gradus oriantur. CARDI. Hæc lux nō ſe diffun
dit per corporalia loca:vt quaſi lux corporea q̄ proximiora loca plus illuminat. Sed
eſt lux:q̄ nec loco clauditur/nec obſtaculo īpęditur/ſicut nec mētis noſtræ cogitatio.
Sed quæ illuminātur:nō poſſunt niſi varia eſſe.qa multa & plura:ſine varietate nec
multa nec plura eſſent/alias idem eſſent. Receptio igiť lucis:varia eſt ī variis mēti-
bus.ſicut receptio vnius lucis ſenſibilis:ī variis oculis varie capitur/ī vno veriori &
lucidiori modo q̄ ī alio iuxta ſuā capacitatē quæ nō poteſt eſſe æqualis ī diuerſis.Re
cipiunt igitur chriſtiformes lucē gloriæ ſufficienter omnes : ſed differēter ſecundū
capacitatē cuiuſq;.Sicut dū prædicator euāgelicus lucē vnā æque ad ſingulos audi-
tores diffundit:nō tamē æque ab oībus capitur/cū nō ſint eiuſdē mētis & capacita-
tis. ALBER. Cū nemo niſi beatus ſit ī regione viuorū/ſitq; ſolus ille beatus q id habet qd appetit/ſitq; vnicū ſolū quies deſideriorum ſcilicet meliori & pfectiori modo
quo id fieri poteſt videre cētrū vitæ ſuæ:ideo miror de eo ꝙ quoſdā ꝓpius ad cētrū
accedere figuraſti/cū remotiores nō cōprehēdāt meliori modo quo hoc fieri poteſt.
CARD. Figuratť fruitio beata ī potatiōe fontis vitæ:eſtq; idē videre & bibere.Vnꝰ
eſt fons viuus totā regionē viuētiū īplens:de quo quātum quiſq; ſitit & deſiderat bi
bit.non poſſunt duo æqualiter ſitire & deſiderare potū.Ideo licet oēs ſufficiētiſſime
bibāt quātum appetunt:nō tamē æqualiter/quādo æqualiter nō ſitiunt. Facit chari
tas ſitire:quæ ī diuerſis diuerſa eſt.Sic CHRISTVS figurabat regnum nuptiis:vbi
ipſe miniſtrat cuiq; id qđ appetit.Saturanť igiť oēs quātum deſiderāt & fameſcunt:
licet alii plus/alii minus capiant. ALBERTVS. Placēt hæc.& video non eſſe nouē
circulos gloriæ ſed īnumerabiles:quādo quiſq; beatꝰ propriū habet.CARDINA.
Licet ſic ſit ꝙ tota latitudo regni vitæ ſit a cētro ad circūferētiā/& hæc latitudo poſ
ſit ad īſtar lineæ quæ ī ſe īfinitas habet lineas ſimiles a cētro ad circūferētiā concipi/
vnumq; ſit cōmune omnium cētrum & circumferētia ſingulorū:tamen illa innume
rabilis multitudo circumferētiarum in nouē gradus partitur/ vt gradatim per regnum illud pulcherrimo decoratum ordine nos ducamur/vbi idē eſt centrum com
mune & particularis circumferētia/ſcilicet ad CHRISTVM.Ibi enim idem eſt cen
trum vitæ creatoris:& circumferentia creaturæ. CHRISTVS enim/deus & ho-
mo:ſt/creator & creatura:& omnium beatarum creaturarū ipſe eſt cētrū.Et attēte aduertas circunferētiam ipſius:eſſe naturæ circūferētialis omnium circumferē-

x ii.

A true and certain manifestation can be made only through truth. Falsity however, which is attributed to the lying and seductive devil errs and deviates. The filiation of God manifests itself in Christ because the truth shows it. And he who truly sees Christ sees the father in him and him in the father.

Therefore circles are grades of vision. A center common to all is seen in every circle, closer in one that is closer to it and more remote in one that is farther from it. Since the center cannot be seen outside of the circle because it is not seen except in the circle, the life of the living or the light of the intellectual lights is not seen outside of the grades of eternal vision and without Christ.

For this reason those who exist in darkness and the shadow of death, lack life just as the unimpaired eye in darkness lacks life because to it to see is to live. Lacking light, the eye can see nothing, although it be a healthy eye. So the soul lacking the manifesting light that is Christ, does not see though it be uncorrupted, nor can it live by the intellectual life. For just as sensible vision requires revealing sensible light in order that it be true and living so does intellectual vision need the intellectual light of truth if it would see or live. And because every number is terminated in the denarium I have imagined the ascension through nine circles to the tenth which is a circle that is a center.

ALBERT: Although I have not captured in the taste of the intelligence all these things that you have competently discussed, nevertheless I see them to be true. I only wonder how the grades arise after the infinity of the central light diffuses itself most liberally.

THE CARDINAL: This light does not diffuse itself through corporeal places in such a way that it illuminates the places closer to it more strongly as does corporeal light. It is a light that is not confined to a place and is not hindered by any obstacle just as the thought of our mind is not. But those things that are illuminated can only be various because the multiple and the plural would be neither multiple nor plural without variety, otherwise they would be the same.

The reception of light is various in various minds, just as the reception of one sensible light is variously received in various eyes, in one in a truer and clearer way than in another according to its capacity, which cannot be equal in diverse things. Therefore those formed in Christ all receive the light of glory sufficiently, but differently according to the capacity of each, just as when the evangelical preacher diffuses one light equally to each listener, it is not nevertheless equally received by each listener, since they are not of the same mind or capacity.

ALBERT: No one is in the kingdom of the living unless he were blessed, and only he who has what he desires is blessed. This is the sole, unique calming of his desires; namely, to see the center of his life in the better and more perfect way which it is possible. Therefore I marvel concerning this that you have represented certain ones as approaching closer to the center, when the more remote ones do not comprehend it in the best way that can be done.

THE CARDINAL: The blessed fruition is represented in the drinking of the fountain of life, and to drink and to see are the same thing. One fountain of life satisfies the whole region of the living; from it each one drinks whatever he is thirsty for and desires. Two [people] cannot thirst and desire drink equally. For this reason although all drink whatever they are thirsty for in a sufficient amount, nevertheless they do not do this equally since they do not thirst equally. Charity, which is diverse in diverse beings, causes this thirst. So Christ has represented his kingdom as the wedding where he himself ministers to each one that which he desires. Therefore all are sated according to their desires and hungers, although some take more and others less (*Matt.* 22).

ALBERT: These things are pleasing and I see that there are not nine circles of glory but innumerable ones, since each blessed person has his own.

THE CARDINAL: Although the kingdom of life extends entirely from the center to the circumference and this extension could be conceived by the image of a line which contains an infinity of similar lines from the center to the circumference, there is one common center of all and circumference of each. Nevertheless this innumerable multitude of circumferences is divided into nine degrees so that by degrees we are led through that kingdom decorated with beautiful order to where the common center and particular circumference are identical—that is, to Christ. For here the center of the life of the creator and the circumference of the creature are identical. For Christ is God and man, creator and creature, he is the center of all blessed creatures.

And consider attentively that his circumference is of the circumferential nature of all circumferences, that is, of all rational creatures. And since he is the same through

tiarum scilicet creaturarum rationalium. Et cum sit idem identitate personali cum centro omnium scilicet creatore: omnes beati per circũferentiam circulorum figurati/ĩ circumferẽtia CHRISTI quæ est similis creatæ naturæ quiescunt/& finẽ attingunt propter circumferẽtiæ naturæ creatæ cum increata natura/hypostaticã vnionẽ/qua nulla maior esse potest. Ex quo vides CHRISTVM oĩbus beatificandis adeo necessarium: ꝙ sine ipso nemo fœlix esse potest. quoniã ipse est vnicus mediator: per quẽ accessus haberi potest ad viuentẽ vitã. ALBERTVS. Magna & pulchra dixisti: quæ vtinã aduersarii christianorum cõsiderarẽt. mox enĩ pacẽ cũ CHRISTO & christianis inirent. Et vt parum ante de substãtia & accidẽtibus dixi: ita mihi occurrit per nouẽ circumferẽtiales designationes ad cẽtrum attingi/vt per nouẽ accidentia ad substantiã. CARDINA. Numerus: discretio est/quæ est vnius ab alio. & hoc per vnũ aut per alterũ aut tertium/& ita consequenter vsꝗ ad denariũ vbi sistitur. quare & oĩs numerus: ibi terminatur. Sic & accidẽtia: nouẽ generib[9] generalissimis distinguntur. & ad notitiã quidditatis seu substãtię conferunt. Nã vt per vnũ accidẽs/aut duo/aut tria/aut quatuor/aut quinꝗ/aut sex/aut septẽ/aut octo/aut nouẽ: vbi ĩpletur numerus qui ĩ denarii vnitate cõplicatur. Numerare: discernere est. res autẽ: maxime per substãtiã discernuntur. & substãtiæ: per quãtitatẽ/qualitatẽ & alia accidẽtia/quæ ĩ nouẽ generibus accidẽtium cõplicãtur. Ob plenã igitur discretionẽ denotandã: talem feci figurationẽ. ALBERTVS. Audiui & angelos nouem choris distingui. CARDINALIS. Angeli: ĩtelligentiæ sunt. & quia varii sunt: oportet intelligẽtiales eorum visiones & discretiones per ordines & gradus ab ĩfimo vsꝗ ad supremũ (qui CHRISTVS & magni consilii angelus dicitur) ĩtellectualiter distingui. ex qua distinctione: tres ordines & in quolibet tres chori reperiuntur. Et minus centrũ est: vt denarius terminus nouem articulorum. Primus ordo est centralior/& intelligibiliũ spirituũ q simplici ĩtuitu ĩ centrum seu omnipotẽs exemplar omnia sine successione siue tẽporali siue naturali/& simul oĩa comprẽhẽdunt. q diuinæ maiestati assistunt: a qua habẽt vt sic videre omnia possint. Nam sicut deus a se habet hãc discretionẽ/vt ĩ sua simplicitate oĩa simul ĩtueatur quia ĩtelligens causa: sic dat illis assistentibus spiritibus/vt ĩ diuina simplicitate sciant oĩa. Qui etiã ideo licet creati sint æterni dicuntur: quia omnia simul compræhendunt. Alius autem ordo est ĩtelligẽtium q omnia simul compræhẽdunt: sed non sine naturali successione/scilicet vt alia ex aliis habẽt naturaliter prouenire. Et licet sine successione tẽporali intelligãt: quia tamen sine naturali ordine non possunt ĩtelligere / ideo subintrat ĩ ipsis quædã cognitionis debilitatio. Ideo non dicuntur æterni vt ĩtellectibiles: sed bene/perpetui/ quia in naturali ordine & successione ĩtelligunt. Tertius etenĩ ordo: rationalis dicitur. Quia licet certa sit eorum compræhensio: minus tamẽ perfecte ĩtelligunt q̃ alii. Primus ordo tres habet choros: qui voluntatem diuinam in deo licet differenter intuentur & eius discretionem imitãtur. Sed tres chori ĩtelligibiles: in ĩtellectibilibus diuinã voluntatem compræhendunt. Et tres chori rationales: ĩ intelligibilibus voluntatem diuinam intuentur. Nouem igitur sunt ordines. & deus ĩ se omnia concludens & continẽs: quasi denarius figuratur. Habet igitur quisꝗ nouem ordinum suã theophaniam siue diuinam apparitionem: & deus decimam a qua omnes emanant. Decem itaꝗ sunt diuersa genera discretionum. scilicet illa diuina quæ ĩ centro figuratur/& ĩ causa omnium: & aliæ nouem ĩ nouem choris angelorum. Et non sunt plures: nec numeri/nec discretiones. Hinc patet cur sic regnum vitæ figurauerim/atꝗ centrum luci solari conformaueri: & tres proximos circulos igneos/alios æthereos/

personal identity with the center of everything, that is, with the creator, all the blessed represented through the circumference of the circle come to rest in the circumference of Christ which is similar to the created nature. And they attain their end on account of the hypostatic union of the circumference of the created nature with the uncreated nature than which nothing greater can be. From this you see that Christ is so necessary for the beatification of all that without him no one can be happy since he is the unique mediator through whom access to the living life can be had.
ALBERT: You have spoken of great and beautiful things which I wish the adversaries of the Christians would consider, for they would soon enter into peace with Christ and the Christians. And as I have spoken a little while ago concerning substance and accidents so it occurs to me that as the center is attained through nine circumferential designations, so substance is attained through nine accidents.
THE CARDINAL: Number is the distinction of one thing from another, through one or another or a third, and so consequently all the way to the number ten where it stops. Therefore all number also stops here. Accidents are distinguished into nine most general classes and in this way contribute to the notion of quiddity or substance, whether through one accident or two or three or four or five or six or seven or eight or nine where the number which is enfolded in the unity of the number ten is completed.

To number is to distinguish. Moreover things are discerned especially through substance and substances through quantity, quality, and other accidents which are enfolded in the nine classes of accidents. Therefore in order to plainly point out this distinction I have made this figure.
ALBERT: I have heard that the angels are also distinguished into nine choruses.[22]
THE CARDINAL: Angels are intelligences and because they are diverse it is necessary that their intelligential visions and their distinctions be intellectually distinguished through orders and grades from the lowest point all the way to the highest which is called Christ, the angel of great counsel. From this distinction three orders and in each of these three choruses are discovered. And the boundary line is the center as the number ten is the boundary line of the nine articles.[23]

The first order of the intelligible spirits is the more central—the ones who comprehend everything in the center or omnipotent exemplar by simple intuition without either temporal or natural succession but simultaneously. These intelligible spirits assist the divine majesty from whom they have the power to see all things. For as God has this distinction from himself, that he sees everything simultaneously in his simplicity because he is the understanding cause of everything, so does he grant to his assisting spirits the power to see everything simultaneously in divine simplicity.[24] Therefore although these spiritual assistants are certainly created they are called eternal because they comprehend all things simultaneously.

Another order is that of the intelligences who comprehend everything simultaneously but not without natural succession as of course some things have naturally arisen out of other things. And although they understand without temporal succession, yet, because they cannot understand without natural order, a certain debilitation of knowledge creeps into them. Therefore they are not called eternal as are the intellectible things, but perpetual, because they understand in natural order and succession.

The third order is called rational because, although the comprehension of its members is certain, they nevertheless understand less perfectly than the others.

The first order has three choruses which intuit the divine will in God, although in different ways, and imitate his discretion. But three intelligible choruses comprehend the divine will in intellectible things. And three rational choruses intuit the divine will in intelligible things. Therefore the nine orders and God, who includes and contains all within himself, are represented as the number ten.[25] Each of the nine orders has its own theophany or its divine manifestation and God is the tenth from which they all emanate. And so there are ten diverse classes of distinction—namely the divine which is imagined in the center and is the cause of all things and the other nine in the nine choruses of angels.

And there are no more in either number or in distinction. Hence it is evident why I have imagined the kingdom of life in this way and have conformed the center to the light of the sun and have depicted the three nearest circles as fire, the next three circles as aether, and the three (outermost) circles which descend into terrestrial blackness, as water.[26]

& tres quasi aqueos / qui in nigro terreo desinunt / depinxerim. ALBERTVS. Cum denarius sit omnem discretionem complicans : cur in quaternario sistit progressio: Nam non nisi quatuor dicuntur causæ seu rerum rationes / & quatuor elementa / & quatuor anni tempora / & ita de multis. CARDINALIS. A maximo exteriori circulo vsq; ad minimũ intimũ & centralẽ si numeras / dicẽdo primo semel vnũ / & deinde numerãdo bis vnũ / deinde ter vnũ / & postea quater vnũ: terminabitur quaternarius ĩ centro. Sic vides vnũ / & duo / & tria / & quatuor simul: facere decẽ. quare progressio ĩ quaternario terminatur: cũ non sit discretio siue numerus / q in ipso non reperiatur. non tamẽ vides: nisi vnum ĩ omni numero. Nec est aut esse potest: nisi vnũ vnum. Plura: non sunt vnũ. Sicut ĩ omnibus circulis: nõ vides nisi circulũ vnius rationis / licet circũferentia vnius plus distet a cẽtro q̃ alterius. Hoc necessario contingit ĩ pluribus: cũ plures circũferẽtias ab eodẽ cẽtro æque distare non sit possibile. Sequitur igitur alteritas pluralitatẽ. quare etsi ĩ oĩbus entibus non sit nisi vna entitas / & omnia entia ĩ ipsa quæ deus est / ita ꝙ non sit opus ad discernẽdum oĩa entia vt entia sunt / nisi habere vnius entitatis discretionẽ: tamẽ cum multitudinẽ sequatur alteritas / ad discretionem omnium entium vt multa sunt / numerus alteritatis discretor est necessarius / sine quo vnum ab altero discerni non potest. ALBERTVS. Non igitur cognoscit deus entia? Cognitio: discretio est / quæ sine numero non videt possibilis. CARDINALIS. Cognoscere dei: est esse. esse dei: est entitas. cognoscere dei: est entitatẽ diuinam ĩ oĩbus entibus esse. Non sic est mens nostra ĩ iis quæ cognoscit sicut deus q cognoscẽdo creat & format. Sed mens nostra cognoscẽdo: creata discernit / vt sua notionali virtute aĩa ambiat. Sicut deus omnium exemplaria in se habet / vt oĩa formare possit: ita mens oĩum exemplaria ĩ se habet / vt oĩa cognoscere possit. deus vis est creatuia: secundũ quã virtutẽ facit oĩa veraciter esse id quod sunt / quoniã ipse est entitas entium. Mens nostra vis est notionalis: secundum quã virtutẽ facit oĩa notionaliter esse. Vnde veritas: est eius obiectum. cui suũ conceptum si assimilat: oĩa ĩ notitia habet / & entia rationis dicuntur. Lapis enĩ ĩ notitia mẽtis nõ est ens reale: sed rationis. Vides igitur deũ non ĩdigere numero: vt discernat. sed mens nostra: sine numero non discernit rerũ alteritates & differẽtias. ALBERTVS. Nonne creator creat etiã alteritatẽ? Si sic. vtiq; cũ non creet qđ non ĩtelligit / alteritas autẽ sine numero non ĩtelligit: per numerũ igit discernit. CARDINA. Oĩa creat deus / etiã alterabilia & mutabilia & corruptibilia: tamẽ alteritatẽ & mutabilitatẽ corruptionẽve non creat. cum ipse sit ipsa entitas: nõ creat ĩteritum / sed esse. Q₂ autem ĩtereant aut alterẽtur: non habẽt a creante / sed sic contingit. deus est causa efficiens materiæ / non priuationis & carẽtiæ: sed opportunitatis seu possibilitatis quã carentia sequitur. ita ꝙ non sit opportunitas absq; carẽtia: quę contigenter se habet. Malũ igitur / & posse peccare / & mori / & alterari nõ sunt creaturæ dei: q est entitas. De essentia igit cuiuscũq; non potest esse alteritas: cũ ĩ ipsa nõ sit entitas / nec sit ĩ ipsa entitate. Nec est de essentia binarii alteritas: licet ab ipso qđ est binarius contigat adesse alteritatẽ. Sicut enĩ plura pisa / vna proiectione sup planũ pauimẽtum proiecta sic se habẽt / ꝙ nullũ pisum aut moueatur aut quiescat æqualiter cum alio / & alius sit locus & motus cuiuslibet: tamẽ illa alteritas & variatio non est a proiiciente oĩa simul æqualiter / sed ex contigẽti. quãdo nõ est possibile ipsa æqualiter moueri / aut eodẽ in loco quiescere. ALBERTVS. Nõne entitatis est vnire & cõnectere? CARDINA. Vtiq;. ALBERTVS. Illa autẽ varia & alia / atq; diuisa esse oportet / quæ cõnecti debent. CARDINALIS. Licet deus qui est nexus / nõ sit causa diuisionis : tñ omnium

x iii.

ALBERT: Since the number ten would enfold all distinction, why does progression lie in the number four? There are said to be only four causes or reasons of things and four elements, four seasons of the year and so on for many things.
THE CARDINAL: If you count from the largest outermost circle all the way to the smallest innermost and central one, first calling one times one and then counting two times one, then three times one and next four times one, the number four is terminated in the center. In this way you see that one and two and three and four together make ten which is why progression is terminated in the number four since there is no distinction or number which is not found in the number four.

Nevertheless you see only one in every number and it is and can be only one. Many things are not one. So in all circles you see only one circle of one ratio although the circumference of one would be more distant from the center than the circumference of another. This necessarily happens when there are many circles since it would not be possible for many circumferences to be equidistant from the same center. Therefore otherness follows plurality.

Hence there is only one entity who is God in all entities and all things are in him—so that there would be no need of distinguishing for all entities that they are entities, only the need to distinguish the one entity that is God. Nevertheless since otherness follows multitude, a number which is a distinguisher capable of distinguishing otherness, without which one thing cannot be distinguished from another, is necessary to distinguish the way in which all things are multiple.
ALBERT: Therefore does not God know beings? Cognition is distinction, which does not seem possible without number.
THE CARDINAL: In God to know is to be. God's being is his entity. God's knowing is the divine entity's being in all things. Our mind is not in those things that it knows as is God's mind, which creates and forms through knowing. But our mind discerns created things through knowing as it embraces all things through its notional power. Just as God has in himself the exemplars of all things so that he can form all things, so does the human mind have the exemplars of all things in itself so that it can know all things.

God is the creative power; according to this power he makes all things truly to be that which they are since he is the entity of entities. Our mind is the notional power; according to this power the mind makes all things exist notionally. Hence truth is its object and when it assimilates its conception to the truth it has all things in itself notionally and they are called beings of reason. For a stone in the notion of the mind is not a real being but a being of reason.[27] You see therefore that God does not need number in order to discern but that our mind does not discern the othernesses and differences of things without number.
ALBERT: Does not the creator create even otherness? If he does, especially since he does not create what he does not understand and otherness is not understood without number, he [God] discerns through number.
THE CARDINAL: God creates all things, even alterable and mutable and corruptible things. Nevertheless he does not create otherness, mutability, and corruption. Since he is being itself he does not create destruction but being. Moreover things perish or are changed because of contingency, not through the Creator. God is the efficient cause of matter, not of privation and lack, but of opportunity or possibility. Lack follows opportunity in such a way that there is no opportunity without lack, which occurs contingently. Therefore evil and the capacity to sin and to die and to be changed are not creatures of God, who is being.

Therefore otherness cannot be part of the essence of anything, since being is not in it and it is not in being. Nor is otherness part of the essence of the twofoldness—although otherness is contingently present from that thing which is binary. When many peas are thrown on the pavement in a single throw no pea is moved or comes to rest in the same way as another and the location and movement of each one differs from that of every other. This otherness and variation does not arise from the thrower who throws all the peas in the same way simultaneously but from contingency since it is not possible for them to be moved equally or to come to rest in the same place.
ALBERT: Is it not the task of being to unite and connect?
THE CARDINAL: Certainly.
ALBERT: It is necessary that those things that must be joined be various and other and diverse.
THE CARDINAL: Although God who is the bond of being is not the cause of division nevertheless he is the creator of all various and diverse things.

variorũ & diuersorũ creator est.Nexus autẽ est ante diuisionẽ:quoniã diuisio vnio nẽ præsupponit.Connectit igiť vnitas q̃ entitas:diuersa & diuisa ĩ vnã concordanti harmoniã.Plura enĩ vt plura/non habẽt esse:nisi vt sunt connexa.Connexio:ab vni tate & æqualitate procedit.Plura igitur entia:ab vnitate seu entitate non habent q̧ non sunt/esse plura.Sed cũ non possint esse multa nisi & altera & diuisa:ideo vt ĩ vni tate subsisterẽt/per entitatẽ quæ est deus connexa sunt/connexione quæ est prior na tura q̃ diuisio.Si igitur acute inspicis:vides entitatẽ esse ipsam vnitatẽ/quæ de se ge nerat æqualitatẽ.a quibus ꝓcedit nexus:qui vnitatis & æqualitatis nexus est.Aequa litas:non potest esse nisi diuersarũ æqualitas hypostaseon ante omnẽ inæqualitatem & alteritatẽ.Quare si ad pluralitatẽ creaturarum vnius vniuersi respicimus in ip sis reperim⁹ vnitatẽ quæ est omnium entitas/& æqualitatẽ vnitatis.Aequaliter enĩ omnia entitatẽ habent:cũ vnũ ens non sit neq̧ plus neq̧ minus ens q̃ aliud.In quib⁹ omnibus & singulis:tota entitas est ĩ æqualitate.Suntq̧ ideo ad vnũ connexa : q̃a in omnib⁹ & singulis est entitas/& æqualitas & nexus ab vnitate & æqualitate ꝓcedẽs. Sic vides primã causam vnã:quia prima.& trinã:quia est vnitas æqualitas & nexus. & nisi hoc verum esset:nõ esset causa ipsa entitas entium.Deus igitur quia creator: nõ potest esse nisi trinus & vnus.Est igitur mundus creatus:vt ĩ ipso videatur crea tor trinus & vnus.qui pater dicitur:cum sit vnitas/ quæ entitas.& filius:quia æqua litas vnitatis.(gignit enĩ vnitas quæ entitas:æqualitatẽ/quæ est essendi æqualitas) et spiritussanctus: q̃a nexus seu amor vnitatis & æqualitatis / prout hoc alibi latius declarauimus. ALBERTVS. Hæc sæpius repeti expetit/q̃a vtilia & rara:quæ spe ro ĩ futurum melius degustabo.Nunc ad cẽtrum simplicissimũ me conuertẽs:video ipsum/prĩcipium medium/& finẽ oĩm circulorum. Nã eius simplicitas est ĩdiuisibi lis & æterna:omnia ĩ sua ĩdiuisibili & strictissima vnitate complicãs.Est initiũ æqua litatis.nisi enĩ omnes lineæ a cẽtro ad circunferentiã sint æquales: vtiq̧ non est cen trum circuli.Indiuisibilitas centri:est simplex initium æqualitatis . & nisi punctalis simplicitas cum æqualitate sit connexa:vtiq̧ non potest esse centrum circuli/de cu ius essentia est ęquidistantia a circũferẽtia.Sic video vnitatẽ/æqualitatẽ/ & vtriusq̧ nexum/in centrali puncto. CARDINALIS.Acute intras.& postq̃ aduertis dictum sapientis q aiebat deum circulum cuius centrũ est vbiq̧:tunc vides q̧ sicut punctus in omni quanto vbiq̧ reperitur:ita deus ĩ omnibus.Non tamẽ propterea sunt plura pũcta quia mens pũctũ vbiq̧ in quãto reperit. Sic nec plures sunt dii: licet ĩ singulis videatur. ALBERTVS.Non bene capio hoc.Declara quæso:quomodo punctus nõ est multiplicatus vt sint plura puncta: licet vbiq̧ ĩ quanto videatur? CARDINA LIS. Si chartam vnã scribendo impleres nihil nisi vnum vbiq̧ scribendo:vtiq̧ licet vbiq̧ videres vnum esse scriptũ/ non esset propterea veraciter plus q̃ vnum vnum vbiq̧ scriptum.Tu enĩ licet pluries scribas vnum ĩ diuersis locis:nõ tamẽ propterea vnũ est mutatũ & plurificatum. ALBERTVS. Certum est me multiplicasse vnius scripturã:non vnum ipsum. CARDINALIS. Vtiq̧ ĩ omnibus albis mens videt al bedinem:non tamẽ ideo sunt plures albedines.Ita in omnibus atomis videt punctũ: non tamen ideo non sunt plura puncta.Et quod clarius intelliges: quando conside ras vnũ simplicissimum ĩ se cõplicare oẽm multitudinẽ . ideoq̧ esse ĩmultiplicabile: cum sit complicatio omnis multiplicationis seu multitudinis.quare ĩ omni multitu dine videtur:quia non est multitudo nisi explicatio vnitatis.sic de puncto q est com plicatio magnitudinis:pariformiter dicẽdum vides. ALBERTVS. Hæc sic esse ĩ tueor. CARDINA. Consequenter aperi mentis obtutum/& videbis deum ĩ omni

The bond exists before division since division presupposes union. Therefore unity which is being connects diverse and divided things in one concordant harmony. Plural things in that they are plural things do not have being except in that they are connected. Connection proceeds from unity and equality. Therefore plural beings do not have plurality from unity or entity because they are not plural beings. But since they could not be many unless they were different and diverse, in order that they subsist in unity they are connected through being which is God, through a connection which is by nature prior to division.

If therefore you examine acutely, you will see that being is unity itself which generates equality from itself from which proceeds the bond which is the bond of unity and equality. Moreover equality cannot exist except as the equality of diverse substances prior to all inequality and otherness. Hence if we consider the plurality of creatures of one universe, we find in them a unity, which is the being of all things, and the equality of unity. For all things have being equally since one being is neither a greater nor a lesser being than another. The whole being is in equality in each thing and everything. Therefore they are connected to the one because being and equality and the bond proceeding from unity and equality is in each thing and everything.

So you see that the first cause is one because it is the first and three because it is unity, equality, and connection. And unless this were true, being itself would not be the cause of beings. Therefore God, because he is the creator, could not exist except as three and one. Therefore the world is created so that in it the creator who is called the father appears as three and one since he is unity which is being, and the son because he is the equality of unity, for unity which is being generates equality, which is the equality of being, and the holy spirit because it is the bond or love of unity and equality, as we have declared more fully elsewhere.[28]

ALBERT: I hope to become better acquainted with this extraordinary and useful doctrine, which tends to be repeated often, in the future. Now, turning myself to the most simple center, I see that it is the beginning, middle, and end of all circles. For its simplicity is indivisible and eternal, enfolding everything in its indivisible and most strict unity. It is the beginning of equality. For unless all lines were equal from the center to the circumference, it certainly is not the center of the circle. The indivisibility of the center is the simple beginning of equality. And unless punctual simplicity is joined with equality, certainly there cannot be a center of the circle whose essence is equidistance from the circumference. Thus I see unity, equality and their connection in the central point.

THE CARDINAL: You penetrate acutely, and when you perceive the dictum of the wise man who said that God is a circle whose center is everywhere, then you see that just as the point is found everywhere in every quantity so God is found in all things. Nevertheless because the mind discovers a point everywhere in quantity, there are not many points on account of this. So too, there are not many gods although God appears in singular things.

ALBERT: I don't understand this well. Tell me, I ask you, why, although the point appears everywhere in quantity, it is not multiplied so that there would be many points?

THE CARDINAL: If you were to fill a piece of paper by writing the number one everywhere, you would do this by writing the same numer—one— everywhere. Although you would see the number one written everywhere, it would not therefore be true that more than one number—one—had been written. For though you might write one many times in different places, the number one is not changed and multiplied on account of this.

ALBERT: Certainly I have multiplied the writing of the number one, not one itself.

THE CARDINAL: The mind sees whiteness everywhere in all white things but nevertheless there are not therefore many whitenesses. So in the same way the mind sees a point in all atoms but nevertheless there are not many points on account of this. You understand this more clearly when you consider that the most simple number one enfolds every multitude within itself. And therefore it [one] is unmultipliable, since it is the enfolding of all multiplication or multitude. Hence it [one] appears in every multitude because multitude does not exist except as the unfolding of unity. So you see the same thing in an analogous way concerning the point which is the enfolding of magnitude.

ALBERT: I consider this to be so.

THE CARDINAL: Consequently you must open up the gaze of your mind and you

multitudine esse/quia est ĩ vno.& ĩ omni magnitudine:quia est ĩ pũcto.ex quo cõstat ꝙ diuina simplicitas subtilior est vno & puncto:qbus dat virtutẽ cõplicatiuã multitudinis & magnitudinis.quare deus est virtus magis cõplicatiua q̃ vnius & puncti. ALBERTVS. Vtiq; maior est dei simplicitas q̃ vnius & puncti. CARDINALIS. Igitur & magis cõplicatiua.nã vis complicatiua est ĩ simplicitate.quæ quãto magis vnita:tãto magis simplex & cõplicatiua.Ideo de⁹ qui est vis qua nulla maior esse potest/est vis maxime vnita & simplex.quare maxime potẽs & cõplicãs.igitur est complicatio cõplicationũ. ALBERTVS. Verissima profers. CARD.Esto igit̃/ens esse omniũ existentiũ cõplicationẽ.tunc cũ nullũ ens sit/nisi ĩ ipso sit entitas:certissimum esse vides deũ eoipso ꝙ entitas est ĩ ente/esse ĩ omnibus.Et licet ens ipsum ĩ oĩbus quę sunt videatur:nõ est tamẽ nisi vnũ ens/sicut de vno & puncto dictũ est.Nec est aliud dicere deũ esse in omnibus:q̃ ꝙ entitas est ĩ ente omnia cõplicante.Sic optime ille vidit qui dixit.Quia deus est:omnia sunt. ALBERTVS. Placeret illius conclusio:nisi obstaret deũ ab æterno fuisse/& creaturas ĩcœpisse. CARDINALIS. Tu decipis. Imaginaris enĩ ante mundi creationẽ deum fuisse/& non creaturas. Sed dũ attendis ꝙ nunq̃ verũ fuit dicere deum fuisse quin & creaturæ essent:vides deũ ante creaturas non proprie dici fuisse.Fuisse enĩ aliquid tẽpore nondũ existẽte/non est possibile: cũ fuisse sit p̃teriti tẽporis.Tẽpus:creatura æternitatis.non em̃ est æternitas quæ tota simul est:sed eius imago/cũ sit ĩ successione. ALBERTVS. Cur dicit̃ tẽpus imago æternitatis? CARDINALIS. Nos æternitatẽ non capimus sine duratione.durationẽ nequaq̃ imaginari possumus sine successione. Hinc successio quæ est tẽporalis duratio/se offert:quãdo æternitatẽ concipere nitimur. Sed mens dicit absolutã durationem quæ est æternitas/naturaliter p̃cedere durationem successiuam.& ita in successiua tanq̃ in imagine videtur duratio in se/a successione absoluta/sicut in imagine veritas. ALBERTVS. Imaginatio igitur adiuuat mentem sibi coniunctam. CARDINALIS. Certissimũ est:intelligentẽ/ex phãtasmatibus/ĩcorruptibiliũ haurire speculationẽ.Sunt autẽ phãtasmata q̃ offert imaginatio.hinc subtiles imaginationes citius succurrũt ratiocinãti & veritatẽ quærẽti.nisi enĩ mens nostra ĩdigeret adiutorio imaginationis/vt ad veritatẽ quæ imaginationẽ excedit/quã solũ q̃rit perueniat/quasi saltator fossæ adiutorio baculi:nõ esset ĩ nobis imaginatio cõiuncta.De his:nũc sic dictũ sit. ALBER. Alibi vt fert̃:latius hæc scripsisti.Nunc reuertẽtes ad circulares descriptiones ludi nostri:dicito si quid mysterii restet.CARD.Tãta sunt ꝙ satis exprimi non possunt. Nã sicut de hierarchicis ordinibus bonorũ spirituum dictũ est:ita & de malis apostaticis spiritibus/& eorũ casu speculator multa ĩueniet: quia de quolibet ordine & choro quidã trãsgressores ceciderunt/& eorũ casus est a certituuine scientiæ ĩ certitudinem ruisse.possunt & cœlorum discretione:aliquatenus venari.nã cœlum visibile/& cœlum ĩtelligibile/& cœlum intellectuale:quidam sancti/esse cõpræhenderunt.& ĩ quodlibet trinã distinctionẽ:vt nouenarius cœlorũ in denario(vbi est sedes dei super cherubim)perficiatur. ALBERTVS. Non dubito numeri/discretionem esse: & in denario compræhẽdi omnẽ numerum & discretionẽ.Ea vero quæ numerãtur & discernuntur per hominẽ: ab ipsa discretione non habẽt esse/sed discerni.nisi enĩ essent:quomodo discernerentur? quare circa virtutẽ discretiuã quæ est post essentiatiuã/pulchra videtur speculatio:quam rogo adiicias. CARDINALIS.Tangã aliquid:vt pareã nobili tuo desiderio.Vis illa discretiua/rationalis aĩa in nobis appellatur.Ratione quidem discernit.ratiocinatio:supputatio/& numeratio est.Nam licet anima/visu visibilia/auditu audibilia/& generaliter sen

x iiii.

will see that God is in all multitude because he is in the number one and in every magnitude because he is in the point. From this it is established that divine simplicity is more subtle than the number one and the point to which it gives the unfolding power of multitude and magnitude. Hence God is a greater enfolding power than that enfolding power of the number one or of a point.
ALBERT: By all means the simplicity of God is greater than that simplicity of the number one or a point.
THE CARDINAL: Therefore so is his [God's] enfolding power greater, for enfolding power lies in simplicity which is more simple and enfolding the more it is united. Therefore God who is the power than which nothing greater can be is the maximally united and simple power, hence he is maximally potent and enfolding. Therefore the power of God is the enfolding of enfoldings.
ALBERT: You put forth things that are most true.
THE CARDINAL: Be it granted that entity is the enfolding of all existing things. Then, since no being is unless entity is in it, you see that it is most certain that God is in all things by the very fact that he is the entity in being. And although being itself appears in all things which are, nevertheless there is only one being, as has been said concerning the number one and the point. To say that God is in all things is nothing other than to say that entity is the being that enfolds all things. So he saw rightly who said that because God is, all things are.
ALBERT: This conclusion would be pleasing except for the objection that God existed from eternity and creatures came into being.
THE CARDINAL: You are deceived. For you imagine that before the creation of the world God was and not creatures. But when you notice that it was never true to say that God was but creatures were not you see that God is not properly said to have existed before creatures. For it is not possible for something to have been when time did not exist since "to have been" is in the past tense. Time is a creature of eternity for it is not eternity, which is entirely simultaneous, but the image of eternity since it exists in succession.
ALBERT: Why is it said that time is the image of eternity?
THE CARDINAL: We do not conceive of eternity without duration. We can in no way imagine duration without succession. Hence succession which is temporal duration manifests itself when we strive to conceive of eternity. But the mind says that absolute duration, which is eternity, naturally precedes successive duration. And thus duration which is in itself free from succession appears in successive duration as though in an image just as truth appears in an image.
ALBERT: Therefore the imagination, which is part of the mind, helps it [to understand the relation of truth to an image].
THE CARDINAL: It is most certain that the intelligence draws its speculation of incorruptible things from phantasms. Phantasms are what the imagination offers. Hence subtle imaginations occur more quickly to the reasoner and someone seeking truth. For unless our mind needed the help of the imagination in order to arrive at the truth which exceeds imagination and which alone it seeks, just as someone jumps over a dark ditch with the help of a staff, the mind would not be linked to the imagination in us. Enough has been said concerning these things for now.
ALBERT: It is said that you have written more extensively on this elsewhere. Now, returning to the description of the circles of our game, tell me if anything mysterious remains.
THE CARDINAL: There are so many things that they cannot be fully explained. For just as much was said concerning the hierarchical orders of good spirits, so the speculator will also discover many things concerning the bad apostate spirits and their downfall. For certain transgressors have fallen from each order and chorus and their fall is to have fallen from the certitude of knowledge into uncertainty.

The divisions of the heavens can also be hunted to some extent, for certain saints have understood there to be a visible heaven and an intelligible heaven and an intellectual heaven and three divisions in each heaven so that a ninefold of heavens is completed inside the tenth place where the seat of God is, above the cherubim.
ALBERT: I do not doubt that distinction belongs to number and that all number and distinction is comprehended in the number ten. But those things that are numbered and distinguished by men do not have being but distinction from distinction itself. For unless they existed how could they be distinguished? Hence there seems to be a beautiful speculation concerning the distinguishing power which follows the power of giving essences. I ask you to add something further on this.
THE CARDINAL: I will touch upon something in order to comply with your noble desire. That power of distinguishing within us is called the rational soul. In fact the soul discerns by reason. Reasoning is counting up and enumerating. For although the soul grasps visible things

ſu ſenſibilia capiat:non tamen diſcernit/niſi ratione.Quando enĩ audimus concinẽtes voces:ſenſu attigimus.ſed differẽtias & concordãtias:ratione & diſciplina menſuramus.quã vim:in brutis nõ reperimus.Non enĩ habẽt vim numerãdi & proportionãdi. Et ideo ĩcapaces ſunt diſciplinæ muſicæ:licet ſenſu voces nobiſcũ attingãt/ & moueantur cõcordãtia vocũ ad delectationẽ.Anima igitur noſtra:rationalis merito dicitur/quia eſt vis ratiocinatiua ſeu numeratiua/ĩ ſe cõplicãs cuncta/ſine quibus perfecta diſcretio fieri nequit.Quãdo enĩ ſenſu auditus mouetur ad motũ delectationis ob dulcẽ harmonicã concordantiã/& intra ſe inuenit rationẽ concordãtiæ in numerali proportione fundari:diſciplinã ratiocinãdi de muſicis concordãtiis per numerũ inuenit.Videtur igitur anima eſſe viua illa vnitas/numeri principiũ: in ſe omnẽ diſcretiuũ numerũ cõplicãs/quæ de ſeipſa numerũ explicat.vt diſcretiuæ lucis viua ſcintilla ſeipſam expãdẽs ſuper illa quæ diſcernere cupit/ & ſeipſam ab iis q̃ ſcire non cupit retrahẽs:ſicut viſum ſenſibilẽ ad viſibile quod videre cupit/conuertit/& a viſibili qđ reſpuit auertit. ALBERTVS. Hoc audire concupiui.Sed cũ ſupra/deũ dixeris vnitatẽ/& modo animã vnitatẽ appelles:quomodo hæc ĩtelligere debeam/dicito.CARDINALIS.Deus eſt vnitas illa quæ & entitas:oĩa vt eſſe poſſunt cõplicans.Anima vero rationalis:eſt vnitas/omnia vt noſci ſeu diſcerni poſſunt cõplicans.In vnitate quæ deus eſt/cõplicatur vnitas animæ rationalis vt eſſe poſſit id qđ eſt:ſcilicet vt eſt anima ĩ ſe notionaliter oĩa cõplicãs. In vnitate igitur q̃ deus eſt: omnia vt & cognoſci poſſunt cõplicãtur/cũ idem ſit ĩ deo vnitas & entitas. Ideo ibi eſſe & cognoſci:ſimiliter idẽ ſunt. Vnitas autẽ quæ eſt anima rationalis nõ eſt idẽ cũ ipſa entitate quæ eſt eſſendi forma:per quã habet & ipſa anima ꝙ eſt. Sed bene conuertitur vnitas animæ cũ ſua propria entitate:licet non cũ abſoluta entitate.qa nec vnitas animæ eſt abſoluta:ſed eſt ipſius animæ ꝓpria/ſicut & ſua entitas. Vnde aĩa rationalis:eſt vis cõplicatiua omniũ notionaliũ cõplicationũ.Complicat enĩ cõplicationẽ multitudinis & cõplicationẽ magnitudinis:ſcilicet vnius & puncti. Nam ſine illis ſcilicet multitudine & magnitudine:nulla fit diſcretio.Complicat cõplicationẽ motuum:quæ cõplicatio quies dicitur.nihil enĩ in motu:niſi quies videt̃.Motus enĩ eſt de quiete in quietẽ.Cõplicat etiã cõplicationẽ tẽporis:quæ nunc ſeu præſentia dicitur.Nihil enĩ in tẽpore:niſi nunc reperitur.Et ita de oĩbus cõplicationibus dicendũ:ſcilicet ꝙ anima rationalis eſt ſimplicitas omniũ complicationũ notionaliũ. Cõplicat enĩ vis ſubtiliſſima animæ rationalis ĩ ſua ſimplicitate omnẽ complicationẽ:ſine qua perfecta diſcretio fieri non poteſt.Quapropter vt multitudinẽ diſcernat:vnitati ſeu cõplicationi numeri ſe aſſimilat:& ex ſe notionalẽ multitudinis numerũ explicat.Sic ſe puncto aſſimilat qui cõplicat magnitudinẽ:vt de ſe notionales lineas/ſuperficies/& corpora explicet.Et ex cõplicatione illorum vel illarũ/ſcilicet vnitate & pũcto:mathematicales explicat figuras/circulares/& polygonias/quæ ſine multitudine & magnitudine ſimul/explicari nequeũt. Sic ſe aſſimilat quieti:vt motũ diſcernat.Et præſentiæ ſeu ipſi nũc:vt tẽpus diſcernat.Et cũ hæ omnes cõplicationes ſint in ipſa vnitæ:ipſa tanq̃ complicatio cõplicationũ/explicatorie oĩa diſcernit & menſurat/& tẽpus/& motũ/& agros/& queq; quãta.Et ĩuenit diſciplinas/ſcilicet arithmeticã / geometricã/muſicã/& aſtronomicã:& illas in ſua virtute cõplicari experitur.Sunt enĩ illæ diſciplinæ:per homines ĩuentæ & explicatæ. Et cũ ſint ĩcorruptibiles & ſemper eodẽ modo manẽtes:vere videt aĩa ſeipſam ĩcorruptibilem/ſemper vere permanentẽ.quoniã non ſunt illæ mathematicæ diſciplinæ/niſi ĩ ea & ĩ eius virtute cõplicatæ:& per eius virtutẽ explicatæ.adeo ꝙ ipſa aĩa rationali non exiſtẽte:illæ

by sight, audible things by hearing, and generally sensible things by the senses, it does not nevertheless discern things except through reason.

When we hear voices singing together we arrive at this through the sense. But we measure differences and concordances through reason and study. We do not find this power in beasts for they do not have the power of numbering and of making proportions. And for that reason they are incapable of the art of music although they hear sounds through the sense as we do and are moved to delight by the concordance of sounds. Therefore our soul is deservedly called rational because it is the calculating or numbering (or the discerning and proportioning) power enfolding all other powers in itself.[29]

Without this rational power perfect distinction cannot be made. For when the listener is moved by the sense of hearing to delight on account of a sweet harmonious concordance and discovers within himself that the reason of concordance is founded in numerical proportion, he discovers the art of calculating musical concordances through number. Therefore the soul seems to be that living unity, the principle of number, enfolding in itself every discrete number, and unfolding number from itself, just as a living spark of distinguishing light expands itself above that which it desires to distinguish and withdraws itself from those things that it does not desire to know, or as the sensible sight turns itself toward the visible thing that it desires to see and turns away from the visible things that it rejects.

ALBERT: I have longed to hear this. But since you said before that God is unity and now you call the soul unity, I ask you how I should understand this.

THE CARDINAL: God is that unity which is also being, enfolding everything that can exist. But the rational soul is unity, enfolding everything that can be known or distinguished. The unity of the rational soul is enfolded in the unity that is God in such a way that it can be that which it is, that is, the soul enfolding everything in itself notionally. Therefore everything as it is and can be known is enfolded in the unity that is God, because in God unity and entity are the same thing.[30] Therefore in God to be and to be known are the same thing. Moreover the unity, which is the rational soul, is not the same thing as the being itself which is the form of being through which the soul itself also has its existence. But the unity of the soul is properly convertible with its own being, although not with absolute being, because the unity of the soul is also not absolute, but is proper to the soul itself just as the being of the soul is.

Hence the rational soul is the enfolding power of all notional enfoldings, for it enfolds the enfolding of multitude and magnitude, that is, of the number one and of a point. For no distinction can be made except through these things, that is multitude and magnitude. It [the rational soul] enfolds the enfolding of motion, which is called rest. For nothing is seen in motion except rest; motion is from rest to rest. The rational soul also enfolds the enfolding of time, which is called "now" or the present. Nothing except "now" is found in time. And the same thing can be said of all enfoldings, namely that the rational soul is the simplicity of all notional enfoldings. For the most subtle power of the rational soul without which a perfect distinction cannot be made enfolds every unfolding in its simplicity.

On account of this, the rational soul assimilates itself to the unity or enfolding of number in order that it discern multiplicity, and it unfolds from itself the notional number of multiplicity. Thus it assimilates itself to the point which enfolds magnitude so that it unfolds from itself notional lines, surfaces, and bodies. And from the enfolding of these things, that is from unity and the point, the rational soul unfolds circular and polygonal mathematical figures which cannot be unfolded without at the same time unfolding multiplicity and magnitude. In the same way it [the rational soul] assimilates itself to rest, so that it discerns motion and it assimilates itself to the present or "now" itself so that it discerns time. And since all these enfoldings are united in it, as it is the enfolding of enfoldings, it discerns all things in an unfolded way and measures time and motion, fields, and all other quantities.

And the rational soul invents the disciplines such as arithmetic, geometry, music, and astronomy and discovers that they are enfolded in its power, for these disciplines are discovered and unfolded by men. And because these disciplines are incorruptible and remain always the same, the soul truly observes itself to be incorruptible, truly always permanent. These mathematical disciplines exist in it and they are enfolded in its power and are unfolded through its power in such a way that if the rational soul itself did not exist they could not exist at all.

nequaꝗ esse possent. Vnde & decem prædicamẽta in eius vi notionali complicãtur. Similiter & quinq; vniuersalia. & quæq; logicalia: & alia ad perfectã notionẽ necessaria. siue illa habeant esse extra mentem siue non: quãdo sine ipsis nõ potest discretio & notio perfecte per animã haberi. ALBERTVS. Quãtum mihi placet intellexisse tẽpus qđ est mensura motus: sublata rationali anima non posse aut esse aut cognosci / cum sit ratio seu numerus motus. & ꝙ notionalia vt notionalia sunt / ab anima hoc habent: quæ est notionaliũ creatrix / sicut deus essentialiũ. CARDINALIS. Creat anima / sua inuẽtione noua instrumẽta vt discernat & noscat: vt Ptholemęus astrolabium / & Orpheus lyram / & ita de multis. Neq; ex aliquo extrinseco inuẽtores crearũt illa: sed ex ꝓpria mẽte. Explicarũt enim in sensibili materia cõceptũ. Sic annus / mẽsis / horæ / sunt instrumẽta mẽsuræ tẽporis / per hominẽ creatæ. Sic tẽpus cum sit mẽsura motus: mẽsurantis animæ est instrumentũ. Non igiť depẽdet ratio animæ a tẽpore: sed ratio mẽsuræ motus quæ tẽpus dicitur / ab anima rationali dependet. Quare anima rationalis nõ est tẽpori subdita: sed ad tẽpus se habet anterioriter sicut visus ad oculũ. qui licet sine oculo nõ videat: tamẽ non habet ab oculo ꝙ est visus / cũ oculus sit organũ eius. Ita anima rationalis licet nõ mẽsuret motũ sine tẽpore: non tamẽ propterea ipsa sub est tẽpori. sed potius ecõuerso: cũ vtatur tẽpore pro ĩstrumẽto & organo ad discretionẽ motuũ faciendã. Nullo igitur tẽpore motus discretiõis animæ mẽsurari potest: ideo nec tẽpore finibilis. quare ꝑpetuus. ALBERTVS. Clarissime video motum animæ rationalis discretiuũ / omnẽ motum & quietem cũ tẽpore mensurantẽ: nõ posse cũ tẽpore mẽsurari. Artes & disciplinæ immutabiles tẽpore: quid aliud sunt ꝗ ratio? Quis dubitat rationẽ circuli supra tẽpus esse: & omnẽ circularem motũ / naturaliter anteire / ideo a tẽpore penitus absolutã / & vbi ratio circuli videtur nõ extra rationẽ? vbi ratio: nisi in anima rationali? Si igitur in seipsa anima rationalis videt rationẽ circuli quæ est supra tẽpus / igiť siue anima rationalis sit ipsa ratio / seu disciplina / seu ars aut scientia / siue nõ sit: vtiq; cõstat ipsam necessario supra tẽpus esse. & hæc satisfaciũt mihi: vt sciam rationalẽ animã nõ posse vllo tẽpore deficere aut interire. Sed cũ videã aliquẽ hominẽ ratiõe carẽtẽ licet sensu vigeat: dubito an anima illius vt alterius bruti sit æstimanda? CARDI. Anima hominis vna est / & rationalis diciť: licet cũ brutis sensitiua sit. nam vt alias me recolo / duci Ioanni in priori colloquio dixisse de trigono & tetragono: vis sensitiua in homine nõ est brutalis animæ / sed rationalis. qđ in exẽplo per beatũ Augustinũ ĩ xiiii. libro de ciuitate dei de Restituto pſbytero: manifestũ factũ est. ALBERTVS. Quomodo? CARDINA. Refert / quomodo hic presbyter Restitut⁹ calamẽsis diœcesis quãdo ei placebat aut rogabať vt faceret / ad simulatas quasi cuiusuis lamentantis hominis voces ita se auferebat a sensibus: & iacebat simillimus mortuo. vt nõ solum vellicãtes atq; pungẽtes minime sentiret: sed aliquãdo etiã igne vrebať admoto / sine vllo doloris sensu / & tanꝗ in defuncto nullus inueniebať anhelitus. hominũ tamẽ voces cũ clari⁹ loquerẽtur: tanꝗ de lõginquo se audire postea referebat. Hoc autẽ voluntate factũ: ostẽdit animã rationalẽ se a corpore retraxisse / ita etiã vt nihil sentiret. Ex quo patet animã rationalem volũtate separatã esse & sensitiuã: & vim rationalẽ dominari potẽtiæ sensitiuę. Vna igiť est anima rationalis & sensitiua in homine. & licet non appareat in aliquo homine exercitiũ ratiõis manifestũ: nõ tamen anima est brutalis. Sicut si corpus adeo esset attenuatũ aut minoratũ ꝙ videri aut tangi nõ facile posset: nõ tamẽ ꝓpterea corpus esse desineret / cũ in nõ corpus resolui nõ possit. Neq; est possibile hominẽ ratione semel habita ĩ infusione rationalis

x.v.

And hence the ten categories are enfolded in its notional power and similarly the five universals and all logical and other conceptions necessary to a perfect notion whether they have existence outside the mind or not, since without them distinction and notion cannot be perfectly had by the soul.
ALBERT: How pleasing it is to me to have understood that time, which is the measure of motion, cannot exist or be known if the rational soul were removed, since time is the measure or number of motion and how pleasing it is to have understood that knowable things in that they are knowable things have their being from the soul which is the creator of knowable things just as God is the creator of beings.
THE CARDINAL: In order that it may distinguish and know, the soul creates new instruments through its inventiveness, for example Ptolemy's astrolabe and Orpheus' lyre and many other such things. These inventors did not create such things out of something extrinsic but from their own minds for they unfolded their conception into sensible matter. The year, the month, the hour are instruments of the measurement of time created by man. Thus time, since it is the measure of motion, is an instrument of the measuring soul. Therefore the reason of the soul does not depend upon time, but the reason of the measure of motion, which is called time, depends upon the rational soul. Hence the rational soul is not subject to time but is anterior to time as the sight is anterior to the eye. Although sight does not see without the eye, nevertheless it does not have from the eye that it is sight since the eye is its organ. Thus although the rational soul does not measure motion without time nevertheless it is not subject to time because of this but rather the opposite since it uses time as an instrument and an organ for making a distinction of motions. The distinguishing movement of the soul can never be measured by time, therefore this movement is not limitable by time. Hence it is perpetual.
ALBERT: I see most clearly that the distinguishing motion of the rational soul, which measures all motion and rest with time, cannot [itself] be measured with time. The arts and disciplines, immutable by time, what else are they than reason? Who doubts that the reason of a circle transcends time and that it is naturally anterior to all circular motion and therefore wholly absolved from time? And where is the reason of a circle seen outside the reason? Where is the reason if not in the rational soul?

If the rational soul sees the reason of a circle in itself which is beyond time, therefore whether or not the rational soul is reason itself or a discipline or art or science, it is necessary that the soul by all means transcends time. And these things are satisfying to me so that I know that the rational soul cannot at any time decline or cease to exist. But when I see some man lacking in reason, although he is strong in his senses, I wonder whether his soul shouldn't be valued like that of another animal?
THE CARDINAL: The human soul is one thing and it is called rational although it is sensitive like the souls of animals. For, as I remember having said elsewhere in the previous colloquium to Duke John concerning the triangle and the quadrangle, the sensitive power in man is not of the animal soul but of the rational soul. This is made manifest in an example given by the blessed Augustine in the 14th book of the *City of God*, which concerns the presbyter Restitus.
ALBERT: How?
THE CARDINAL: He [Augustine] reported how this presbyter Restitus of the diocese of Calamis would imitate the sounds of some lamenting man and so take leave of his senses and lay down as if he were dead, whenever it pleased him or when he was asked. Not only would he not feel pinches and prickings at all but also sometimes he would actually be burned by the application of fire without any painful sensation and no breath was discovered in him. It was just as if he were dead. Nevertheless the man later reported that he clearly heard voices as if from a distance when they spoke.

This voluntary act shows that the rational soul had withdrawn itself from the body so that it actually felt nothing. From this it is evident that the rational and the sensitive soul are separated by will and that the rational power dominates the sensitive power. Therefore the rational soul and the sensitive soul are one in man.

And although the exercise of the reason does not appear manifest in some men, nevertheless their souls are not those of animals. It is just as if the body were so weak or small that it could not be seen or touched well; it would not cease to be a body for this reason since it cannot be resolved into a non-body. Nor is it possible that a man,

animæ: posse penit[9] postea spoliari / licet nõ videaẽ aliquis ratiõis vsus. Nã hic vsus in vno est clarior / in alio obscurior: ideo nunq̃ potest esse mimim[9] / & penitus nulli[9] / etiãsi adeo paru[9] ꝙ discerni ab aliis nõ posset. Hoc ex regula doctæ ignorantiæ constat / quæ habet: ꝙ in recipiẽtibus magis & minus nõ est deuenire ad maximũ & minimũ simpliciter. ALBERTVS. Cũ stultitia quã in multis experimur hominibus / ingerat dubiũ an sit in ipsis ratio: videẽ per simile hoc dubiũ solui posse hoc modo, habẽt quidã integros oculos & nihil discernũt: non tamẽ ꝑpterea virtute visiua carent sed vsu. qui vt appareat: meliorẽ organi exigit dispositionẽ. Et sicut aliquando oculus recipit meliorẽ dispositionẽ / & tũc vsus vidẽdi apparet / aliquãdo manet indisposit[9] / & nõ aduenit: ita de stultitia quæ sanitate organi aduenĩẽte sine quo vsus rationis nõ potest adesse / vsu ratiõis apparẽte / cessat: & nõ cessat defectu organi nõ sublato. Hoc verũ æstimo ꝙ sicut nunq̃ reperiẽ oculus adeo indisposit[9] quin aliquã lucẽ sentiat / licet nihil discernat: ita de stulto asserendũ. Et si hæc sic sint vt asseris: restant tamẽ adhuc quædã quæ me turbãt. cũ anima sit causa motus corporis quomodo hoc fieri possit sine mutatione? etsi mouẽdo mutaẽ anima: vtiq̃ tẽporalis est. Omne enĩ q̃d mutatur: instabile / & nequaq̃ ꝑpetuũ esse potest. CARDINA. Oportet vt dicamus animã mouere & nõ mutari: vti Aristoteles dicebat deũ dasideratũ mouere. Manet enĩ in se fixum illud bonũ ab oĩb[9] desideratũ: & ad se oĩa mouet quæ bonũ desiderãt. Anima rationalis suã operationẽ intẽdit producere. Intẽtiõe firma persistente: mouet manus & instrumẽta dũ dolat lapidẽ statuarius. Intẽtio videẽ in anima imutabiliter ꝑsistere: & mouere corpus & instrumẽta. Sic natura quã mũdi animã quidã appellãt: stãte imobili & instabili intẽtiõe exequẽdi imperiũ creatoris / omnia mouet. Et creator: stante æterna imobili & imutabili intentiõe / oĩa creat. Et quid est intẽtio: nisi conceptus seu verbũ rationale in quo omniũ rerũ exẽplaria? Est enim finalis termin[9]: infinitatẽ oĩs posse fieri determinãs. Vna igiẽ æterna & simplicissima dei intẽtio stans & ꝑmanẽs: causa est oĩm. Sic in anima rationali: vna est ꝑpetua & finalis intẽtio acquirere sciẽtiã dei / hoc est in se habere notionaliter hoc bonũ quod oĩa appetũt. Nunq̃ enim illã mutat rationalis anima / vt rationalis est. Sũt & aliæ secũdæ intẽtiones: quæ quãdo ab illa prima intẽtione deuiant mutãtur / primo desiderio firmo ꝑmanẽte. Et ob mutationẽ intentionũ taliũ / non mutatur anima rationalis: quia in prima intẽtiõe fixa ꝑmanet. Et immutabilitas illius primæ intẽtionis: causa est mutationis taliũ secũdarũ intẽtionũ. ALBERTVS. Duxisti me paucis: vt videam / intẽtione in deo & anima rationali per quã & secũdũ quã operanẽ & mouent stabiliter permanẽte: oĩa fieri & moueri. Nec est hæsitatio: si intentio firma persistit / deũ & animã rationalẽ mouere / & nõ moueri nec mutari. Stãte enim intentione, vtiq̃ stat intẽdens qui ab intẽtione non mouetur. Nec in deo aliud est intẽtio: q̃ deus intẽdens. Sic nec in rationali aĩa: intẽtio est aliud / q̃ intendẽs anima. Et id q̃d de secũdis intẽtiõib[9] dixisti / valde necessariũ est aduerti: & tollit plura dubia. CARDINALIS. Dũ intẽdo videre visibile: admoueo oculos. dũ intẽdo audire: admoueo aures. & dũ intẽdo ambulare: admoueo pedes. & generaliter dũ intẽdo sentire: admoueo sensum. Dũ intẽdo videre quæ sensi: admoueo imaginationẽ seu memoriã. Ad oĩa igitur corporalia: mediante organo corporeo pergo. Sed dũ ad incorporea me cõuertere volo: remoueo me ab istis corporeis. & quãto veri[9] illa speculari intẽdo: tãto verius me a corporeis retraho. Vt dũ volo videre animã meam quæ nõ est obiectũ visus sensibilis: melius clausis sensibilib[9] oculis ipsam videbo. Et facio animã instrumentũ incorporea vidẽdi. Vt dũ disciplinas cõpræhẽdere intẽdo: ad virtutẽ

Docta ignorantia.

once having obtained reason in the infusion of the rational soul, can later be robbed entirely of reason, although no use of his reason may be apparent in him.

This use of reason is more obvious in one [man] and more obscure in another. Reason can never be the smallest and wholly nothing, although it can be so very small that it could not be discerned by others. This is established from the rule of learned ignorance which holds that in things receiving more or less the simple maximum and minimum cannot be arrived at.

ALBERT: Since the folly that we experience in many men raises doubt as to whether there is reason in them, it seems to me that this doubt can be resolved by a comparison in this way. Some men have healthy eyes and discern nothing, nevertheless they do not on account of this lack the power of seeing but rather they lose the use of that power which needs, so that it may appear, a better disposition of the organ. Sometimes the eye does receive the better disposition and then the use of its vision appears. Sometimes the eye remains indisposed and its sight does not appear. So it is concerning folly. When health is added to the organ without which the use of reason cannot be present, and when the use of reason appears, folly ceases. And it does not cease when the defect of the organ is not removed. I believe that this is true because, just as the eye is never found so indisposed that it does not sense some light, although it sees nothing, so it can be asserted concerning a fool.

And if these things are as you assert them, nevertheless there still remain some things that bother me. Since the soul is the cause of the motion of the body how could this [motion occur] without the mutation? And if in moving the soul is changed, certainly it is temporal. For everything that is changed is unstable and can never be perpetual.

THE CARDINAL: It is necessary that we say that the soul moves and is not changed as Aristotle said that God moves things as He desires (*Met.* 1072a-1073a). For that good desired by all things remains fixed in itself and it moves those things that desire the good towards itself. The rational soul intends to produce through its operation. The sculptor moves his hand and instruments when he shapes the stone while his intention remains firm. The intention seems to persist immutably in the soul and to move the body and instruments. So nature, which some call the soul of the world, standing immobile and in stable intention of carrying out the command of the creator, moves all things. And the creator creates all things while his intention remains eternal, immobile and immutable.

And what is intention except the rational concept or word in which are the exemplars of all things? It [intention] is the fixed limit, determining the infinity of all possible becoming. Therefore the one eternal and most simple intention of God is the standing and permanent cause of all things. So in the rational soul there is the one perpetual and final intention to acquire knowledge of God, that is to have in itself notionally this good which all things desire. The rational soul in that it is rational never changes that intention.

There are other secondary intentions, which, when they deviate from that first intention, are changed, while the first desire remains firm. And the rational soul does not change on account of the change of such secondary intentions, because it persists in the first fixed intention. And the immutability of that first intention is the cause of the mutation of such secondary intentions.

ALBERT: You have led me with a few words so that I see that all things are made and moved while the intention in God and the rational soul through which and according to which they work and move persists stably. Nor is there any doubt that the firm intention persists that God and the rational soul move and are not moved or changed. For if the intention persists, certainly he who intends, who is not moved outside of his intention, persists. In God the intention is not other than God intending. And so in the rational soul intention is not other than the soul intending. And that which you have said concerning secondary intentions is certainly necessary to notice and it destroys many doubts.

THE CARDINAL: When I intend to look at a visible thing I move my eyes toward it. When I intend to hear something audible I direct my ears to it. And when I intend to walk towards something I move my feet towards it. Generally, when I intend to perceive I direct my senses. When I want to see what I have perceived, I direct my imagination or memory. Therefore I proceed towards all corporeal things by means of corporeal organs. But when I want to turn myself towards incorporeal things, I remove myself from these corporeal things and the more truly I intend to speculate upon these incorporeal things, the more truly I withdraw myself from corporeal things. And when I want to see my soul, which is not an object of sensible sight, I see it better with the sensible eyes closed. And I make the soul the instrument for seeing incorporeal things. When I intend to understand the disciplines I turn myself to the understanding power of the soul.

animæ intelligẽtialẽ me cõuerto.Et dum intẽdo videre omniũ rerũ rationẽ & causam:ad intellectibilẽ animæ simplicissimã/fortissimãq; cõuerto virtutẽ. Vnde anima melius videt incorporalia q̃ corporalia:quia incorporalia ad se ingrediẽs videt/corporalia vero a se egrediẽs.Et nihil in oĩbus his nisi vnũ intẽdit:scilicet omniũ & sui causam per suã rationalẽ fortitudinẽ videre & cõprahẽdere.vt dũ oĩm & suiipsius causam & rationẽ in sua viua ratiõe esse sentit: summo bono/pace perpetua/& delectatiõe fruat. Rationalis enĩ spirit⁹ natura scire desiderãs: quid aliud quærit q̃ omniũ causam & rationẽ?nec quiescit:nisi ipsam sciat. qđ fieri nequit: nisi suũ sciendi desideriũ/scilicet rationis suæ æternã causam/in se/ipsa scilicet virtute rationali videat & sentiat.ALBERTVS.Magna dicis & certa.supremo cũ ferat desiderio anima rationalis vt discernat & sciat: quãdo ad id puenit vt causam tãti desiderii ĩ seipsa scilicet discretiua videat virtute/vtiq; in se habet scientiã datoris desiderii. Et nihil appetere potest/qđ nõ in seipã videat. Quid enĩ amplius desiderari posset/per scire desiderantẽ:quãdo causatũ suæ causæ scientiã in se intuetur?Tunc enĩ suæ creationis rationẽ & artẽ habet:quæ est oĩs desiderii sciẽdi perfectio & cõplementũ. quo nihil rationali naturæ/scire auidissimæ:beatius feliciusq; aduenire potest.Oĩm enĩ scibiliũ artiũ habere peritiã : modicũ est respectu artis oĩm artiũ creatiuæ. Solũ mihi difficile videt:creaturã quantũcũq; rationalẽ & docilẽ/creatiuã artem capere posse/quã solus deus habet.CARDI.Ars creatiua quã felix aĩa assequet:non est ars illa p essentiã quæ deus est/sed illius artis cõmunicatio & participatio.Sicut acquirere albedinẽ participatiõe albedinis absolute/p essentiã talis & nõ p essentiã nõ acquisitæ/nõ est trãsmutatio albi in ipam albedinẽ : sed cõformatio acquisitæ cum nõ acquisita.vbi acquisita nihil ex se potest:nisi in virtute non acquisitæ.Non enim album dealbat nisi ĩ virtute albedinis:a qua habet vt sit albũ aut cõforme albedini/alba formãti.ALBER.Placent hæc:dicẽte scriptura de filio dei.cũ apparuerit in gloria:similes ei erimus. nõ ait:q; erimus ipse. Sed quia dixisti de sensu aĩæ rationalis: quomodo intelligis sensum esse in intellectuali natura? CARDI. Sæpe prætereũtes nõ sentim⁹/nec visu/nec auditu:quia nõ sum⁹ ad hoc attẽti.sed quãdo sum⁹ attẽti: sentim⁹.nos in aĩa nostra rationẽ & scientiã scibiliũ virtualiter possidem⁹:nõ tamẽ actu sentim⁹ hui⁹ veritatẽ/nisi attẽte ad hoc vidẽdũ cõuersi fuerim⁹.Licet enĩ musicæ scientiã habeã:tamẽ cũ geometriæ vaco/nõ sentio me musicũ.Attẽta igit cogitatio:me sentire facit intelligibilia/quæ nõ senserã. Sicut enim centrũ oĩm circulorũ est in pfundo occultatũ/in cui⁹ simplicitate vis est oĩa cõplicãs:sic in centro aĩæ rationalis cõplicant oĩa in ratiõe cõprahẽsa.sed nõ sentiunt:nisi attẽta cogitatione vis illa cõcitetur & explicet.ALBER.Optime ad oĩa/& gratissime respõdes.Nunc vt video:ad finẽ pperas.verũ aliquid quæso circa occultũ & patulũ adiicias. Videt enim ex figura descriptionis:vis oĩs in cẽtro occultari.CARDI.Deũ esse abscõditũ ab oculis oĩm sapientũ scribit:& omne inuisibile in visibili occultat. Visibile est oculis manifestũ:& indiuisibile ab oculis remotũ.Principia:minima(dicit Aristoteles) quãtitate/& maxima virtute.Virt⁹ spiritualis & ĩuisibilis ẽ.& tãtæ potẽtiæ est virtus scintillæ ignis:quãtæ totus ignis.Tãta virt⁹ in vno modico grano sinapis/quãta in multis granis ĩmo & in oĩbus quæ esse possunt . Finis manifesti est occultũ: & extrĩseci intrinsecũ.Pelliculæ & cortices pter carnes & medullas: & ille pter intrinsecam vitalẽ inuisibilẽ virtutẽ.Elemẽtatiua virtus:in chaos occultat.& in vegetatiua:occultat sensitiua.& in illa:imaginatiua.& in illa:logica seu rationalis.in rationali:intelligẽtialis.in intelligẽtiali:intellectibilis.in intellectibili:virtus virtutũ.

And when I intend to see the reason and cause of all things I turn myself toward the most simple and strong intellectual power of the soul.

Hence the soul sees incorporeal things better than corporeal things because it sees incorporeal things when entering into itself but corporeal things when leaving itself. And it intends only one thing in all these activities, and that is to see and comprehend the cause of all things and of itself through its rational strength so that when it perceives that the cause and reason of all things and of itself exists in its living reason, it enjoys the highest good; perpetual peace and delight.

For what else does the rational spirit, desiring by nature to know, seek but the cause and reason of all things? It does not rest unless it knows it [the cause and reason of all things]. This cannot be done unless it sees and perceives its own desire of knowing, namely the eternal cause of its own reason, in itself, that is, in the rational power itself.

ALBERT: You say great and certain things. Since it [the rational soul] is carried by a supreme desire to discern and to know, it by all means has knowledge within itself of the giver of this desire when by means of its distinguishing power it arrives at the point that it sees the cause of so great a desire in itself. And it [the rational soul] can desire nothing that it does not see within itself. For what could be further desired by him who desires to know, when what is caused contemplates in itself the knowledge of its cause? For then it has the reason and art of its creation; which is the perfection and complement of all desire to know. Nothing more blessed and felicitous can happen to the rational nature most eager for knowledge. To have knowledge of all knowable arts pales in comparison to the creative art of all arts. It only seems difficult to me that the creature, however rational and easily taught, can grasp the creative art which only God has.

THE CARDINAL: The creative art which the happy soul will attain is not that art through essence which is God, but the communication of and participation in His art, just as the acquisition of whiteness by participation in absolute whiteness which is such through essence and not through acquisition is not the transmutation of white into whiteness itself. It is rather the conformation of the acquired with the non-acquired where the acquired has no power from itself except in the power of the non-acquired. For white does not whitewash except in the power of whiteness from which it has [the capacity] to be white or conform to the whiteness forming white things.

ALBERT: These things are pleasing since scripture says concerning the son of God "when he appears in his glory, we will be similar to him"; it does not say that we will be him (I *John* 3:2). But you have spoken of the sense of the rational soul. In what manner do you understand the sense to be in the intellectual nature?

THE CARDINAL: Often we do not sense passing things either by vision or by hearing because we are not attentive, but when we are attentive we sense. We possess in our soul in a potential way the reason and knowledge of knowable things. Nevertheless we do not actually sense the truth of it unless we are consciously converted towards seeing this. For although I have knowledge of music, nevertheless I do not perceive myself as a musician when I am occupied with geometry. Therefore a conscious reflection makes me sense intelligible things which I had not sensed. For just as the center of all circles whose simplicity is the power enfolding all things is hidden in profundity, so all things comprehended in the reason are enfolded in the center of the rational soul, but they are not sensed unless that power is stimulated and unfolded by conscious reflection.

ALBERT: You respond excellently and agreeably to all my questions. Now, I see you hasten towards the conclusion. I ask that you add something about the hidden and the manifest, for it seems from the figure described that all power is hidden in the center.

THE CARDINAL: It is written that God is hidden from the eyes of all wise men and that every invisible thing is hidden within a visible one (*Matt* 11:25; *Luke* 10:21). The visible is manifest to the eyes and the invisible is removed from the sight. The principles, Aristotle says, are those of minimal quantity and maximal power (*De gen animal*. 788a). Power is spiritual and invisible. And the power of a spark of fire is of a potency as great as the whole fire. There is as much power in one small grain of mustard as in many grains or rather in all the grains that can exist.

The purpose of that which is manifest and extrinsic is that which is hidden and intrinsic. Skins and barks exist because of flesh and marrow and flesh and marrow exist because of the intrinsic, invisible vital power. Elemental power is hidden in chaos and sensitive power is hidden in vegetative power, and in that vegetative power the imaginative power, in the imaginative power, the logical or rational, in the rational the intelligential, in the intelligential the intellectible, and in the intellectible the power of powers.

Hæc in figura circulorũ: mystice legas. Circul⁹ circũdãs & extrĩsecus: figurat ipm cõfusum chaos. Secũdus: virtutẽ elemẽtatiuã / quæ est ꝓxima ipsi chao. Tertius: mineralem. & hi tres circuli terminãtur in quarto qui est circul⁹ / vegetatiuã figurãs. Post illũ est quintus circul⁹: sensitiuã figurãs. Deinde sextus: imaginatiuã siue phãtasticã figurãs. Et hi tres circuli scilicet quart⁹ / quĩtus / & sextus in sequẽti quarto terminanť / scilicet logicam seu rationalẽ figurãte: & septim⁹ est. Deĩde est octauus: figurãs intelligẽtialẽ. & nonus: figurãs intellectibilẽ. Et hi tres scilicet / septim⁹ / octauus / & nonus in sequẽti quarto qui est decim⁹ terminãtur. ALBERTVS. Pulchra nũc recitasti: quomodo de cõfuso ad discretũ fit ꝓgressio. Et quia hac cõsideratione de omni ĩpfecto ad perfectũ ascẽditur: de cõfusis tenebris ad discretã lucẽ / de insipido ad sapidũ per medios sapores / de nigro ad albũ per medios colores / ita de odoribus / & cũctis in quibus ad perfectũ deueniť. Atq; in / per te posito exẽplo: de corporali natura ad spiritualẽ: cui⁹ experientiã homo in seipso repperit / & cur microcosmos nomineť / inuenit. Ideo de ratiõe huius ꝓgressionis adeo mirabilis & fœcũdæ / ad omne scibile applicabili: nõ pigriteris adhuc pauca saltẽ subiũgere. CARDINALIS. Sicut denario oĩs discretio contineť: ita necessario oĩs ꝓgressio in quaternario. Nã vnũ & duo & tria & quatuor: decẽ sunt. In quo cũ discretio subsistat: ideo & discretiõis ꝓgressio. Neq; possunt plures q̃ tres esse tales ꝓgressiões: quãdo tertia denario cõcludiť. quæ necessario sic se ad inuicẽ habẽt: ꝙ supremũ primæ sit infimum secũdæ. & supremũ secũdæ: sit infimũ tertiæ. vt sit vna cõtinua / pariter & trina ꝓgressio. Igiť sicut prima ꝓgressio recedẽs ab ĩpfecto / finitur in quaternario: ita secunda incipit in quaternario & finiť in septenario. Et ibi tertia incipit. quæ denario perficiť. Hui⁹ cupis rationẽ audire: quã sic intelliges. Ordo cũ sit de necessitate oĩm operũ dei / vt recte apostol⁹ aiebat dicẽs / quæcũq; a deo sunt ordinata sunt: sine principio medio & fine nec esse nec intelligi potest. Est autẽ ordo pfectissimus & simplicissimus: quo nullus aut pfectior aut simplicior esse potest. qui est in omni ordinato / & in quo oĩa ordinata: modo quo in generali ꝓpositiõe in exordio p̃misimus. In eo autẽ ordine qui est oĩm ordinũ exẽplar: necesse est mediũ esse simplicissimũ / cũ ordo sit simplicissimus. Erit igiť adeo æquale mediũ: ꝙ & ipsa æqualitas. qui ordo nõ potest per nos aliqua discretione capi / nisi in ordinatissima ꝓgressione: quæ ab vnitate incipit / & ternario terminať. In qua mediũ simplicissimũ: est æquale mediũ prĩcipii & finis. Duo enim / mediũ est præcisum & æquale / vnius & triũ: & præcisa tertia totius ordinis & ꝓgressiõis. Aliter nos illũ simplicissimũ diuinũ ordinẽ nisi præmissa progressiõe discernere nõ possumus. Et cũ mediũ / sit æquale mediũ sicut & indistinctum ab æqualitate: ita & in essentia manet idẽ cũ principio & fine. Diuersarũ enim essentiarũ: nõ potest esse præcisa æqualitas. Omnis autẽ ordo qui habet ꝙ est ordo a iam dicto simplicissimo ordine: nõ potest habere simplex & æquale mediũ. Est enim oĩs ordo / excepto simplicissimo: cõposit⁹. Omne autẽ qđ cõponiť: ex inæqualib⁹ cõponiť. Impossibile est enĩ plures partes cõponibiles: p̃cise æquales esse. Nõ enĩ essent aut plures aut partes. Neq; æqualitas: est plurificabilis. Ideo in primo ordine simplicissimo: vna est trium hypostasium æqualitas. quia ĩpossibile est plures esse æqualitates: quãdo pluralitas sequiť alteritatẽ & inæqualitatẽ. Si igiť nõ potest esse in ordinato seu creato ordine simplex & æquale mediũ: ideo nec in ternaria ꝓgressiõe cõcluditur / sed vltra ꝓgrediť in cõpositionẽ. Quaternarius autẽ est immediate a prima ꝓgressiõe exiens. & nõ exiret: nisi ordinata esset ꝓgressio. Quare id qđ ordinata ꝓgressio de prima ordinatissima exiens requirit: necessario in ipã quia ternaria / exi

You may read this mystically in the figure of circles. The enclosing and extrinsic circle represents the confused chaos. The second circle represents elemental power which is nearest to chaos itself. The third circle represents mineral power. And these three circles are terminated in a fourth circle representing the vegetative. After it is the fifth circle representing the sensitive. Next is the sixth circle representing the imaginative or fantastic. And these three circles, that is the fourth, fifth, and sixth, are terminated in a fourth circle that represents the logical or rational; this circle is the seventh circle. Next is the eighth circle representing the intelligential, and the ninth, representing the intelligible. And these three, that is, the seventh, eighth, and ninth, are terminated in the fourth circle, which is also the tenth circle.

ALBERT: You have now related something beautiful, how a progression from confusion to distinction is made. In this way the ascent from all imperfection to perfection is made, from confused darkness to distinct light, from the tasteless to the tasty through intermediate tastes, from black to white through intermediate colors, and so also for odors and everything in which perfection is reached. In your own example man experiences the progression from the corporeal nature towards the spiritual in himself and thus discovers the reason why he is named "the microcosm." Therefore please don't hesitate to add to this at least a few words concerning the reason for this progression which is so marvelous and fecund and applicable to all knowable things.

THE CARDINAL: As all distinctions are contained in the number ten, so all progressions are necessarily contained in the number four. For one, two, three and four are ten. Therefore distinction and the progression of distinction subsist in the number ten. And there cannot be more than three such progressions, since the third progression ends in the number ten. These progressions necessarily have such a relationship to one another that the highest number of the first progression is the lowest number of the second progression and the highest number of the second progression is the lowest of the third, so that there is one continuous and also threefold progression. Therefore just as the first progression, receding from imperfection, is terminated in the number four, so the second [progression] begins in the number four and is terminated in the number seven. And here begins the third, which is perfected in the number ten.

You desire to hear the reason for this, which you should understand thus: Order necessarily applies to all the works of God as the Apostle rightly said when he stated that all things that are ordered by God cannot be or be understood without a beginning, middle, and end (*Romans*, 13:1). Moreover, it is a most perfect and a most simple order, more perfect and simple than any other order can be. It is in all ordered things and in it all ordered things exist in the way that we have premised in the general proposition at the beginning. In that order, which is the exemplar of all orders, it is necessary that the middle be more simple, since the order is the most simple. Therefore the middle will be so equal that it will be equality itself.

This order cannot be grasped by us through any distinction except in the most ordered progression which begins in one and is terminated in three. The middle equal to the beginning and end is the most simple middle in this [order], for two is the equal and precise middle of one and three and an exact third of the entire order and progression. We cannot discern that most simple divine order except in the aforementioned progression. And as the middle is an equal middle and indistinct from equality, so in essence it remains the same thing as the beginning and the end. For precise equality cannot be of diverse essences. Every order that has its being from the previously mentioned most simple order cannot have a simple and equal middle, for every order, with the exception of the most simple, is composite. Moreover everything that is composed, is composed from unequal things. It is impossible for many component parts to be precisely equal for they would not be either plural or parts. Nor is equality capable of being made plural. Therefore in the first most simple order, there is one equality of three hypostases, because it is impossible for there to be many equalities since plurality follows otherness and inequality. If therefore there cannot be a simple and equal middle in an ordained or created order, then it is not terminated in the ternary progression, but it proceeds farther into composition.

The number four issues immediately from the first progression and it would not come forth unless it were an ordered progression. Hence an ordered progression which issues forth from the first most ordered progression necessarily exists in it [the first progression] because the first progression is ternary.

Therefore the progression has a composite middle, namely two and three, which together are the middle of the whole progression. For one plus two plus three plus four are ten. Yet two

stit.Ideo habet cõpositũ mediũ/scilicet duo & tria:quæ simul sunt mediũ toti⁹ progressiõis.Sũt enĩ vnũ & duo & tria & quatuor simul:decẽ.duo vero & tria/quinq₃: medietas scilicet de decẽ.Sic se habẽt quatuor quinq₃ sex septẽ:& septẽ octo nouẽ decẽ. & ita vides antedicti rationẽ.ALBER.Magna est rationis vigorositas:vt video. sed miror de eo ꝙ dixisti:nihil ex æqualib⁹ cõponi.Nõne ex duob⁹binariis: quaternarius est cõposit⁹?CARDI.Nequaq̃. Oĩs enĩ numer⁹ est aut par aut impar. Et cũ cõponitur:nõ nisi ex numero cõponiť scilicet ex pari & ĩpari/siue ex vnitate & alteritate.Quãtitatẽ quaternarii eẽ ex duob⁹binariis/nõ nego:sed ei⁹substãtiã dico nõ nisi ex pari & ĩpari.Oportet enĩ inter partes quæ debẽt cõponere aliqd:ꝓportionẽ esse.ideo & diuersitatẽ.Ob hoc recte boetius aiebat:ex parib⁹ nihil cõponi.Harmonia enĩ ex acuto & graui adinuicẽ ꝓportionatis:cõponitur.Ita & oĩa.Vnde quaternarius:ex ternario & altero cõponitur.Ternari⁹ est ĩpar: alter par. sicut binari⁹ ex vno & altero.Alteritas: par diciť/ꝓpter casum ab vnitate indiuisibili ĩ diuisibilitatem/quæ in pari est.Sic quaternari⁹: ex ternario scilicet ĩpari & indiuisibili/& altero altero scilicet diuisibili cõponitur.Oĩs enĩ numerus/ex numero cõponiť:quia ex vno & altero.vnũ & alterũ numer⁹ est.De his meminim⁹ nos alias latius scripsisse: maxime in libello de mẽte.Nũc hęc sic repetita sint:vt rationem seu virtutẽ animæ discretiuã/ĩ numero qui ex mẽte nostra est/meli⁹ cognoscas.ac ꝙ vis illa discretiua ex eodẽ & diuerso/& vno & altero cõposita diciť vt numer⁹: quia numerus discretiõe mẽtis nostræ numer⁹ est.& ei⁹numerare:est vnũ cõmune multiplicare & plurificare qđ est vnũ in multis/& multa in vno/& vnũ ab altero discernere.Pythagoras aduertẽs nullã posse fieri nisi ꝑ discretionẽ scientiã:de oĩbus per numerũ philosophatus est.Neq₃ arbitror queq̃: rationabiliorẽ philosophandi modũ assecutũ.quẽ quia Plato imitat⁹ est:merito magnus habeť.ALBER. Hæc/sic vt asseris admitto. Nũc ergo cũ dies ad vesperã tẽdat:hoc colloquiũ valere/memoriaq₃ dignũ delectabili cõclusiõe facito. CARDI. Conabor.& nõ incidit mihi quomodo melius quæ dixi valere faciam:q̃ si de valore loquar.ALBER.Optime.CARDI. Bonũ/& nobile/ atq₃ pretiosum est esse: ideo omne qđ est/nõ est valoris expers.Nihil penit⁹ esse potest:quin aliqd valeat.Neq₃ reperiri potest quicq̃ minimi valoris:ita ꝙ minoris esse nequeat.Neq₃ adeo magni valoris quicq̃ est:quin maioris esse possit. Solus autẽ valor qui est valor valorũ/& qui in oĩbus quæ valẽt est/& in quo quæ valent existunt: in se omnẽ valorẽ cõplicat/& plus aut min⁹ valere nequit. Hũc igiť absolutũ valorẽ/oĩs valoris causam:in cẽtro circulorũ oĩm occultatũ cõcipito.& extremũ circulum:valorẽ extremũ/& ꝓpe nihil facito. & quomodo in denariũ vnitrina ꝓgressiõe augeť/modo sæpe tacto/cõsidera:& dulcẽ speculationẽ subintrabis.ALBER.Puto si ad pretiũ valoris/sermonẽ cõtraheres:magis nos instrueres.CARDI.Forte de pecunia dicere intẽdis.ALBER.Sic volo.CARDI. Demũ faciã. Sed nũc attẽde: quomodo valor rerũ omniũ/nõ est nisi esse ipm omniũ. Et sicut in simpliciter maximo valore vno/& penit⁹ incõposito & indiuisibili/verissime oĩs omniũ valor existit: ita in entitate simplicissima/oĩm esse.Sicut enĩ in valore alicuius floreni est valor mille paruulorũ denariorũ/& in duplo meliori floreno duorũ miliũ/& ita in infinitũ: ita in optimo quo melior esse non posset/infinitorũ denariorũ valorẽ esse necesse esset. Et sicut hoc vides verum:ita veraciter & realiter verũ esset. ALBER.Vtiq₃ sic est. CARDI.Dũ autẽ tu in teipso hoc verũ vides: quid valet ille tuæ mentis oculus/in sua virtute valorẽ omnẽ discernẽs?Nam in ipso visu:valor omniũ & valores singulorum sunt.sed nõ vt in valore valorũ.Nõ enim ꝓpterea quia mens videt id qđ oĩa

Liber de mente.

Valor.

and three are five—that is, half of ten. The same relation obtains between four, five, six, and seven, and seven, eight, nine, and ten [that is, the sum of five and six is equal to half of the sum of four, five, six, and seven and the sum of eight and nine is equal to half of the sum of seven, eight, nine, and ten]. And so you see the aforementioned line of reasoning.
ALBERT: As I see, the force of this reasoning is great, but I am surprised concerning that which you have said, that nothing is composed out of equal numbers. Is not the number four composed of two two's?
THE CARDINAL: Not at all. For every number is either even or odd. And when it is composite, it is composed from number, that is from the even and odd or from unity and otherness. I do not deny that the quantity of the number four is that of two two's but I say that its substance does not exist except out of even and odd. For it is necessary that there be some proportion and therefore diversity between the parts that must combine. On account of this Boethius rightly said that nothing is composed of even things (*De arith.* 1.2). Harmony is composed out of mutually proportioned high-pitched and low-pitched sounds, and so it is for all things. Hence the number four is composed of the number three and another number, the number three is odd and the other number even, just as two is composed out of one and another number. Otherness is called even on account of the fall from indivisible unity into divisibility which is in even numbers. So the number four is composed from the number three which is odd and indivisible, and the other number that is divisible. Every number is composed from number because it comes from one number and another. One number and another make a third number. I remember having written more widely concerning these things in other places, especially in the book *On the Mind*.[31]

Now these things should be repeated in such a way that you may better understand that reason or the distinguishing power of the soul is in number which is from our mind, and that that distinguishing power is said to be composed out of the same and the different, and the one and the other as number, because number is number from the discretion of our mind. And the numbering of the mind is the multiplication and plurification of a common one, which is one in many things and many things in one, and the discerning of one thing from another.

Pythagoras, observing that no science can be made except through distinguishing, philosophized concerning all things through number. I do not think that anybody attained any more rational mode of philosophizing than this. Plato, because he imitated it, is rightly considered great.
ALBERT: I admit that this is as you assert. Now since the day proceeds toward evening I ask that you say farewell to this colloquium and make it worthy of memory by a delightful conclusion.
THE CARDINAL: I will try and it occurs to me that there is no better way to say farewell to what I have said than to speak of value.[32]
ALBERT: Very good.
THE CARDINAL: Being is good and noble and valuable. For this reason everything that is, is not without value. For nothing can wholly exist without being worth something. Nor can anything be found of such minimal value that something of lesser value cannot exist. And nothing is of so great a value that there cannot be anything of greater value. Only the value that is the value of values which is in all things that have value and in which all things that have value exist, enfolds in itself all value and is unable to have value that is more or less. Conceive therefore that this absolute value, the cause of all value, is hidden in the center of all circles. And make the outermost circle the outermost value and close to nothing. And consider how value is increased to the number ten in ternary progression in the manner often touched upon and you will enter into sweet speculation.
ALBERT: I think that if you concentrate your discourse on the price of the value, you would instruct us greatly.
THE CARDINAL: Perhaps you want me to speak of money.
ALBERT: That's what I want.
THE CARDINAL: I'll do just that. Now consider how the value of all things is nothing but the being of these same things. And just as in the one greatest value which is simply and entirely incomposite and indivisible, every value of everything most truly exists, so the being of everything is in the most simple being. For just as in the value of a florin there is the value of a thousand little denarii and in the higher value of the double florin there is the value of two thousand denarii, and so on *ad infinitum*, so in the optimal florin than which none other could be higher there would necessarily be the value of an infinity of denarii. This would be truly and really true, just as you see it to be true in this example.
ALBERT: Certainly it is so.
THE CARDINAL: When you observe this truth in yourself, what value has that eye of your mind, discerning in its power the value of all things? In its vision the value of all things and the values of singular things exist, but not as they exist in the value of values. Because the mind sees that which

valet: ideo ipsa oia valet. Nõ eni sunt i ipsa valores vt in sua essentia: sed vt in sua notione. est enim valor ens reale: sicut & valor mẽtis est ens aliqđ & ens reale. Et ita est in deo: vt i essentia valoris. & est ens notionale / quia cognosci potest: & ita est i intellectu vt in cognoscẽte valorẽ / nõ vt in maiori valore / aut vt in causa & essentia valoris. Nã per hoc ꝙ itellectus noster cognoscit minorẽ aut maiorẽ valorẽ: ꝑpterea tamen nõ est maior aut minor valor. Quia hæc cognitio: essentiã valori nõ ꝓstat. ALBER. Nonne hæc cognitio maioris valoris q̃ sit valor cognoscẽtis: adauget valorẽ cognoscẽtis? CARDI. Valor cognitiõis cognoscẽtis auget in eo ꝙ plura cognoscit: siue illa sint maioris / siue minoris valoris q̃ sit valor cognoscẽtis. Nõ enim valor cogniti intrat i valorẽ cognoscẽtis / vt faciat valorẽ cognoscẽtis maiorẽ: licet melioret cognitio. Sicut enim cognoscere malũ nõ facit cognoscẽtẽ peiorem / aut cognoscere bonũ meliorẽ: facit eũ tamẽ melius cognoscẽtem. ALBER. Intelligo. Nã sic dicimus aliquẽ valentẽ doctorẽ: licet plures nõ docti plus eo valeãt. tamẽ valor intellectualis naturæ / magnus valde est: quia i ipsa est discretio valorũ quæ est mirabilis / & cũcta discretiõe carẽtia excellẽs. CARDI. Dũ ꝓfunde cõsideras: intellectualis naturæ valor / post valorẽ dei suprem⁹ est. Nã in eius virtute: est dei & omniũ valor notionaliter & discretiue. Et q̃uis intellect⁹ nõ det esse valori: tamẽ sine itellectu valor discerni etiã quia est / nõ potest. Semoto enim intellectu: nõ potest sciri an sit valor. nõ existẽte virtute rationali & ꝓportionatiua: cessat æstimatio. qua nõ existẽte: vtiq͂ valor cessaret. In hoc apparet ꝓciositas mẽtis: quoniã sine ipa / oia creata valore caruissent. Si igit̃ deus voluit opus suũ debere æstimari aliquid valere: oportebat iter illa intellectualẽ creare naturã. ALBER. Videtur ꝙ si deum ponim⁹ quasi monetariũ: erit intellectus quasi nũmularius. CARDI. Non est absurda hæc assimilatio: quãdo cõcipis deũ quasi omnipotentẽ monetariũ / qui de sua excelsa & omnipotẽti virtute ꝑducere potest omnẽ monetã. Ac si quis tãtæ potẽtiæ esset ꝙ de manu sua / quãcũq͂ vellet monetã ꝑduceret / & statueret nũmulariũ habentẽ in sua virtute omniũ monetarũ discretionẽ & numerãdi scientiã / monetãdi arte tãtũ sibi reseruata: nũmularius ille nobilitatẽ monetarũ & valorẽ / numerũ / pondus / & mẽsurã quã a deo moneta haberet patefeceret / vt preciũ ipsius monetæ & valor / atq͂ per hoc potẽtia monetarii nota fieret: apta esset similitudo. ALBER. Magna esset huius potẽtia monetarii: qui i ea cõtineret omniũ monetarũ thesaurũ. Et ab illo posset ꝑducere nouas / & antiquas / aureas / argẽteas / & cereas / maximi / & minimi / & medii valoris monetas: manẽte semp thesauro æque infinito / inexhauribili / & incõsumptibili. Magnaq͂ esset nũmularii discretio discernendi has oẽs quantũcũq͂ varias monetas: & numerandi / põderandi / & mẽsurandi omnẽ omniũ valorẽ. sed ars dei in infinitũ vinceret artem nũmularii: quia ars dei faceret esse / ars nũmularii faceret tantum cognosci. CARDI. Nõne sic vides aliũ essendi modũ monetæ in arte omnipotentis monetarii / aliũ in monetabili materia / aliũ in motu & instrumẽtis vt monetatur / alium vt est actu monetata? Et hi oẽs modi: circa esse ipsius monetæ cõsistũt. Deĩde est alius modus qui circa illos essendi modos versatur: scilicet vt est in ratiõe discernẽte monetam. Id qđ facit monetã seu numisma: imago seu signum est eius / cui⁹ est. qđ si est monetarii: ipsius habet imaginẽ / puta faciei eius similitudinẽ. vt CHRISTVS nos docet: quãdo ostẽso numismate / interrogauit cuius esset imago. & respõsum est ei: Cæsaris. Facies notitia est. per faciem discernimus vnũ ab alio. Vna est igitur facies monetarii: in qua cognoscit̃ / & quę ipsum reuelat / qui aliter esset inuisibilis atq͂ incognoscibilis. Et huius faciei similitudo cũ sit in oibus numismatibus: nõ nisi noti-

has the value of all things, it does not on account of this itself have the value of all things. For values are not in it [the mind] in an essential way but rather in a notional way. Value is a real being and the value of the mind is another kind of real being. Value is in God as the essence of value. And value is in the mind as notional being because it can be known and so it is in the intellect as that which knows value. But the greater value that is in God is not in the mind, nor is the cause and essence of value. Although our intellect knows the greater or lesser value through this notional value, the notional value is nevertheless not, on account of this, a greater or lesser value because cognition does not convey essence to value.
ALBERT: Does not this cognition of value greater than that of the knower increase the value of the knower?
THE CARDINAL: The value of the cognition of the knower is increased in that he knows more things, whether they be of greater or lesser value than the value of the knower. The value of that which is known does not enter into the value of the knower in such a way that it makes the value of the knower greater, although knowledge may be improved. The knowledge of evil does not make the knower worse or the knowledge of good make him better, nevertheless it makes him a better knower.
ALBERT: I understand. So we say that someone is a worthy doctor although many who are not learned are worth more than him. Nevertheless the value of the intellectual nature is a great value because the distinction of values is in it. It [the intellectual nature] is marvelous and surpasses everything lacking the capacity to make distinctions.
THE CARDINAL: When you profoundly consider you see that the value of the intellectual nature is supreme after the value of God. For the value of God and of all things are in its power notionally and by distinctions. And although the intellect does not give being to value, nevertheless without the intellect, even the existence of value cannot be discerned. If the intellect is removed, it cannot be known whether value exists. If the rational and proportioning power does not exist, judgment ceases and if judgment did not exist, value would cease. In this the preciousness of the mind appears, since without it every created thing would be lacking in value. Therefore if God wished that his work be judged to be worth something it was necessary for him to create the intellectual nature among his works.
ALBERT: It appears that if we assume that God is the mint-master then the intellect would be the coin-broker.
THE CARDINAL: This metaphor is not absurd when you conceive of God as an omnipotent coiner of money who, from his high and omnipotent power can produce all money. And if someone would be of such great power that he would produce from his hand whatever kind of money he wished and would establish a coin-broker having in his power the distinction of all monies and the knowledge of their numbering, while reserving to himself [the omnipotent mint-master] only the art of coinage, that coin-broker would disclose the nobility of the monies and he would reveal the value, number, weight, and measure which the money had from God, so that the price and value of his money and through it the power of the mint-master would be known. The similitude would be an apt one.
ALBERT: The power of this mint-master, who contains in his power the treasure of all coinages, would be great. From that treasure he could produce new and old monies, gold and silver coinages, waxen coinages, coinages of greatest and least and middling value, with the treasure always remaining the same, infinite, inexhaustible and unconsumable. And great would be the discretion of the coin-broker, discerning all the various kinds of coinages and numbering, weighing, and measuring every value of all of them. But the art of God would infinitely surpass the art of the coin-broker because the art of God would make things exist, the art of the coin-broker would only make them knowable.
THE CARDINAL: Do you not see one mode of being of money in the art of the omnipotent coiner, another in the material out of which the money is made, another in the motion and instruments through which the money is made, and another in the money when actually made? And all these modes of being are centered around the being of money itself.

Then there is another mode which concerns those modes of being as it is the mode that is in the reason discerning money. The coin is the image or sign of him who makes the money or coins. If it is the coin of the mint-master, it has his own image, for example, the likness of his face. Christ taught this when, being shown a coin, he asked whose image it was and was answered "Caesar's" (*Matt*. 22:20 sqq.).

The face is a sign of knowledge and through the face we distinguish one person from another. Therefore, one [such sign] is the face of the mint-master in which he is known and which reveals him who would otherwise be invisible and unknowable. And while the likeness of this face is on

tiam seu faciẽ monetarii cuius est moneta / ostẽdit. Neq̃ aliud est imago: q̃ nomẽ sit prascriptũ. Sic enim dicebat CHRISTVS. Cui⁹ est imago hæc: & supscriptio eius? Respõderunt. Cæsaris. Facies igitur / & nomẽ / & figura substãtiæ / & filius monetarii: idẽ sunt. Filius igiẽ est imago viua / & figura substãtiæ / & splẽdor patris: per quẽ pater monetari⁹ facit / seu monetat / siue signat oĩa. Et cum sine signo tali nõ sit moneta: id vnũ qđ in omni moneta figuratur est exẽplar vnicũ / & formalis causa omnium monetarũ. Vnde si monetarius fuerit vnitas seu entitas: æqualitas quæ naturaliter ab vnitate generatur / est causa formalis entiũ. In æqualitate igiẽ vna & simplici: vides veritatẽ omniũ quæ sunt aut esse possunt / vt sunt per entitatẽ signata. Vides & in ipsa æqualitate vnitatẽ: vt in filio patrẽ. Omnia igiẽ quæ sunt aut esse possunt: in illa figura substãtiæ patris creatoris cõplicãtur. Est igitur creator monetarius in oĩbus monetis / per figurã substantiæ eius: sicut signatũ vnum in multis signis. Nã si in oĩbus numismatibus respexero ad quidditatẽ signati: nõ nisi vnũ video cuius est moneta. Et si ad signa monetarũ me cõuerto / plura numismata video: quia vnum signatũ in plurib⁹ signis signatũ video. Sed aduerte quomodo monetabile signatũ signo: est numisma seu moneta. Puta æs signatũ / est moneta: signatũ scilicet signo similitudinis signãtis. monetabilis materia: signo fit numisma. Et dicitur materia signata seu figurata: quæ recipit determinationẽ possibilitatis essendi nũmum. Sic video signatũ ante signũ / in signo / & post signũ. Ante signũ: vt est veritas quæ est ante suam figurã. In signo: vt veritas in imagine. Et post signũ: vt signatum a signo est signatũ. Primũ signatũ: est infinita actualitas. Vltimũ signatũ: est infinita possibilitas. Mediũ signatum est duplex: aut vt primũ est in signo / aut vt signum est in vltimo. Primũ signatum qđ infinitã dixi actualitatẽ: dicitur ipsa absoluta necessitas quæ est omnipotẽs / omnia cogens / cui nihil resistere potest. Vltimũ signatũ scilicet infinita possibilitas: dicitur & absoluta & indeterminata possibilitas. Inter illos essendi extremos modos: sunt alii duo. vnus est contrahẽs necessitatẽ ĩ cõplexũ / & vocaẽ necessitas cõplexiõis / vt necessitas essendi hoĩem. Illa enĩ essendi necessitas ad hoĩem cõtracta: cõplicat ea q̃ ad istũ essendi modũ sunt necessaria / q̃ hũanitas dicĩ. ita de oĩbus. Alius eleuãs possibilitatẽ ĩ actũ p determinationẽ: & vocaẽ possibilitas determinata / vt est ille florenus / aut iste homo. Considera igitur monetã aliquã puta papalem florenũ / & facito ipsum in tuo cõceptu viuũ vita intellectuali / & q̃ in se mẽtaliter respiciat: tũc se speculãdo / hæc & cũcta quæ dicta aut dici possunt / reperiet. nullum animal est adeo obtusum: q̃ se ab aliis non discernat / & in sua specie alia eiusdẽ speciei non cognoscat. Sed viuẽs vita intellectuali: oĩa intelligibiliter / hoc est omniũ in se notiones reperit. Cõplicat enim vis intellectiua: oĩa intelligibilia. omnia quæ sunt / intelligibilia sunt: sicut oĩa colorata / sunt visibilia. excedunt aliqua visibilia visum vt excellens lux: & aliqua adeo minuta sunt q̃ nõ immutãt visum / & illa directe nõ videnẽ. Videtur enim excellentia lucis solaris negatiue: quia id quod videtur non est sol / cũ tanta sit lucis eius excellẽtia / q̃ videri nequeat. Sic id qđ videẽ non est indiuisibilis punctus: cum ille sit minor q̃ qđ videri potest. Eo modo intellectus videt negatiue infinitã actualitatẽ seu deũ: & infinitã possibilitatẽ seu materiã. Media affirmatiue videt: in ĩtelligibili & rationabili virtute. Modos igitur essendi vt sunt intelligibiles: intellectus intra se vt viuũ speculũ contẽplatur. Est igitur intellectus ille nũmus: qui & nũmularius. Sicut deus illa moneta: quæ & monetarius. Quare intellectus reperit sibi cõgenitam virtutẽ: omnem monetã cognoscẽdi & numerandi. Quomodo autẽ viuus ille nũmus qui intellectus / in se oĩa intellectualiter

all coins, it shows only the cognitive sign or face of the minter whose coin it is. Nor is the image anything other than the name written upon it. Thus Christ said, "Whose image is this and what is written upon it?" and they answered "Caesar's."

Therefore the face and the name and the substantial form and the son of the mint-master are the same. Therefore the son is the living image and the substantial form and the splendor of the father through whom the father or coiner makes money and puts his sign on everything. Since it would not be money without such a sign, that which is signed on all coins is the unique exemplar and the formal cause of all coinages.[33] Hence if the coiner were unity or being, equality, which is naturally generated from unity, is the formal cause of beings. Therefore in the one and simple equality you see the truth of all things which are or can be, as they are signed through being.

And you see unity in equality itself as the father in the son. Therefore all things which are or can be are enfolded in that substantial form of the father-creator. Therefore the creator and coiner is in all coined things through his substantial form just as a single signified thing is in many signs. For if I consider the quiddity of that which is in all coins, I see only the one whose money it is. And if I turn myself to the signs of monies, I see many coins, because I see one signified thing signified in many signs. Notice how something coinable signified by a sign is coinage or money.

For example a signed piece of copper is a coin that is signed with the sign of the likeness of the signer. The coinable matter is made into money by the sign. And that material which receives the determination of the possibility of being a coin, is called stamped or figured. So I see what is stamped prior to the sign, in the sign, and after the sign: prior to the sign in that it is the truth which exists prior to its image, in the sign as the truth in an image, and after the sign as what is stamped is stamped by the sign. The first stamp is infinite actuality, the last stamp is infinite possibility. The middle stamp is twofold either as the first is in the sign or as the sign is in the last. The first stamp which I have called infinite actuality is called absolute necessity itself, which is omnipotent, compelling all things and which nothing can resist. The last stamp is called infinite possibility and absolute and indeterminate possibility as well.

In between these extreme modes of being there are two other modes. One is the drawing together of necessity into the complex and is called the necessity of combination, as the necessity of being man. For that necessity of being contracted to man enfolds those things that are necessary to such a mode of being which is called humanity. And so it is for all things. The other mode of being elevates possibility into act through determination and is called determinate possibility as for example in this florin or that man. Consider therefore some kind of money—for example the papal florin—and make it live in your understanding through intellectual life. Because the intellectual life looks inside itself mentally, through speculating within itself, it will discover this and everything that has been or can be said. No animal is so stupid that it does not distinguish itself from others and does not recognize in its species others who are of the same species. But he who is living in the intellectual life discovers all things intellectually—that is, all the notions of things in himself.

For the intellective power enfolds all intelligible things. All things that are, are intelligible just as all colored things are visible. Some visible things exceed sight, as for example blinding light and some indeed are so minute that they do not affect vision and they are not directly seen. The excellence of solar light is seen negatively because that which is seen is not the sun since the excellence of its light is so great that it could not be seen. So also, that which is seen is not the indivisible point since it is smaller than that which can be seen.

In the same way the intellect sees infinite actuality or God and infinite possibility or matter negatively. Middle range things it sees affirmatively in intelligible and rational strength. Therefore the intellect contemplates the modes of being that are intelligible within itself as in a living mirror. Therefore the intellect is that money which is also the money-handler just as God is that money which is also the mint-master. Hence the intellect discovers the power that is congenital to it, that of recognizing and numbering all money.

quærens reperiat: exemplum qualecunq; capere potes in iis quæ ego in intellectum prospiciens/propalaui. Quæ acutius q̃ ego subintrans: præcisius videre & reuelare poterit. Et hæc: sic de monetario & nũmulario/dicta sint. ALBER. Abũde quæ simpliciter protuli: adaptasti. Istud solum pro mea instructione audias. Videtur enim q velis dicere: si floren⁹ papalis viueret vita ĩtellectuali/q vtiq; se florenũ cognosceret. & ideo se esse monetã illius: cuius signum & imaginẽ haberet. Cognosceret eñ q a seipso esse floreni nõ haberet: sed ab illo qui suam imaginẽ ei impressisset. & per hoc q in omnibus viuis intellectibus similem videret imaginem: eiusdẽ omnes monetas esse cognosceret. Vnam igitur faciem in signis omniũ monetarũ vidẽs: vnam æqualitatem per quã omnis moneta esset actu constituta/videret oĩs possibilis eiusdem monetæ causam. etiã probe videret cũ sit moneta monetata: q fieri potuit moneta/& fuit prius monetabilis anteq̃ actu monetata. & ita in se videret materiam: quã impressio signi determinauit esse florenum. & cum sit moneta eius cuius est signum: tunc esse suum haberet a veritate quæ est in signo/non a signo materiæ impresso/q q; vna veritas in variis signis/varie materiam determinat. Non enim possunt esse plura signa: nisi concomitetur pluralitatem varietas. nec potest veritas in variis signis: nisi varie materiam determinare. Ex quo euenit/non posse nisi omne numisma cum alio numismate concordare: cũ sint nũmi cõcordantes/in eo q eiusdem sunt monetæ. & differẽtes: cum inter se sint varii. Talia quidem & multa alia: in se viuus ille florenus videret. CARDINA. Plane cũcta quæ dixi: resumpsisti. Singularius tamen memoriæ cõmenda: quomodo non est nisi vna/vera/& præcisa ac sufficientissima forma omnia formans/in variis signis varie resplendens/& formabilia varie formans/determinansq; seu in actu ponens.

SECVNDI DE LVDO GLOBI FINIS.

Legisti quicunq; globi studiose libellum,
Quem Baiohario scripsimus ante duci.
Hunc quoq; qui sequitur castis secessibus hauri:
In quo iam rerum copia maior erit.
Nam velut abstrusis paulatim viribus arbor
Spargitur occulto lata per arua pede:
Sic opus æternum diuinæ mentis in arctis
Mansurum foliis/ætheris arce venit.
Num queat ingenium rerũ cognoscere causas:
Cernitur hic/vbi mens se & sua iura videt.
Conscẽdat sed enim tãti in speculaminis arcem
Quis: nisi quem summo tollat amore deus?
I decus egregium fratri coniunctus honesto
Dux Alberte ducum gloria. plaude patri.
Extrema est quoniã manus hoc ĩpressa libello/
Aureaq; in lucem prodere scripta parat.

Moreover, you can grasp any example of how this living coin, which is the intellect, intellectually discovers all things by seeking them in itself, in the things that I have divulged by looking into the intellect. Someone entering into these things more acutely than I could see and reveal them more precisely. And so these things may be said concerning the minter and the money handler.
ALBERT: You have abundantly dealt with those things that I simply brought forth. Please listen to only one more point to instruct me. It seems that what you want to say is that if a papal florin were to live the intellectual life, it certainly would know itself to be a florin and for this reason to be the money of him whose sign and image it would have. For it would know that it did not have the being of the florin from itself but from him who had impressed his image upon it. And through the fact that it would see a similar image in all living intellects, it would know that all monies would be of the same person.

Therefore, seeing one face in the signs of all coinages, it would see one equality through which all money would be constituted in act as the possible cause of all possible identical money. Besides it would see rightly since it would be coined money that it could be made into money and was previously coinable before it was actually minted. And so it would see in itself the material which the impression of the sign determined would be a florin. And because it is his money whose sign it is then it would have its being from the truth which is in the sign, not from the sign impressed in the matter, because one truth determines matter diversely in various signs.

There cannot be plural signs unless variety accompanies plurality, nor can the truth determine matter through various signs except variously. From this it follows that one coinage cannot be harmonized with another coinage except completely because coins are concordant in that they are coins of the same money and different in that they are different from each other. Indeed that living florin would see in itself such things and many others.
THE CARDINAL: You have clearly summarized all that I have said. However, commit to memory this specific point: there is but one true and precise and most sufficient form forming all things, shining forth variously in various signs, and variously forming, determining, or putting into act formable things.

NOTES

1. The word *rythmimachia* which I here translate *number games* appears to refer to some kind of medieval number game. Though Lefèvre D'Étaples uses this word, the incunabulum of 1488 and the two manuscripts used by Gabriel employ *rithmatia*. The exact origins and form of this game are not clear. Gerda von Bredow points out in her first note to her German translation of the *De ludo globi*, that John of Salisbury refers to a game which he too calls *rithmatia* in his *Policraticus* 1, 5 and in a letter (*Vom Globusspiel*, p. 98). More recently, Wolfgang Breidert has traced the sources and form of this game in greater detail (apparently it was Pythagorean in origin) in his "Rhythmomachie und Globusspiel," *Mitteilungen und Forschungsbeiträge der Cusanus-Gesellschaft* 10, Mainz: Matthias-Grünewald, 1973, pp. 155-171.
2. On the peculiar shape of the *globus* and its motion, see the Introduction, pp. 24-26; Gerda von Bredow, *Das Globusspiel*, notes 5 and 12.
3. Introduction, pp. 17-18; 27-28.
4. The Gabriel edition reads "universaliter" for the Paris "verisimiliter." I use "universaliter" because it seems to me that Cusanus is here articulating a rule that applies to "all things necessarily greater or lesser"; in this sense it is "universal." The context does not imply verisimilitude or probability.
5. The Paris, 1514 edition reads "trinitas" for Leo Gabriel's "aeternitas." "Aeternitas" clearly fits the context.
6. Introduction, p. 28.
7. Introduction, pp. 31-32.
8. Cf. Aristotle, *Categories* 14. 15a-b.
9. The Paris, 1514 edition reads "terminatio"; I choose to use Leo Gabriel's "determinatio."
10. Introduction, pp. 32-34.

11. The Paris, 1514 edition reads "vides" rather than "video."
12. There is an important variation in the text of this sentence. *Cod. Krakow* reads ". . . ut illa praedicta experimentaliter cognoscis in primis nos *non* libere moveri, sed ex necessitate naturae sensibilis et corporae." *Cod. Cusanus* reads "tamen" for Krakow's "non." The Paris edition contains neither word. It seems clear from the context and from the conclusion of the sentence, that the *Cod. Krakow* reading is the most convincing one: "we are *not* freely moved in the first things, *but from the necessity of the sensible nature and of corporeal things."*
13. Introduction, p. 34.
14. The *De coniecturis* and the *Compendium* both contain explicit and extended treatments of man as maker and ruler over his own human world, but as the Introduction indicates, this is a theme that runs through all of Cusanus's major works subsequent to the *De coniecturis*.
15. I here include in the translation a clause contained in *Cod. Krakow*, but not in the Paris edition: "Fuit autem propositum meum hunc ludum noviter inventum, quem passim omnes facile capiunt et libenter ludunt, (*propter crebrum risum, qui ex vario et numquam certo cursu contingit*) et numquam certo cursu contingit in ordinem proposito utilem redigere."
16. There are variant readings for this sentence. *Cod. Cusanus* and the Paris edition read "locus," instead of "globus" in the final clause; the *Cod. Krakow* reads "globus." The last clause can therefore be read "for each person's *place* rests on its own point and atom which no other could ever attain." I have followed the *Cod. Krakow's* "globus" since it seems to best continue the imagery of the previous sentences, upon which the meaning of the sentence in question depends.
17. Paris, 1514 reads "studioso," Leo Gabriel "virtuoso." I follow Paris, 1514 because "studioso" seems to fit the context somewhat better, though "virtuoso" can be appropriately used as well.
18. Again here, Paris, 1514 reads "studioso" and Gabriel "virtuoso" and again both words can be suitably used.
19. The identity of the poet to whom Cusanus refers here is not evident. Moreover, the idea that fortune is omnipotent is fairly widespread in classical literature and is carried over into medieval Christian literature, though for Christian poets the vagaries and whimsies of fortune tend to be dominant rather that her omnipotence. On this subject see H.R. Patch's *The Goddess Fortuna in Medieval Literature*, Cambridge, Mass. Harvard University Press, 1927.
20. Paris 1514 reads "mysterium"; Gabriel "mysticationem," which I follow.
21. The Paris 1514 edition reads "motum"; Gabriel, "vitam," which I follow.
22. Dionysius the Areopagite, *De caelesti hierarchia*, 6, 2.
23. The Paris, 1514 edition reads "et minus"; Gabriel "terminus," which I follow.
24. In this sentence I follow Gabriel's reading: ". . . ut in divina simplicitate simul omnia videant."
25. The Paris, 1514 edition reads "concludens"; Gabriel "includens," which I follow.
26. Introduction, pp. 29-31.
27. Cf. Aristotle, *De anima*, 431b.
28. Cusanus's seminal discussions of God as one and three are found in the *De docta ignorantia*. Chapters VII-X of Book I are fundamental.
29. I add here the phrase "sive discretiva ac proportionativa" included by Gabriel and found in the *Cod. Krakow.*
30. The Paris, 1514 edition reads "omnia ut et cognosci"; Gabriel "omnia ut esse ut cognosci."
31. See also *De coniecturis*, Chapters IV-X.
32. Throughout this final section, Cusanus is punning on the verb "valeo." It can mean to bid farewell and it can also mean to be worth. Cusanus clearly intends his reader to take it in this double sense.
33. The Paris, 1514 edition reads "figuratur"; the Gabriel edition "signatur" which I follow.

5. List of Variants

Between the Paris, 1514 edition of Lefèvre D'Étaples and the 1967 edition of Leo Gabriel

I include here only those variants that affect the meaning of the text. Errors in spelling or punctuation in the two versions are not included, nor are orthographical differences.

Paris, 1514	Leo Gabriel
Fol. CLII	
line 8: rythmimachiam	p. 222, line 8: rithmatiam
Fol. CLIIv	
lines 9-10: non enim faceret motum quem videtis: eliocoidem/vertiginosum seu spiralem aut curvae involutum	p. 224, lines 3-5: non enim faceret motum quem videtis elicum seu spiralem aut curvae involutum
line 29: ad motem naturalem	p. 224, line 31: ad motem et naturalis
Fol. CLIII	
line 17: extremitas mundi ex punctis	p. 228, line 15: extremitas mundi et punctis
line 19: possunt	p. 228, line 18: possint
line 22: si possibile esset	p. 228, line 22: si possibile foret
lines 37-38: hoc quidem videre videor	p. 230, line 11: hoc quidem mihi videt
line 43: possibile esset	p. 230, line 19: possibile foret
line 44: esset visibilis	p. 230, line 20: foret visibilis
Fol. CLIIIv	
line 28: verisimiliter	p. 232, line 28: universaliter

Fol. CLIIII

line 2: haec est participabilis	p. 234, line 25: haec est enim participabilis
lines 5-6: qua maior non est	p. 234, line 31 qua maior esse nequit
line 9: video imaginem trinitas	p. 236, lines 1-2 video imaginem aeternitas

Fol. CLIIIIv

line 25: sine violentia et fatigatione	p. 240, line 32: sine violentia et fatiga
line 40: ille esset perfecte rotundus	p. 242, line 22: ille foret perfecte rotundus
line 43: motus vivificandi animali	p. 242, line 27: motus vivificandi animal

Fol. CLV

no variants

Fol. CLVv

line 38: cogitatio, consideratio, et terminatio	p. 250, line 14: cogitatio, consideratio, et determinatio

Fol. CLVI

line 15: et in hoc vides	p. 252, line 18: et in hoc video
line 27: et non esset aliter perfectissima unitas	p. 254, line 5: et non esset alias perfectissima unitas
line 41: sed imperium superiorum	p. 254, line 24: sed imperium superioris
line 45: alioqui nihil inveniret	p. 254, line 29: alias nihil inveniret

Fol. CLVIv

line 2: hunc esse impulsium. Contentus sum igitur	p. 256, line 6: hunc esse impulsivum. Contentor igitur
line 5: nos libere moveri	p. 256, line 6: nos non libere moveri

line 6: libere cum liberum	p. 256, line 8: libere cum liber

Fol. CLVII

line 46: si velit optime contentus est	p. 262, line 31: si velit, optime contentatur

Fol. CLVIIv

lines 4-5: attente igitur ad vertito	p. 264, line 5: attende igitur adesto
line 23: per quod	p. 264, line 33: quomodo
line 27: creavit enim possibilitatem	p. 266, line 6: creativit possibilitatem
line 32: quae possibilitas	p. 266, line 12: qui possibilitas
line 40: non enim esset mens	p. 266, line 23: non enim foret mens
line 44: non enim ex seipso	p. 268, line 1: non ex se ipso

Fol. CLVIII

line 25: haec quae coepisti	p. 270, line 9: haec, quae incepisti
line 29: recenter inventum	p. 270, line 14: noviter inventum
line 30: liber ludunt, et numquam certo cursu	p. 270, lines 16-17: liber ludunt propter crebrum risum, qui ex vario et numquam certo cursu contingit et numquam certo cursu
line 38: quiesceret	p. 270, line 29: quiescat
line 41: locus	p. 272, line 1: globus
line 42: atomo sua propria quam	p. 272, line 2: suo proprio quem

Fol. CLVIIIv

line 9: huic	p. 272, line 22: huius

line 13: ignobilior	p. 272, line 28: nobilior
line 18: Christi	p. 272, line 3: Dei
line 21: ut video	p. 272, line 9: tu vides quam
line 31: studioso	p. 274, line 23: virtuoso
line 40: impediatur	p. 276, line 6: impediat
line 41: studioso	p. 276, line 8: virtuoso

Fol. CLIX

line 1: centro	p. 276, line 16: centre
line 7: possumus	p. 276, line 25: possuimus
line 26: si	p. 278, line 17: sic
lines 26-27: sic fiant omnia ut fieri folent alioquin	p. 278, line 17: sic fiant omnia sicut fiunt alioquin
line 37: non iis extrinsecis	p. 280, line 5: non in iis extrinsecis

Fol. CLIXv

line 6: perducit	p. 280, line 27: producit

Fol. CLX

(This folio contains the greater part of a poem in praise of the *De ludo globi* which Lefèvre D'Étaples appended to his edition of the work. Leo Gabriel does not include the text of his poem in his edition).

Fol. CLXv

line 16: impertiar	p. 286, line 17: impartiar
line 21: mysterium: quod	p. 286, line 25: mysticationem, quam

line 25: esset	p. 288, line 3: foret
line 30: deduxeris	p. 288, line 11: deduxisti
line 31: tu probe mente	p. 288, line 12: tu bene mente
line 35: alioqui non esset	p. 288, line 19 alias non est
line 41-41: exemplatum omnem	p. 288, line 28: exemplatum. et ante omnem
lines 42-43: Ideo si essent	p. 288, lines 29-30: Ideo et si forent
line 43: esset	p. 288, line 30: forent

Fol. CLXI

line 4: obsistit	p. 290, line 2: restistit
line 5: exemplar	p. 290, line 3: exemplaris
line 6: exemplar	p. 290, line 4: exemplaris
line 9: esset	p. 290, line 9: foret
line 14: admisisti	p. 290, line 15: admittis
line 15: esset	p. 290, line 16: esse
line 16: quem	p. 290, line 17: qui
lines 37-38: videturque ei ac si	p. 292, line 15: videtur sibi

Fol. CLXIv

line 25: motum	p. 294, line 32: vitam
line 44: noster	p. 296, line 26: nostri

Fol. CLXII

line 7: in tenebris	p. 298, line 9: in tenebra
line 8: est illi vivere	p. 298, line 10: est sibi vivere
line 45: creator et creatura et omnium beaturum creaturarum	p. 302, line 3: creator et creatura quorum omnium beaturum creaturarum

Fol. CLXIIv

line 1: rationalium	p. 302, line 5: rationabilium
line 23: Et minus	p. 304, line 5: Et terminus
line 29: ut in divina simplicitate sciant omnia	p. 304, lines 13-14: ut in divina simplicitate simul omnia videant
line 34: sed bene perpetui	p. 304, line 22: sed perpetui
line 35: tertius etenim ordo	p. 304, line 23: tertius ordo
line 40-41: deus in se omnia concludens	p. 304, line 30: Deus in se omnia includens

Fol. CLXIII

line 5: minimum intimum	p. 306, line 10: minimum interiorem
line 39: licet ab ipso	p. 308, line 26: licet eo ipso

Fol. CLXIIIv

lines 4-5: non habent quod non sunt esse plura	p. 310, lines 11-12: non habent quod sunt plura
lines 8-9: Aequalitas non potest	p. 310, line 17: Aequalitas autem non potest
line 9: aequalitas	p. 310, line 18: aequalium
line 14: est entitas et aequalitas et nexus ab unitate et aequalitate procedens	p. 310, lines 25-26: est entitas et entitas aequalitatis et nexus de unitate et aequalitate procedens

line 34:
ubique

p. 312, line 22:
undique

lines 35-36:
nihil nisi unum ubique scribendo utique licet ubique

p. 312, lines 24-25:
nihil nisi li unum undique scribendo, utique licet undique

line 37:
ubique scriptum

p. 312, line 27:
undique scriptum

Fol. CLXIIII

line 14:
tu decipis

p. 316, line 1:
tu deciperis

lines 15-17:
Sed dum attendis quod nunquam verum fuit decere deum fuisse quin et creaturae essent vides deum ante creaturas non proprie dici fuisse.

p. 316, lines 2-5:
Sed dum attendis Deum prius non fuisse antequam omnia faceret, quia facere et ese Dei unum sunt, vides quod numquam verum fuit dicere Deum fuisse quin et creaturae essent.

line 20:
capimus

p. 316, line 10:
concipimus

line 30:
quasi saltator fosae adiutorio baculi

p. 316, lines 23-24:
quasi saltator fossati baculo

lines 36-37:
certituudine scientia et in certitudinem ruisse. possunt et coelorum discretione: aliquate nus venari

p. 318, lines 2-5:
certitudine scientia in incertitudinem ruisse. Possunt et caelorum discretiones aliqualiter venari.

line 38:
quodlibet

p. 318, line 6:
quolibet

Fol. CLXIIIIv

line 6:
vis ratiocinativa seu numerativa sive discretiva ac proportionativa in se complicans

p. 318, lines 25-27:
vis ratiocinativa seu numerativa sive discretiva ac proportionativa in se complicans

line 14:
Hoc audire

p. 320, line 7:
Haec audire

line 20:
omnia ut et cognosci

p. 320, line 15:
omnia ut esse et cognosci

lines 36-37: scilicet unitate et puncto	p. 322, line 5: scilicet unitatis et puncti

Fol. CLXV

line 46: hominem ratione	p. 326, line 25-26: hominem penitus ratione

Fol. CLXVv

no variants

Fol. CLXVI

line 2: fortissimamque converto	p. 332, line 2: fortissimamque me converto
lines 21-22: per essentiam talis et non per essentiam non acquisitae	p. 332, line 30: per essentiam talis et non acquisitae
line 36: properas verum aliquid quaeso	p. 334, line 20: properas aliquid quaeso

Fol. CLXVIv

line 10: de confusis tenebris	p. 356, line 22: de confusa tenebra

Fol. CLXVII

no variants

Fol. CLXVIIv

no variants

Fol. CLXVIII

line 6: in omni moneta figuratur	p. 350, line 3: in omni moneta signatur

Fol. CLXVIIIv

line 1: exemplum qualecumque	p. 352, line 31: exemplum aliquale
line 11: etiam probe videret	p. 354, line 11: etiam bene videret

6. BIBLIOGRAPHY OF WORKS CITED

1.

CUSANUS'S WORKS: TEXTS AND TRANSLATIONS

Texts:

Nicolai Cusae accurata recognitio trium voluminum operum ed. Iacobus Faber Stapulensis, 3 Vols. Paris, 1514 (anastatic reprint, Frankfurt: Minerva, 1962).

Nicolaus Cusanus. *Opera Omnia*. Iussu et auctoritate Literarum Heidelbergensis ad codicum fidem edita. Leipzig: Felix Meiner, 1932– .

Vol. I, *De docta ignorantia*. ed. Ernst Hoffmann and Raymond Klibansky. Leipzig, 1932.

Vol. II, *Apologia doctae ignorantiae*. ed. Raymond Klibansky. Leipzig, 1932.

Vol. III, *De coniecturis*. ed. Josef Koch and Karl Bormann. Hamburg, 1972.

Vol. V, *Idiota de sapientia*, *Idiota de mente*, *Idiota de staticis experimentis*. ed. Ludwig Baur. Leipzig, 1937.

Vol. XI/1, *De beryllo*. ed. Ludwig Baur. Leipzig, 1940.

Vol. XI/3, *Compendium*. ed. Bruno Decker and Karl Bormann. Hamburg, 1946.

Nicolaus Cusanus. *Philosophisch-Theologische Schriften*. Ed. Leo Gabriel, 3 Vols. Vienna: Herder, 1967.

Translations:

Anonymous. *The Idiot*. 1650. Reprinted in 1940 with a preface by W.R. Dennes. San Franciso: California State Library Occasional Papers. Reprint Series No. 19, 1940.

von Bredow, Gerda. *Vom Globusspiel (De ludo globi)*. Hamburg: Felix Meiner, 1952.

Dolan, John P., ed. *Unity and Reform: Selected Writings of Nicholas de Cusa*. South Bend: University of Notre Dame Press, 1962.

Hopkins, Jasper. *A Concise Introduction to the Philosophy of Nicholas of Cusa*. Minneapolis: University of Minnesota Press, 1978 (contains a translation of the *De possest*).

______. *Nicholas of Cusa on God as Not-other: A Translation and an Appraisal of* De li non-aliud. Minneapolis: University of Minnesota Press, 1979.

______. *Nicholas of Cusa on Learned Ignorance: A Translation and an Appraisal of* De docta ignorantia. Minneapolis: The Arthur J. Banning Press, 1981.

______. *Nicholas of Cusa's Debate with John Wenck: A Translation and an Appraisal of De Ignota Litteratura and Apologia Doctae Ignorantiae*. Minneapolis: The Arthur J. Banning Press, 1981.

Miller, Clyde Lee. *Nicholas de Cusa Idiota de Mente. The Layman: About Mind.* New York: Abaris Books, Janus Series 7, 1979.

Randall, Giles. *The Single Eye, Entitled the Vision of God*. London: Streater, 1646.

Salter, Emma G. *The Vision of God*. With an introduction by Evelyn Underhill. New York: Dutton, 1928.

2.

OTHER PRIMARY SOURCES AND SCHOLARLY STUDIES

(I have not cited specific editions of standard ancient and medieval thinkers, except where I quote passages from their works in the text of the introduction).

Alberti, Leon Battista. *The Family in Renaissance Florence: A Translation of I Libri della Famiglia*. Translation, with introduction, by Renée N. Watkins. Columbia, S.C.: University of South Carolina Press, 1969.

Baeumker, Clemens. "Das pseudo-hermetische 'Buch der vierundzwanzig Meister' (*Liber XXIV Philosophorum*): Ein Beitrag zur Geschichte des Neupythagoreismus und Neoplatonismus im Mittelalter." *Beiträge zur Geschichte der Philosophie und Theologie des Mittelalters* 25, 1928, pp. 194-214.

Baur, L. "Cusanus Texte III, Marginalien 1. Nicolaus Cusanus und Ps. Dionysius im Lichte der Zitate und Randbemerkungen des Cusanus." *Sitzungsberichte der Heidelberger Akademie der Wissenschaften, Philosophisch-historiche* Klasse. Heidelberg: Carl Winter, 1941.

Biechler, James. *The Religious Language of Nicholas of Cusa*. The American Academy of Religion Dissertation Series No. 8. Missoula, Montana: Scholars Press, 1975.

Breidert, Wolfgang. "Rhythmomachie und globusspiel: Bemerkungen zu zwei mittelalterlichen Lehrspielen." *Mitteilungen und Forschungsbeiträge der Cusanus-Gesellschaft* 10. Mainz: Matthias-Grünewald, 1973.

Cassirer, Ernst. *The Individual and the Cosmos in Renaissance Philosophy*. Translated by Mario Domandi. Oxford: Basil Blackwell, 1963.

Chevalier, P. et al., editors. *Dionysiaca*, 2 Vols. Paris-Bruges, 1937-1949.

Colomer, Eusebio. *Nikolaus von Kues und Raymund Lull aus Handschriften der Kueser Bibliothek*. Berlin: Walter De Gruyter & Co., 1961.

Coulter, James A. *The Literary Microcosm: Theories of Interpretation of The Later Neoplatonists*. Leiden: E.J. Brill, 1976.

Courtenay, William J. "Covenant and Causality in Pierre D'Ailly." *Speculum* 46, 1971, pp. 94-119.

______. "The King and the Leaden Coin: The Economic Background of *Sine Qua Non* Causality." *Traditio* 28, 1972, pp. 185-209.

Cranz, F. Edward. "Cusanus, Luther, and the Mystical Tradition," in *The Pursuit of Holiness*. Ed. Charles Trinkaus with Heiko Oberman. Leiden: E.J. Brill, 1974, pp. 93-103.

Crescini, Angelo. *Il Problema Metodologico alle Origini della Scienza Moderna*. Rome: Edizioni Dell'Ateneo, 1972.

Danzer, Robert. "Cusanus-Bibliographie, Fortsetzung (1961 bis 1964), und Nachträge." *Mitteilungen und Forschungsbeiträge der Cusanus-Gesellschaft* 3, 1963, pp. 223-237.

Denifle, H. "Meister Eckharts lateinische Schriften und die Grundanschauung seiner Lehre." *Archiv für Literatur und Kirchengeschichte des Mittelalters II*, 1886, pp. 417-615.

Duhem, Pierre. "Thierry de Chartres et Nicolaus de Cues." *Revue des Sciences philosophiques et théologiques*. Vol. 3, Paris, 1909, pp. 525-531.

Falckenberg, R. *Grundzüge der Philosophie des Nikolaus Cusanus mit besonderer Berucksichtigung der Lehre von Erkennen*. Breslau: Koebner, 1880 (anastatic reprint Frankfurt: Minerva, 1968).

Gabriel, Astrik L. "'Via antiqua' and 'via moderna' and the Migration of Paris Students and Masters to the German Universities in the Fifteenth Century." *Miscellanea Medievalia*, Vol. 9: *Antiqui und Moderni*. Ed. A. Zimmermann. Berlin: Walter De Gruyter & Co., 1974.

Grant, Edward. "Medieval and Seventeenth-Century Conceptions of an Infinite Void Space beyond the Cosmos." *Isis* 68, 1969, pp. 39-60.

______. *A Source Book in Medieval Science*. Cambridge, Mass.: Harvard University Press, 1974.

______. "The Condemnation of 1277, God's Absolute Power, and Physical Thought in the Late Middle Ages." *Viator* 10. Los Angeles: University of California Press, 1979.

______. *Much Ado About Nothing: Theories of Space and Vacuum from the Middle Ages to the Scientific Revolution*. Cambridge, England: Cambridge University Press, 1981.

Harries, Karsten. "The Infinite Sphere: Comments on the History of a Metaphor." *Journal of the History of Philosophy* 13, 1975, pp. 5-15.

Haubst, Rudolph. *Das Bild des Einen und Dreieinen Gottes in der Welt nach Nikolaus von Kues. Trier Theologische Studien* 4. Trier: Paulinus, 1952.

______. *Die Christologie des Nikolaus von Kues*. Freiburg: Herder, 1956.

______. "Studien zu Nikolaus von Kues und Johannes Wenck aus Handschriften der Vatikanischen Bibliothek." *Beiträge zur Geschichte der Philosophie und Theologie des Mittelalters* 38, No. 1. Münster-Westfalen: Aschendorff, 1955.

Heninger, S.K. "Pythagorean Cosmology and The Triumph of Heliocentrism." *Le Soleil à la Renaissance: Sciences et Mythes*. Colloque International 1963. Université Libre de Bruxelles. Travaux de l'Institut pour L'Étude de la Renaissance et de l'Humanisme, II. Brussels/Paris: Presses Universitaires, 1965, pp. 35-53.

______. *The Cosmographical Glass: Renaissance Diagrams of the Universe*. San Marino, Cal.: The Huntington Library, 1977.

Huizinga, Johan. *Homo Ludens: A Study of the Play Element in Culture*. Boston: The Beacon Press, 1955.

Kleinen, Hans, and Robert Danzer. "Cusanus-Bibliographie (1920-1961)." *Mitteilungen und Forschungsbeiträge der Cusanus-Gesellschaft* 1, 1968, pp. 95-126.

Klibansky, Raymond. "Copernic et Nicolas de Cues." *Léonard de Vinci et l'expérience scientifique au seizième siècle*, Paris: Presses Universitaires de France, 1953.

Koyré, Alexander. *From The Closed World to the Infinite Universe*. New York: Harper and Row Torchbooks, 1958.

Kristeller, P.O., "A Latin Translation of Gemistos Plethon's *de fato* by Johannes Sophianos dedicated to Nicholas of Cusa." *Nicolò Cusano agli Inizi del Mondo Moderno. Atti del Congresso internazionale in occasione del V centenario della morte di Nicolò Cusano. Bressanone, 6-10 settembre, 1964*. Florence: Sansoni, 1970.

Mahnke, D. *Unendliche Sphäre und Allmittelpunkt. Beiträge zur Genealogie der Mathematischen Mystik* 8. Halle: Niemeyer, 1937.

Marsh, David. *The Quattrocento Dialogue: Classical Tradition and Humanist Innovation*. Cambridge, Mass.-London: Harvard University Press, 1980.

McTighe, Thomas. "Nicholas of Cusa's Theory of Science and its Metaphysical Background." *Nicolò Cusano agli Inizi del Mondo Moderno. Atti del Congresso internazionale in occasione del V centenario della morte di Nicolò Cusano. Bressanone, 6-10 settembre, 1964*. Florence: Sansoni, 1970, pp. 317-339.

Meuthen, Erich. *Die letzen Jahren des Nikolaus von Kues: Biographische Untersuchungen nach neuen Quellen. Wissenschaftliche Abhandlungen der Arbeitsgemeinschaft für Forschung des Landes Nordrhein-Westfalen* 3. Köln-Opladen, 1958.

Oberman, Heiko A. "Some Notes on the Theology of Nominalism with Attention to its Relation to the Renaissance." *Harvard Theological Review* 53. 1960, pp. 47-76.

Oberman, Heiko A. *The Harvest of Medieval Theology: Gabriel Biel and Late Medieval Nominalism*. Grand Rapids: William B. Erdmans Publishing Co., 1967.

Patch, H.R. *The Goddess Fortuna in Medieval Literature*. Cambridge, Mass.: Harvard University Press, 1927.

Pico della Mirandola, G. *On the Dignity of Man, On Being and the One, Heptaplus.*. Introduction by Paul J.W. Miller. New York: Bobbs-Merrill Co., Inc., Library of Liberal Arts 1965.

Plato. *The Collected Dialogues*. Edited by E. Hamilton and Huntington Cairns. Bollingen Series 71. Princeton: Princeton University Press, 1961.

Plotinus. *The Enneads*. 6 Vols. Translated by A.H. Armstrong. Cambridge, Mass.: Harvard University Press, 1967.

Proclus. *In Platonis Rem Publicam Commentarii*. 2 Vols. Edited by W. Kroll. Leipzig, 1899-1901, reprinted Amsterdam, 1954.

Rose, Paul Lawrence. *The Italian Renaissance of Mathematics: Studies on Humanists and Mathematicians from Petrarch to Galileo*. Geneva: Librairie Droz, 1975.

Sabbadini, R. "Niccolò da Cusa e i conciliari di Basilea alla scoperta dei codici." *Rendiconti della R. Accademia dei Lincei, Scienze morali*. Ser. 5, Vol. 20, 1911.

Senger, H.G. *Die Philosophie des Nikolaus von Kues vor dem Jahre 1440. Untersuchungen zur Entwicklung einer Philosophie in der Frühzeit des Nikolaus (1430-1440). Beiträge zur Geschichte der Philosophie und Theologie des Mittelalters. Neue Folge* 3. Münster: Aschendorff, 1971.

Sigmund, Paul E. *Nicholas of Cusa and Medieval Political Thought*. Cambridge, Mass.: Harvard University Press, 1963.

Tateo, Francesco. *Tradizione e realtà nell'umanesimo italiano*. Bari: Dedalo Libri, 1967.

The Shorter Oxford English Dictionary. 3rd edition. Oxford: The Clarendon Press, 1973. "bowls."

Thorndike, Lynn. *Science and Thought in the Fifteenth Century*. New York: Hafner, 1963.

Traut, Wolfgang, and Manfred Zacher. "Cusanus-Bibliographie, 2. Fortsetzung (1964-1967) und Nachträge." *Mitteilungen und Forschungsbeiträge der Cusanus-Gesellschaft* 6, 1967, pp. 178-202.

Trinkaus, Charles. *In Our Image and Likeness: Humanity and Divinity in Italian Humanist Thought*. 2 Vols. Chicago: The University of Chicago Press, 1970.

Vansteenberghe, Edmond. *Le Cardinal Nicolas de Cues (1401-1464): L'Action – La Pensée*. Paris, 1920 (anastatic reprint, Frankfurt: Minerva, 1963).

______. "Quelques lectures de jeunesse de Nicholas de Cues." *Archives d'histoire doctrinale et littéraire du moyen âge* 3, 1928, pp. 275-284.

______. "Le 'de ignota Litteratura' de Jean Wenck de Herrenberg." *Beiträge zur Geschichte der Philosophie des Mittelalters*. Vol. 8, No. 6. Münster: Aschendorff, 1910.

Vazquez, Mario. "Cusanus-Bibliographie, 3. Fortsetzung (1967-1973) Ergänzungen." *Mitteilungen und Forschungsbeiträge der Cusanus-Gesellschaft* 10, 1973, pp. 207-234.

Wackerzapp, H. *Der Einfluss Meister Eckharts auf die ersten philosophischen schriften des Nikolaus von Kues*. Ed. J. Koch. Münster-Westfalen: Aschendorff, 1962.

Watanabe, Morimichi. *The Political Ideas of Nicholas of Cusa with special reference to his De concordantia catholica*. Geneva: Librairie Droz, 1963.

Watts, Pauline M. *Nicolaus Cusanus: A Fifteenth Century Vision of Man*. Leiden: E.J. Brill, 1982.

Wind, Edgar. *Pagan Mysteries in the Renaissance*. New York: W.W. Norton and Co., Inc., 1968.

THE JANUS LIBRARY

Lorenzo Valla, DE VOLUPTATE (ON PLEASURE).
Maristella Lorch and A. Kent Hieatt

Rene Descartes, LE MONDE (THE WORLD).
Michael Sean Mahoney

Immanuel Kant, DER STREIT DER FAKULTÄTEN
(THE CONFLICT OF THE FACULTIES).
Mary J. Gregor

Thomas Hobbes, DE CORPORE (PART FIRST).
Aloysius Patrick Martinich; with an inquiry into Hobbes's
Theory of Language, Speech, and Reasoning by
Isabel C. Hungerland and George R. Vick

Immanuel Kant, DER EINZIG MÖGLICHE BEWEISGRUND
(THE ONE POSSIBLE BASIS FOR A DEMONSTRATION OF
THE EXISTENCE OF GOD).
Gordon Treash

Etienne Bonnot de Condillac, LA LOGIQUE (LOGIC).
W. R. Albury

Nicholas de Cusa, IDIOTA DE MENTE.
Clyde Lee Miller

Johannes Reuchlin, DE ARTE CABBALISTICA.
Martin Goodman

Johannes Kepler, MYSTERIUM COSMOGRAPHICUM.
E. J. Aiton and A. M. Duncan

Immanuel Kant, FORTSCHRITTE DER METAPHYSICK
(PROGRESS IN METAPHYSICS).
Ted B. Humphrey

Nicholas Malebranche, ENTRETIENS SUR LA
METAPHYSIQUE ET SUR LA RELIGION
(DIALOGUES ON METAPHYSICS AND RELIGION).
Willis Doney

Nicholas de Cusa, DE LUDO GLOBI
(THE GAME OF SPHERES).
Pauline Moffitt Watts

Forthcoming:

Luca Pacioli, DIVINA PROPORTIONE.

Charlier de Gerson, CONSOLATIO DE THEOLOGIA.
Clyde Lee Miller